Accounting
A Basic Approach

Accounting
A Basic Approach

Michael D. Tuttle
St. Clair Community College

Elizabeth Walls
University of New Mexico

Wm. C. Brown Company Publishers
Dubuque, Iowa

wcb group

Wm. C. Brown
Chairman of the Board

Mark C. Falb
Corporate Vice President/ Operations

Book Team

G. W. Cox
Editor

Lynne M. Meyers
Production Editor

Marla A. Schafer
Designer

Robert H. Grigg
Production Services

wcb

Wm. C. Brown Company
Publishers, College Division

Lawrence E. Cremer
President

Raymond C. Deveaux
Vice President, Product Development

David Wm. Smith
Assistant Vice President/National Sales Manager

David A. Corona
Director of Production Development and Design

Matthew T. Coghlan
National Marketing Manager

Janis Machala
Director of Marketing Research

William A. Moss
Production Editorial Manager

Marilyn A. Phelps
Manager of Design

Mary M. Heller
Visual Research Manager

Cover design by Julia A. Scannell

Contents

Illustrations   xi
Preface   xiv

1 Introduction
The Nature of Accounting 2

Objectives   2
Need for Accounting   4
Users of Accounting Information
   5
Language of Business   5
Bookkeeping and Accounting
   5
Business Entity Concept   6
Assets, Liabilities, and Owner's
   Equity   6

The Accounting Equation   8
Business Transactions   8
Effect of Transactions on the
   Accounting Equation   8
Revenue and Expense   12
Double-Entry Accounting   15
Summary   16
Key Terms   17

2 The Accounting Cycle
The Recording Process 18

Objectives 18
The Account 20
The Recording Process 25
Source Documents 25
The Journal 25
Journalizing Transactions 27

Proving the Journal 31
The General Ledger 32
The Chart Accounts 34
Posting 35
Summary 42
Key Terms 43

3 The Accounting Cycle
The Reporting Process 44

Objectives 44
The Trial Balance 46
Balancing the Accounts 46
Discovery and Solution of Errors 50

The Income Statement 52
The Balance Sheet 54
Summary 58
Key Terms 59

4 Accounting for a Personal Service Enterprise 60

Objectives 60
Cash System of Accounting 62
Records Kept by a Doctor 63
The Combined Journal 69
Recording Transactions in the Combined Journal 70

Posting from the Combined Journal 72
Accounting for Other Personal Service Enterprises 77
Summary 78
Key Terms 79

5 The Accounting Cycle
The Adjusting and Closing Process 80

Objectives 80
Account Adjustments 82
Adjusting Entries 83
The Worksheet 87
Preparing the Financial Statements 92
Journalizing and Posting the Adjusting Entries 93

Journalizing and Posting the Closing Entries 94
Open and Closed Accounts 101
Postclosing Trial Balance 102
Summary 104
Key Terms 105

6 Control of Cash   106

Objectives   106
Composition of Cash   108
The Bank Account   109
The Bank Statement   115
The Bank Reconciliation   117

The Petty Cash Fund   121
Cash Short and Over   124
Summary   125
Key Terms   126

7 Special Journals   128

Objectives   128
Function of Special Journals
   130
Cash Receipts Journal   131
Cash Payments Journal   134
Sales Journal   140

Purchases Journal   142
Other Journals   143
Advantages of Special Journals
   144
Summary   145
Key Terms   145

8 Accounting for a Merchandising Firm   146

Objectives   146
Accrual System of Accounting
   148
Merchandise Inventory   149
Accounting for Sales and
   Purchases   149
Sales   149

Purchases   154
Subsidiary Ledgers and Control
   Accounts   163
Journalizing and Posting
   Procedures   165
Summary   173
Key Terms   174

9 Accounting for Uncollectible Accounts and Promissory Notes   176

Objectives   176
Uncollectible Accounts   178
Writing Off Uncollectible Accounts
   178
Worksheet Adjustments for
   Uncollectible Accounts   183
Promissory Notes   184

Computing Interest   185
Notes Receivable   186
Notes Payable   190
Accrued Interest   194
Summary   195
Key Terms   196

10 Accounting for Depreciation and Inventory 198

Objectives   198
Accounting for Depreciation
200
Long-Lived Assets and
  Depreciation   200
Methods for Determining
  Depreciation   202
Comparison of Depreciation
  Methods   203
Worksheet Adjustments for
  Depreciation   206
Disposal of Long-Lived Assets
  206

Accounting for Inventory   211
Importance of Inventory   211
Determining Inventory on Hand
  211
Determining Cost of Inventory
  212
Comparison of Methods   214
Estimating Inventory   216
Summary   218
Key Terms   219

11 Adjusting and Closing Process for a Merchandising Firm   220

Objectives   220
The Worksheet   222
Adjustments   222
Merchandising Inventory   223
Financial Statements   227

Adjusting and Closing Entries
  232
Postclosing Trial Balance   234
Reversing Entries   234
Summary   238
Key Terms   238

12 Accounting for Payroll Employees   240

Objectives   240
Necessity of Payroll Records
242
Employer-Employee Relationship
  242
Types of Remuneration   243
Employee Earnings   243
Fair Labor Standards Act   243
Gross Earnings   243

Deductions from Earnings   244
Payroll Records   250
Accounting for the Payroll   254
Use of Pegboard or Automated
  Systems   255
Summary   257
Key Terms   257

13 Accounting for Payroll Employer 260

Objectives   260
Employer's Payroll Taxes   262
Recording Taxes   264
Reporting and Paying Taxes   265

Payment of Voluntary Deductions 270
Accrual of Taxes and Wages 271
Summary   274
Key Terms   274

14 Automated Processing of Accounting Data 276

Objectives   276
Introduction to Automated Accounting Systems   278
System Analysis   278
System Design   278
System Implementation   279
Methods of Processing Data 279
Manual Data Processing   280
Mechanical Data Processing   280
Punched Card Data Processing 280
Electronic Data Processing   280

Characteristics of Automated Systems   281
Input Stage   281
Processing Stage   286
Output Stage   286
Electronic Data Processing: The Computer   287
Automated Processing of Payroll Records   289
Automated Processing of Other Business Records   290
Summary   291
Key Terms   292

15 Forms of Ownership 294

Objectives   294
Single Proprietorships   296
Organization   296
Advantages and Disadvantages 296
Accounting Procedures   297
Partnerships   299
Organization   299
Advantages and Disadvantages 300

Accounting Procedures   301
Dissolution of a Partnership   304
Corporations   306
Organization   306
Advantages and Disadvantages 308
Accounting Procedures   308
Summary   313
Key Terms   315

Glossary   317
Index   327

Illustrations

Figures

Figure 2.1 A two-column general journal.   26
Figure 2.2 Entries in a general journal.   27
Figure 2.3 Journalizing the transactions of Dr. Wanda Ford.   29
Figure 2.4 A compound journal entry.   31
Figure 2.5 Correcting a journal error.   32
Figure 2.6 Standard two-column account form.   33
Figure 2.7 Four-column balance form.   33
Figure 2.8 Chart of accounts.   34
Figure 2.9 Posting the debit portion of a journal entry.   35
Figure 2.10 Posting the credit portion of a journal entry.   36
Figure 2.11a General journal of Dr. Ford's transactions.   37
Figure 2.11b General ledger accounts.   39
Figure 2.12 Flow of data through the recording process.   41

Figure 3.1 Two-column account form balancing.   47
Figure 3.2 Balancing of four-column form.   48
Figure 3.3 Debit and credit account balances.   50
Figure 3.4 Income statement.   53
Figure 3.5 Balance sheet, account form.   55
Figure 3.6 Statement of owner's equity.   56
Figure 3.7 Balance sheet, report form.   56
Figure 3.8 Relationship of the income statement and the balance sheet.   57
Figure 3.9 A net loss in the owner's equity section of the balance sheet.   58

Figure 4.1 Patient service record form.   64
Figure 4.2 Statement of patient transactions.   65
Figure 4.3 Medicare request form.   66
Figure 4.4 Patient account statement.   67
Figure 4.5 Dr. Ford's chart of accounts.   68
Figure 4.6 Combined journal.   71
Figure 4.7 Dr. Ford's ledger accounts.   73
Figure 4.8 Trial balance.   76

Figure 5.1 Worksheet for Dr. Wanda Ford. 88
Figure 5.2 Trial Balance columns of the worksheet. 90
Figure 5.3 Adjustment columns. 90
Figure 5.4 Adjusted Trial Balance columns. 90
Figure 5.5 Income Statement columns. 91
Figure 5.6 Balance Sheet columns. 91
Figure 5.7 Income statement for Dr. Wanda Ford. 92
Figure 5.8 Balance sheet for Dr. Wanda Ford. 93
Figure 5.9a Adjusting entries in the general journal. 94
Figure 5.9b Ledger accounts after posting the adjusting entries. 95
Figure 5.10a Closing entries in the general journal. 97
Figure 5.10b Ledger accounts after posting the closing entries. 97
Figure 5.11 The closing process. 100
Figure 5.12 Balance form closed account. 101
Figure 5.13 Two-column closed account, one entry. 101
Figure 5.14 Two-column closed account, two entries. 101
Figure 5.15 New accounting period entry on balance form. 102
Figure 5.16 New accounting period entry on two-column form. 102
Figure 5.17 Postclosing trial balance. 103

Figure 6.1 Signature card. 109
Figure 6.2 Sample check. 110
Figure 6.3 Check register. 110
Figure 6.4 Deposit slip. 111
Figure 6.5 Machine-printed deposit receipt. 112
Figure 6.6 American Bankers Association number. 113
Figure 6.7 Magnetic ink character recognition number. 113
Figure 6.8 Check endorsements. 114
Figure 6.9 Bank statement. 116
Figure 6.10 Simple bank reconciliation. 119
Figure 6.11 More involved bank reconciliation. 120
Figure 6.12 Petty cash voucher. 122
Figure 6.13 Petty cash disbursements record. 122
Figure 6.14 Statement of petty cash disbursements and accompanying journal entry. 123

Figure 7.1 Cash receipts journal for a professional enterprise. 133
Figure 7.2 Cash receipts journal for a merchandising firm. 133

Figure 7.3 Transactions recorded in a cash receipts journal. 134
Figure 7.4 Dr. Ford's ledger accounts after posting of December cash receipts transactions. 135
Figure 7.5 Cash payments journal for a professional enterprise. 137
Figure 7.6 Cash payments journal for a merchandising firm. 137
Figure 7.7 Dr. Ford's ledger accounts after posting of December cash payments transactions. 138
Figure 7.8 Single-column sales journal. 141
Figure 7.9 Three-column sales journal. 141
Figure 7.10 Single-column purchases journal. 142
Figure 7.11 Multicolumn purchases journal. 143

Figure 8.1 A bank credit card. 150
Figure 8.2 Bank credit card invoice. 151
Figure 8.3 Cash register tape (left). Prenumbered sales slip (right). 152
Figure 8.4 Sales ticket. 153
Figure 8.5 Sales invoice used by a wholesale firm. 153
Figure 8.6 Invoice verification form. 155
Figure 8.7 Credit memorandum. 160
Figure 8.8 Debit memorandum. 161
Figure 8.9 Three-column subsidiary ledger form. 163
Figure 8.10 Schedule of accounts receivable. 164
Figure 8.11 Schedule of accounts payable. 164
Figure 8.12 Three-column sales journal. 165
Figure 8.13 One-column purchases journal. 166
Figure 8.14a Posting from a cash receipts journal. 167
Figure 8.14b Posting from a cash payments journal. 167
Figure 8.14c Posting from a sales journal. 167
Figure 8.14d Posting from a purchases journal. 168
Figure 8.14e Posting to a general ledger. 168
Figure 8.14f Posting to an accounts receivable ledger. 170
Figure 8.14g Posting to an accounts payable ledger. 171

Figure 9.1 A promissory note. 184
Figure 9.2 Notes receivable register. 190
Figure 9.3 Notes payable register. 192

Figure 11.1 Worksheet for Signature B. 224
Figure 11.2 Multiple-step income statement. 228
Figure 11.3 Classified balance sheet. 230
Figure 11.4 Adjusting entries for Signature B. 232

Figure 11.5 Closing entries for Signature B. 233
Figure 11.6 Expense and Revenue Summary and Capital accounts after posting. 234
Figure 11.7 Postclosing trial balance for Signature B. 235
Figure 11.8 Bank credit card accounts after posting. 235
Figure 11.9 Reversing entry for the bank credit card expense adjustment. 236
Figure 11.10 Bank credit card accounts after posting of reversing entry. 236
Figure 11.11 Interest accounts after posting. 237
Figure 11.12 Reversing entry for the accrued interest expense adjustment. 237
Figure 11.13 Interest account after posting of note payment. 237

Figure 12.1 Social Security Employee Tax Table (1981 figures). 245
Figure 12.2 Form W-4, Employee Withholding Allowance Certificate. 247
Figure 12.3 Wage-bracket table. 248
Figure 12.4 Percentage Method Income Tax Withholding Table. 248
Figure 12.5 Tables for Percentage Method of Withholding. 248
Figure 12.6 Payroll register. 250
Figure 12.7 Paycheck and stub. 252
Figure 12.8 Employee earnings record. 253
Figure 12.9 Pegboard system of payroll accounting. 256

Figure 13.1 Federal Tax Deposit Form 501. 265
Figure 13.2 Employer's Quarterly Federal Tax Return. 266
Figure 13.3 Federal Tax Deposit Form 508. 267
Figure 13.4 Employer's Annual Federal Unemployment Tax Return. 268
Figure 13.5 Form W-2, Wage and Tax Statement. 269
Figure 13.6 Form W-3, Transmittal of Income and Tax Statements. 270

Figure 14.1 Many types of computers are used to electronically process accounting data. 281
Figure 14.2 A data card. 282
Figure 14.3 A data card recording the number 2. 283
Figure 14.4 A data card recording the number 25. 283
Figure 14.5 A data card showing the punch combinations for recording letters. 283

Figure 14.6 A data card containing the fields necessary for a sample invoice. 284
Figure 14.7 Punched tape. 285
Figure 14.8 Flow of data through an automated data processing system. 286
Figure 14.9 Some common flowchart symbols. 288
Figure 14.10 Flow of data within a computer system. 289

Figure 15.1 Balance sheet prior to opening a formal set of accounting records. 298
Figure 15.2 Owner's equity section of a balance sheet for a single proprietorship. 298
Figure 15.3 Capital statement for J. M. Thomas. 299
Figure 15.4 Owner's equity section of a balance sheet when a capital statement is prepared. 299
Figure 15.5 Income statement showing the division of income for a partnership. 303
Figure 15.6 The organizational structure of a corporation. 307
Figure 15.7 Income statement for a corporation. 311
Figure 15.8 Owner's equity section of a balance sheet for a corporation. 311
Figure 15.9 A statement of retained earnings. 312

Tables

Table 9.1 Aging schedule of accounts receivable 182
Table 10.1 Declining-balance method 204
Table 10.2 Sum-of-the-years'-digits method 205
Table 10.3 Comparison of three depreciation methods 205
Table 10.4 Calculation of group depreciation rate 210
Table 10.5 Comparison of inventory cost valuation methods 214

Preface

Introduction

Accounting: A Basic Approach has been written to meet the needs of several types of students:

1. Those who have no previous accounting experience and wish to acquire the basic concepts and procedures of accounting for either personal or business use.
2. Those who need to develop procedural accounting skills in preparation for entering the job market.
3. Those who want to increase or broaden their knowledge of the basic accounting concepts as a means of advancing in their chosen careers.
4. Those who wish to broaden their accounting background before taking additional accounting courses.

To achieve these objectives, this textbook provides a thorough coverage of the total accounting process from the analyzing and recording of business transactions to the preparation of periodic financial reports.

Format of Chapters

This text is divided into fifteen chapters, each of which focuses on a particular aspect of the accounting process. The accounting equation, the theory of debits and credits, and the analyzing and recording of transactions are covered in chapters 1 and 2. Chapters 3 and 4 describe the cash basis of accounting and the preparation of periodic financial reports as they relate to a service business. Chapter 5 is a discussion of the adjusting and closing process for a service business. The control of cash is explained in chapter 6, and chapter 7 introduces the concept of special journals. In chapter 8 the accrual basis of accounting is discussed together with the accounting procedures related to a merchandising operation. Specific procedures used in accounting for uncollectible accounts, promissory notes, depreciation, and inventory are covered in chapters 9 and 10. The adjusting and closing process for a merchandising firm is explained in chapter 11. Chapters 12 and 13 provide an explanation of the basics of payroll accounting. The function of automated data processing as it relates to accounting activities is discussed in chapter 14. Chapter 15 describes the various types of business ownership and some of the special accounting procedures common to each of them.

Current accounting terminology is used throughout the text, and each chapter contains detailed explanations and illustrations to reinforce the concepts presented. Some special features have been included to increase the effectiveness of each chapter: (1) learning objectives at the beginning of each chapter, (2) chapter summaries that contain page references to the concepts in the chapters, and (3) a list of key terms and their definitions at the end of each chapter.

Several Aids Accompany Text

A number of instructional aids have been prepared in conjunction with this text.

Workbook/Working Papers

A separate workbook containing questions, problems, and working papers for each chapter has been prepared for the student. A special feature of the workbook is the inclusion of a mastery test for each chapter with the answers provided at the back of the workbook.

Practice Sets

There are two practice sets that accompany the text. Each practice set is based on the business transactions of a hypothetical firm during a two-month period. The transactions are recorded on duplicates of actual business forms to help acquaint the student with day-to-day accounting procedures. The first practice set is designed for a service business; the second for a merchandising firm. The two practice sets are independent of each other but are designed so that they can be used in sequence, thus giving students practical experience in keeping records for both a service and a merchandising business.

Answers to the accounting problems in the practice sets are contained in the instructor's versions of these ancillaries.

Instructor's Manual

The Instructor's Manual is a comprehensive supplement to the text and workbook. It contains teaching suggestions, information on time utilization, information on careers in accounting, and three suggested course outlines. Other features of importance are chapter tests and a final examination. As an aid to the instructor, solutions for the exams and the workbook problems are also included.

Acknowledgments

The authors of *Accounting: A Basic Approach* are indebted to many persons for their help in preparing the material for this book. We wish to express our gratitude to those who gave generously of their time and experience by reviewing the manuscript and offering valuable suggestions and constructive criticism. Our thanks go also to the many teachers and administrators who participated in the survey that led to the writing of this textbook. Special thanks go to the members of the staff at Wm. C. Brown Company Publishers for their assistance, support, and encouragement: William Cox, Robert Stern, Kathy Loy, Julie Mueller, Lynne Meyers, Bob Grigg, and Pat Hendricks. We also wish to thank Sandy Baxendale for her tireless efforts in typing the manuscript.

Michael D. Tuttle

Elizabeth I. Walls

Accounting
A Basic Approach

Objectives   Upon completion of this chapter, you should be able to:

1. Explain the need for a system of accounting for a business, an individual, and an organization.
2. Analyze the effects of various business transactions on the accounting equation.

1 Introduction The Nature of Accounting

3. Define the following accounting terms:

accounting equation

accounts payable

accounts receivable

assets

business entity concept

creditor

double-entry accounting

expense

liabilities

net income

net loss

notes payable

notes receivable

owner's equity

revenue

Need for Accounting

Accounting provides a system for collecting and reporting information about the financial activities of a business, an individual, or an organization. Generally, such information is needed for making decisions, planning, and exercising control over financial activities.

Business needs a system of accounting for the following reasons:

1. To provide management with data needed for decision making and for efficient operation of the firm.
2. To prepare tax returns and reports.
3. To prepare special reports for certain agencies of the local, state, and federal government, which serve as regulatory bodies. For example, a mover of household goods, because of the nature of its business, must report to the Interstate Commerce Commission.
4. To prepare periodic reports that show the firm's financial position and the results of its operations.

Because most individuals engage in business activities at some time in their lives, they must be concerned with the financial aspects of such activities. Individuals need accounting information in order to:

1. Keep better personal records.
2. Understand financial reports.
3. Undertake financial planning and budgeting.
4. Make wiser investments.
5. Prepare tax returns.

Individuals who plan to work in the clerical and secretarial fields have an even greater need for acquiring accounting skills and knowledge. They may be required to perform accounting functions on the job since accounting in some way affects all offices. With few exceptions, nearly all office workers handle some financial data that is a part of accounting. It is essential, therefore, that clerical and secretarial workers develop some basic accounting skills and broaden their knowledge of accounting concepts and terminology. A practical background in accounting can prove invaluable to anyone planning to enter clerical or secretarial careers.

Organizations, both profit and nonprofit, need a system of accounting for the following reasons:

1. To prepare tax returns.
2. To prepare financial reports for interested parties, such as contributors of funds.
3. To make decisions about the distribution or investment of funds.

Users of Accounting Information

Among the users of accounting information are owners and managers of businesses, creditors, government agencies, consumers, investors, and labor unions.

Owners can use accounting information to decide whether to expand or cut back on business operations or to change the form of ownership of a business. **Creditors** are persons or businesses to whom a debt is owed. They often use such information to determine whether or not to extend credit or whether to limit the amount of credit granted. Government agencies use accounting information for taxation and regulation purposes. Consumers need to be informed about the financial stability of a company. Investors rely on information not only to help them decide whether or not to invest in a company but also to help them decide whether to keep or sell their investments. Labor unions make use of information about a firm's ability to pay increased wages and its ability to provide permanent employment.

Each of these users requires different kinds of information; however, they share a basic interest in the results of financial operations during a certain period or a summary of total possessions and debts at the end of that period.

Language of Business

Accounting has often been termed "the language of business." It is the medium through which financial information is communicated from one person to another. Logically, anyone entering the business world must possess a working knowledge of the language in order to communicate with others. This language includes the terminology, principles, and concepts of accounting. The task of learning the terminology is complicated because many words used in accounting are the same as words used in nonbusiness situations, though their meanings differ. Therefore, familiarity with the accounting meanings of these words is a prerequisite to understanding accounting information. In addition, certain basic principles and concepts must be understood in order to use the "language" efficiently.

Bookkeeping and Accounting

Many uninformed persons often confuse bookkeeping with accounting. While the two are closely related, bookkeeping deals mainly with the recording of the financial transactions of a business. A bookkeeper is responsible for recording business data in a prescribed manner and for keeping accounting records. A large portion of the work of a bookkeeper is clerical in nature. Today more and more of this work is being performed by mechanical and electronic means.

On the other hand, accounting includes the design of the system of recording, the preparation of reports, and the analysis and interpretation of data and reports. An accountant designs an accounting system to meet the particular needs of a business and oversees the operation of the system. In addition, accountants are concerned with the preparation of financial statements, tax returns, budgets, and cost studies. Accountants must be able to direct and review the work of bookkeepers. In general, they must possess a higher level of knowledge and analytical skills than is required of a bookkeeper.

Business Entity Concept

In keeping the financial records of a company, it is essential to separate the company's business activities from the owner's personal financial affairs. Such a procedure is in keeping with the **business entity concept**. This concept states that a business is assumed to be a separate and distinct entity from the person or persons who own it. Therefore, a separate set of records must be kept. It is also assumed that a person who owns more than one business keeps a separate set of records for each business.

For example, Mr. James McIntire owns a business, Travel Unlimited. The accounting records for Travel Unlimited should include only information about the business entity itself. These records should not include information about any other business Mr. McIntire may own. Nor should they include information about the personal business affairs of Mr. McIntire.

Assets,
Liabilities, and
Owner's Equity

The financial structure of all businesses is based on three interrelated elements—assets, liabilities, and owner's equity. The financial activities of a business will affect one or more of these basic elements.

Assets are anything of value owned by a business. These assets may take many forms. Some are physical items of property, such as cash, equipment, land, and buildings. Other assets exist as claims against the property of another person or business for payment of goods purchased or services rendered. In accounting, these types of assets are identified by the word *receivable* (e.g., accounts receivable, notes receivable). An **account receivable** is an amount due from a customer who has purchased goods or services on credit. Goods are purchased or services are rendered "on account," and the customer agrees to pay within a given time—usually thirty days. A **note receivable** is a customer's written promise to pay a specific sum of money on a future date. The note serves as evidence of the customer's promise to pay. The payment period of a note can vary from thirty days up to one year.

As an example, assume that a business has the following assets:

Cash	$ 3,000
Accounts Receivable	500
Equipment	1,500
Land	5,000
Building	15,000
Total	$25,000

Total assets for this business amount to $25,000.

The types and quantities of assets needed to conduct a business vary with the company. However, cash is always a necessary asset, and all other assets are assigned a monetary value.

Liabilities are the debts of a business. These debts materialize when an owner buys goods or services on a credit basis or borrows money. They represent obligations of the owner to disburse cash (or other assets) or provide services in the future for payment of debts. Rarely does a business operate without liabilities.

Liabilities can be thought of as the creditors' claims to or interest in the assets of the business. In accounting, these liabilities are identified by the word *payable* (e.g., accounts payable, notes payable). An **account payable** is an amount owed to a creditor. Goods or services are purchased on a credit basis, and payment must be made within a short time. A **note payable** is a written promise to pay a specific amount of money to a creditor or lender on a future date.

If the business cited in the above example has accounts payable totaling $1,500 and notes payable of $5,000, its total liabilities are $6,500. In other words, persons outside the business have a claim against the assets of the business amounting to $6,500.

Owner's equity refers to the owner's interest in the business or claim upon the assets of the business. The difference between what the business owns (assets) and what it owes (liabilities) represents the owner's equity. *Net worth, proprietorship,* and *capital* are terms that are also used to designate owner's equity.

Equity actually includes two different kinds of claims against the assets of a business—the claims of owners and creditors. In most instances, the creditors' claims to the assets take priority over those of the owner. The owner then has a claim to whatever value of assets remains. The leftover amount is called owner's equity. In the example, the firm's assets are $25,000 and creditors' claims (liabilities) are $6,500. Therefore, the owner's equity is $18,500 ($25,000 − $6,500). If there were no liabilities, the owner's equity would be equal to the amount of the assets, or $25,000.

The Accounting Equation	As stated previously, assets, liabilities, and owner's equity are interrelated. This relationship is expressed in the form of an equation: Assets = Liabilities + Owner's Equity (A = L + OE). The relationship shown by the equation states that total claims against the assets are always equal to the total assets. The two sides of the equation must always be equal since the rights to all the assets of a business are owned by someone, either the creditors or owners or both.

If the amounts of any two of the basic elements are known, the third can be determined. As an illustration, assume that Helen Miller has $5,000 invested in a restaurant, The Pizza Place, and has liabilities of $2,340.

$$\text{Assets} = \text{Liabilities} + \text{Owner's Equity}$$
$$\$5,000 = \$2,340 + \quad ?$$

To find her owner's equity, subtract the liabilities from the assets ($5,000 − $2,340 = $2,660).

$$\text{Assets} = \text{Liabilities} + \text{Owner's Equity}$$
$$\$5,000 = \$2,340 + \$2,660$$

The missing element in the equation can always be determined in one of two ways: either by adding the two known elements or by subtracting one of the known elements from the other. When these procedures are followed, the equality of assets and equities is always maintained even though the equation is expressed in different ways:

1. Assets = Liabilities + Owner's Equity (A = L + OE)
2. Liabilities = Assets − Owner's Equity (L = A − OE)
3. Owner's Equity = Assets − Liabilities (OE = A − L)

Business Transactions	A *business transaction* involves an exchange of values that affects the elements of the accounting equation. For example, the original investment of cash by an owner in his or her business represents an exchange of cash for ownership rights. A purchase of equipment on account represents an exchange of equipment for a promise to pay. These exchanges are expressed in terms of dollar amounts, and they have a direct effect on assets, liabilities, and owner's equity. All business transactions can be described in terms of their effect on the elements of the accounting equation.

Effect of Transactions on the Accounting Equation	As an example, some typical business transactions of Dr. Wanda Ford will be used to illustrate the effect of different types of transactions on the accounting equation. Note that a transaction can result in two pluses (increases), two minuses (decreases), or a plus and a minus (an increase and a decrease).

Transaction a

Dr. Ford established her medical practice by depositing $5,000 in a bank account in the name of Dr. Wanda O. Ford. The effect of this transaction is to increase the assets (Cash) by $5,000. The owner's equity (Wanda Ford, Capital) is increased on the other side of the equation by the same amount. (Owner's equity is usually identified by the owner's name followed by the word *Capital*.)

Assets	=	Liabilities	+	Owner's Equity
Cash				Wanda Ford, Capital
(a) +$5,000	=			(a) +$5,000

Transaction b

Dr. Ford purchased medical equipment for which she paid $1,450 in cash. This transaction changes the form of the assets but does not change their total value. No additional money has been invested. Part of one asset (Cash) has been exchanged for another asset (Medical Equipment). Cash has been decreased by $1,450, while Medical Equipment has been increased by that same amount. Therefore, there is no change in the owner's equity.

	Assets		=	Liabilities	+	Owner's Equity
	Cash	+ Medical Equipment				Wanda Ford, Capital
Bal	$5,000					$5,000
(b)	− 1,450	+$1,450				
Bal	$3,550 +	$1,450	=			$5,000

Transaction c

Dr. Ford bought office furniture for $450 on a credit basis from the Wilson Furniture Company. This transaction creates a liability, Accounts Payable. The effect on the accounting equation is to increase both assets (Office Furniture) and liabilities (Accounts Payable) by $450. Dr. Ford has additional assets worth $450 even though the furniture will not be paid for until a later date. (Items purchased on a credit basis are recorded as assets at the time of purchase not at the time of payment.) Liabilities have been increased because Dr. Ford now owes $450 to a creditor. The owner's equity remains unchanged because Wilson Furniture Company has acquired a claim on the assets equal to the increase in assets.

	Assets			=	Liabilities	+	Owner's Equity
	Cash	+ Medical Equipment +	Office Furniture		Accounts Payable		Wanda Ford, Capital
Bal	$3,550	$1,450					$5,000
(c)			+$450		+$450		
Bal	$3,550 +	$1,450 +	$450	=	$450	+	$5,000

Transaction d   Dr. Ford purchased additional medical equipment worth $500 by giving her personal note to the Standard Equipment Company. A transaction of this type has the same effect on the accounting equation as transaction c. Assets (Medical Equipment) have been increased even though no money has changed hands. Likewise, liabilities (Notes Payable) have been increased. By giving her note, Dr. Ford has created a different type of a liability—a note payable rather than an account payable. Standard Equipment Company has acquired a claim on the assets equal to the increase in assets so there is no change in the owner's equity.

		Assets		=	Liabilities		+	Owner's Equity
	Cash +	Medical Equipment +	Office Furniture		Accounts Payable +	Notes Payable		Wanda Ford, Capital
Bal	$3,550	$1,450	$450		$450			$5,000
(d)		+ 500				+$500		
Bal	$3,550 +	$1,950 +	$450	=	$450 +	$500 +		$5,000

Transaction e   Dr. Ford paid $150 of what she owed Wilson Furniture Company. This transaction decreases both the assets and the liabilities. Even though the asset (Cash) is being decreased by $150, the liability (Accounts Payable) is also being decreased by the same amount. Thus, the equation remains in balance.

		Assets		=	Liabilities		+	Owner's Equity
	Cash +	Medical Equipment +	Office Furniture		Accounts Payable +	Notes Payable		Wanda Ford, Capital
Bal	$3,550	$1,950	$450		$450	$500		$5,000
(e)	− 150				− 150			
Bal	$3,400 +	$1,950 +	$450	=	$300 +	$500 +		$5,000

Transaction f   Dr. Ford has made an additional investment of $1,000. With the additional investment of cash, two basic elements are affected, assets (Cash) and owner's equity (Wanda Ford, Capital). In the preceding transactions, no changes have been reflected in the owner's equity. However, since assets have increased by $1,000, the owner's equity in the assets also increases by the same amount. Since nothing else has changed, the equation is still in balance.

	Assets			=	Liabilities		+	Owner's Equity
	Cash +	Medical Equipment +	Office Furniture		Accounts Payable +	Notes Payable		Wanda Ford, Capital
Bal	$3,400	$1,950	$450		$300	$500		$5,000
(f)	+ 1,000							+ 1,000
Bal	$4,400 +	$1,950 +	$450	=	$300 +	$500	+	$6,000

Additional investments in a business by the owner are not always represented by cash. For example, an owner may make an additional investment of equipment, land, or an automobile.

Transaction g Dr. Ford made another investment in her practice, medical equipment worth $1,000. This transaction affects the accounting equation in the same way as transaction f. Only the form of the assets differs (i.e., an increase in equipment rather than cash). Both assets (Medical Equipment) and owner's equity (Wanda Ford, Capital) increase.

	Assets			=	Liabilities		+	Owner's Equity
	Cash +	Medical Equipment +	Office Furniture		Accounts Payable +	Notes Payable		Wanda Ford, Capital
Bal	$4,400	$1,950	$450		$300	$500		$6,000
(g)		+ 1,000						+ 1,000
Bal	$4,400 +	$2,950 +	$450	=	$300 +	$500	+	$7,000

Transaction h Dr. Ford has withdrawn $500 for personal use. (The withdrawal of cash or other assets from a business by the owner is a common practice as you will learn later.) This type of transaction affects two basic elements, assets (Cash) and owner's equity (Wanda Ford, Capital). In this instance, both elements are decreased. By withdrawing cash, the owner has $500 less in assets; therefore, the owner's equity is also $500 less. Since both cash and owner's equity are decreased by the same amount and liabilities remain unchanged, both sides of the equation remain equal.

	Assets			=	Liabilities		+	Owner's Equity
	Cash +	Medical Equipment +	Office Furniture		Accounts Payable +	Notes Payable		Wanda Ford, Capital
Bal	$4,400	$2,950	$450		$300	$500		$7,000
(h)	− 500							− 500
Bal	$3,900 +	$2,950 +	$450	=	$300 +	$500	+	$6,500

These illustrations show how different types of business transactions can affect the basic accounting elements. Transactions b and e represent types of transactions that can change the assets and liabilities but not the owner's equity. Transactions a, f, g, and h represent types of transactions that *can* change the owner's equity. Additional owner investments of assets can increase the equity (transactions f and g). The withdrawal of cash or other assets by the owner can decrease the equity (transaction h). These are not, however, the only ways in which the owner's equity can be changed. It can increase through the receipt of revenue from the sale of goods or services. It can decrease when expenses are incurred in operating the business.

Revenue is defined as the inflow of cash or receivables in exchange for goods or services. Revenue results in an increase in assets and a corresponding increase in owner's equity.

Expenses are defined as the costs incurred by a firm in order to produce revenue. Some examples of expenses are salaries, rent, and advertising. Expenses can decrease both assets and owner's equity, or they can increase liabilities and decrease owner's equity.

Accounting records are usually kept for a certain period of time. If revenues exceed expenses during that period, the excess represents a **net income** or **net profit.** This net profit represents an increase in owner's equity. If, however, expenses for the period exceed revenues, a **net loss** results. The owner's equity is decreased as a result of the net loss. The increase or decrease is not recorded in the owner's equity until the end of the accounting period.

Revenue and expense amounts could be recorded directly in owner's equity since they do eventually increase or decrease the equity. However, if that procedure is followed, it is often difficult to determine the source of the increases (i.e., additional investment of assets or the receipt of revenue). It is equally difficult to determine the causes of the decreases (i.e., a withdrawal of assets by the owner or expenses incurred). The preparation of financial reports also becomes more complicated. For these reasons, it is practical and convenient to keep revenue and expenses separate from the owner's equity.

These individual revenue and expense accounts still represent owner's equity accounts, but they are considered to be *temporary owner's equity accounts.* The revenue and expense amounts are used for calculating the profit or loss for the firm for one accounting period only. The profit or loss for the period is eventually transferred as an increase or decrease in the owner's equity. This procedure is explained in detail in chapter 5.

The accounting equation can now be expanded to include revenue and expense: Assets = Liabilities + Owner's Equity ± (Revenue − Expense) or $A = L + OE \pm (R - E)$.

The effects of revenue and expense transactions on the accounting equation can be seen in the following analyses.

Transaction i

Dr. Ford received $1,500 from patients for services performed. This transaction causes an increase in the assets (Cash) of $1,500. Revenue is produced in the same amount. Owner's equity is increased by the receipt of the revenue; however, the $1,500 is not recorded directly in the owner's equity. It is recorded temporarily as an increase to revenue (Professional Fees).

	Assets			=	Liabilities		+	Owner's Equity	±	Revenue
	Cash +	Medical Equip. +	Office Furniture		Accounts Payable +	Notes Payable	+	Wanda Ford, Capital		Professional Fees
Bal	$3,900	$2,950	$450		$300	$500		$6,500		
(i)	+ 1,500									+$1,500
Bal	$5,400 +	$2,950 +	$450	=	$300 +	$500 +		$6,500	+	$1,500

Transaction j

Dr. Ford performed services totaling $150 for a patient on a charge basis. By allowing the patient to charge $150, Dr. Ford has acquired a new asset, Accounts Receivable. At the same time, revenue is produced even though no cash has been received. This transaction affects the accounting equation in the same manner as transaction i—assets and revenue have both increased. The only difference is the form the asset takes (i.e., an account receivable instead of cash).

	Assets				=	Liabilities		+	Owner's Equity	±	Revenue
	Cash +	Accts. Rec. +	Medical Equip. +	Office Furniture		Accounts Payable +	Notes Payable	+	Wanda Ford, Capital		Professional Fees
Bal	$5,400		$2,950	$450		$300	$500		$6,500		$1,500
(j)		+$150									+ 150
Bal	$5,400 +	$150 +	$2,950 +	$450	=	$300 +	$500 +		$6,500	+	+$1,650

Goods or services sold on account are considered as revenue at the time the sale is made. When an account receivable is later collected, the amount collected is not considered as revenue again. It merely reflects a shift in the form of the assets, cash for an account receivable. To count it as revenue when the cash is actually received would be to count the same dollar amount as revenue twice.

Transaction k Dr. Ford paid $500 rent for the month. This expense results in a $500 decrease in the assets (Cash) and a corresponding decrease in the owner's equity. Owner's equity decreases because the firm has incurred an expense. However, that expense is not recorded as a direct decrease in the owner's equity. It is recorded temporarily to expenses (Rent Expense).

	Assets			=	Liabilities		+	Owner's Equity	± (Revenue −	Expenses)
Cash	Accts. Rec.	Med. Equip.	Office Furn.		Accts. Pay.	Notes Pay.		W. Ford, Capital	Prof. Fees	Rent Expense
Bal $5,400	$150	$2,950	$450		$300	$500		$6,500	$1,650	
(k) − 500										−$500
Bal $4,900 +	$150 +	$2,950 +	$450	=	$300 +	$500 +		$6,500 +	$1,650 −	$500

Transaction l Dr. Ford purchased $150 worth of office supplies on account from the Hollis Supply Company. Both a liability and an expense have been incurred. Liabilities (Accounts Payable) have increased because Dr. Ford owes more money. Owner's equity decreased because she now has incurred another expense. That expense is also temporarily recorded to expenses (Office Supplies Expense).

	Assets			=	Liabilities		+	Owner's Equity	± (Revenue −	Expenses)	
Cash	Accts. Rec.	Med. Equip.	Office Furn.		Accts. Pay.	Notes Pay.		W. Ford, Capital	Prof. Fees	Rent Exp. −	Off. Sup. Exp.
Bal $4,900	$150	$2,950	$450		$300	$500		$6,500	$1,650	$500	
(l)					+ 150						−$150
Bal $4,900 +	$150 +	$2,950 +	$450	=	$450 +	$500 +		$6,500 +	$1,650 −	$500 −	$150

The subsequent payment of this account payable is not considered as an additional expense. Cash outlays to acquire assets or pay liabilities do not represent expenses since expenses are directly related to the earning of revenue.

The following summarizes the foregoing transactions and their effect on the accounting equation:

	Cash	+	Accts. Rec.	+	Med. Equip.	+	Office Furn.	=	Accts. Pay.	+	Notes Pay.	+	W. Ford, Capital	Prof. Fees	Rent Exp.	Off. Sup. Exp.
			Assets					=	Liabilities			+	Owner's Equity ± (Revenue − Expenses)			
(a)	+$5,000												+$5,000			
(b)	− 1,450				+$1,450											
(c)							+$450		+$450							
(d)					+ 500						+$500					
(e)	− 150								− 150							
(f)	+ 1,000												+ 1,000			
(g)					+ 1,000								+ 1,000			
(h)	− 500												− 500			
(i)	+ 1,500													+$1,500		
(j)			+$150											+ 150		
(k)	− $500														+$500	
(l)									+$150							+$150
	$4,900 +		$150 +		$2,950 +		$450 =		$450 +		$500 +		$6,500 +	$1,650 −	$500 −	$150

$8,450 $8,450

Double-Entry Accounting

Each of the preceding transactions had a double effect on the accounting equation. With each transaction the equality or balance of the equation was maintained. Any change recorded in any one of the accounting elements was accompanied by an offsetting change in one or more of the other elements. This dual effect is known as **double-entry accounting** and forms the basis for the recording of every business transaction. This system assures that the balance between assets, liabilities, and owner's equity is maintained. At the same time, it provides a means for verifying the arithmetic accuracy of the recorded transactions. Using this double-entry system, an accountant can detect errors in recording and arithmetic calculations. If the equation is out of balance, an error obviously exists.

Summary

Accounting is considered to be the language of business. It provides the means for communicating information about the financial activities of a business. Accounting consists of certain terminology, principles, and concepts that need to be understood before effective communication is possible (p. 5).

Three basic elements make up the financial structure of all businesses—assets, liabilities, and owner's equity. Assets are the things of value owned by a company. Liabilities are the debts of a company. The owner's equity represents the owner's claim upon the assets of the business. The relationship of these three elements is expressed in the form of the equation $A = L + OE$ (pp. 6–8). This equation is expanded to include two other elements, revenue and expenses: $A = L + OE \pm (R - E)$ (p. 12). Revenue is the inflow of cash or receivables in exchange for goods or services. Expenses are the costs incurred to produce revenue (p. 12).

Business transactions are analyzed to determine what changes (increases or decreases) they cause in the five elements of the equation. Each transaction has a double effect on the accounting equation; yet the equality of the equation is always maintained. This dual effect is known as double-entry accounting and forms the basis for the accounting system (p. 15).

Key Terms

accounting equation The relationship between assets, liabilities, and owner's equity. Assets = Liabilities + Owner's Equity.

accounts payable Amounts owed to creditors.

accounts receivable Amounts due from customers who purchase goods or services on a credit basis.

assets Anything of value owned by a business.

business entity concept The concept that a business is a separate and distinct entity from the person or persons who own it. A separate set of records should be kept for each business.

creditor A person or business to whom a debt is owed.

double-entry accounting Theory upon which the accounting system is based. Every business transaction affects at least two elements of the accounting equation.

expense A cost incurred by a firm in order to produce revenue.

liabilities The debts of a business, which represent creditors' claims to the assets of a business.

net income The amount by which total revenue exceeds total expenses for an accounting period.

net loss The amount by which total expenses exceed total revenue for an accounting period.

notes payable Written promises to pay a specific sum of money to a creditor or lender on a future date.

notes receivable Customers' written promises to pay a specific sum of money on a future date.

owner's equity Owner's interest in the business or claim to the assets of the business; the difference between what the business owns and what it owes. Often referred to as net worth, proprietorship, or capital.

revenue The inflow of cash or receivables in exchange for goods or services.

Upon completion of this chapter, you should be able to:

1. Record transactions in a general journal.
2. Post entries from a general journal to a general ledger.

2 The Accounting Cycle The Recording Process

3. Define the following accounting terms:

account	general ledger
accounting cycle	journal entry
chart of accounts	journalizing
compound journal entry	posting
credit	proving the journal
debit	source document
general journal	

In chapter 1 the theory of double-entry accounting was introduced, along with the basic accounting elements and the accounting equation. Transactions were analyzed and recorded in terms of their effect on the accounting equation. Pluses and minuses were used to show the changes (increases or decreases) in the elements of the equation. However, such a format is not practical for the daily recording of the transactions of a business. It is a slow, time-consuming process even for relatively small businesses. In this chapter, a more efficient procedure for recording transactions will be discussed.

The Account

The device customarily used for individually recording and summarizing the changes in assets, liabilities, owner's equity, revenue, and expenses is called an **account.** The use of an account can best be shown by a simplified form called a T account. This simplified version is used for instructional purposes only. It is not a replica of an actual form. Some of the different types of account forms are described in detail on page 31.

A separate account is kept for each asset, liability, owner's equity, revenue, and expense. The name of the particular item that the account represents is written across the top of the T. The left side of the T is called the **debit** side. The right side is known as the **credit** side. Any amount entered on the left side is called a debit, and any amount entered on the right side is called a credit. In accounting, debit is commonly abbreviated as Dr. and credit as Cr.

Account Name	
Debit	Credit
(Dr.)	(Cr.)

Every business transaction affects at least two accounts, and the sum of the debits is always equal to the sum of the credits. In other words, for every debit there must be an offsetting credit. This dual effect is in keeping with the double-entry theory upon which accounting is based.

Assets = Liabilities + Owner's Equity ± (Revenue − Expenses)
Debits = Credits

The recording process still involves recording increases and decreases, but these changes are now recorded as debits or credits to a specific account. However, the terms *debit* and *credit* are not synonymous with the words *increase* and *decrease*. Some accounts are increased on the debit side and decreased on the credit side. Other accounts are increased on the credit side and decreased on the debit side.

To determine the relationship between debits and credits and increases and decreases, recall the accounting equation, $A = L + OE \pm (R - E)$. The rule for increasing and decreasing each kind of account is based on the equation and represents the one and only arbitrary rule in accounting: In asset and expense accounts, increases are recorded by debits and decreases are recorded by credits. In liability, owner's equity, and revenue accounts, increases are recorded by credits and decreases are recorded by debits.

This rule is illustrated in the T form as follows:

Assets		=	Liabilities		+	Owner's Equity		$\pm$	(Revenue		$-$	Expense)	
Debit	Credit		Debit	Credit		Debit	Credit		Debit	Credit		Debit	Credit
Increase	Decrease		Decrease	Increase		Decrease	Increase		Decrease	Increase		Increase	Decrease
(+)	(−)		(−)	(+)		(−)	(+)		(−)	(+)		(+)	(−)

According to this rule, those accounts appearing on the left side of the equation are increased on the debit side of the account. Those appearing on the right side of the equation are increased on the credit side of the account. The noticeable exception regards expense accounts. Even though expense accounts appear on the right side of the equation, they are increased by debiting. The following illustrates the reason for this and shows the relationship between the owner's equity and the revenue and expense accounts in more detail.

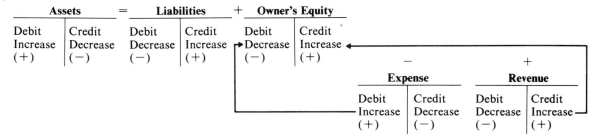

The credit side of a revenue account represents increases in owner's equity and can be thought of as an extension of the credit side of the owner's equity account. The debit side of an expense account represents decreases in owner's equity and can be thought of as an extension of the debit side of the owner's equity account.

The balance of an account usually appears on the side on which increases are recorded. Therefore, the balances for asset and expense accounts normally appear on the debit side. The balances for liabilities, owner's equity, and revenue accounts normally appear on the credit side.

To illustrate the process of increasing and decreasing accounts by debiting and crediting, the transactions discussed on pages 7 through 12 will be recorded. In these examples, the simplified T account replaces the accounting equation.

Transaction a

Investment of $5,000 cash to establish a medical practice.

Cash		Wanda Ford, Capital	
(a) +5,000			(a) +5,000

An increase in an asset is offset by a corresponding increase in the owner's equity. In recording the transaction, Cash is debited to show the increase in assets. Wanda Ford, Capital is credited to show the corresponding increase in the owner's equity.

Transaction b

Purchase of medical equipment for $1,450 cash.

Cash		Medical Equipment	
(a) +5,000	(b) −1,450	(b) +1,450	

One asset (cash) is exchanged for another (equipment) of the same value. The transaction is properly recorded by debiting a new asset account (Medical Equipment) and crediting Cash.

Transaction c

Purchase of office furniture worth $450 on account from Wilson Furniture Company.

Office Furniture		Accounts Payable	
(c) +450			(c) +450

An increase in assets is balanced by an increase in liabilities of the same amount. Office furniture is debited to show the increase in assets. Accounts Payable is credited to show the increase in liabilities.

Transaction d

Purchase of additional $500 worth of medical equipment by giving a personal note to the Standard Equipment Company.

Medical Equipment		Notes Payable	
(b) +1,450			(d) +500
(d) + 500			

An increase in assets is offset by an increase in liabilities. Assets are increased by debiting Medical Equipment. Liabilities are increased by crediting Notes Payable.

Transaction e

Payment of $150 to Wilson Furniture Company on account.

Cash		Accounts Payable	
(a) +5,000	(b) −1,450	(e) −150	(c) +450
	(e) − 150		

The $150 decrease in assets is offset by a $150 decrease in liabilities. The asset Cash is reduced by crediting the account. The liability, Accounts Payable, is reduced by a debit to that account.

Transaction f   Additional investment of $1,000 cash.

	Cash				Wanda Ford, Capital	
(a)	+5,000	(b)	−1,450		(a)	+5,000
(f)	+1,000	(e)	− 150		(f)	+1,000

With the additional investment, both assets and owner's equity are increased. These increases are properly recorded by debiting Cash and crediting Wanda Ford, Capital.

Transaction g   Additional investment of medical equipment worth $1,000.

	Medical Equipment			Wanda Ford, Capital	
(b)	+1,450			(a)	+5,000
(d)	+ 500			(f)	+1,000
(g)	+1,000			(g)	+1,000

With this additional investment, assets and owner's equity are again increased. Medical Equipment is debited to record the increase, and Wanda Ford, Capital is credited.

Transaction h   Withdrawal of $500 cash for personal use.

	Cash				Wanda Ford, Drawing	
(a)	+5,000	(b)	−1,450	(h)	+500	
(f)	+1,000	(e)	− 150			
		(h)	− 500			

Dr. Ford's assets have been reduced. At the same time, her owner's equity in the assets has also been decreased. This change is reflected by a credit to Cash and a debit to Wanda Ford, Drawing. Although this reduction in owner's equity could be entered directly as a debit to the Capital account, a separate account called the *drawing account* is used. By keeping withdrawals in a separate account, the owner can determine quickly the total amounts withdrawn without having to analyze the Capital account. Debiting the Drawing account to reflect the decrease in owner's equity has the same effect as debiting the Capital account. The drawing account is a temporary owner's equity account because it shows withdrawals for one accounting period only. At the end of the accounting period, the total amount of withdrawals for the period is transferred as an increase or decrease to the owner's Capital account.

Transaction i

Receipt of $1,500 cash for professional services.

	Cash				Professional Fees	
(a)	+5,000	(b)	−1,450		(i)	+1,500
(f)	+1,000	(e)	− 150			
(i)	+1,500	(h)	− 500			

The receipt of revenue has resulted in an increase in an asset. That increase is balanced by a corresponding increase in the owner's equity. Cash is debited to show the increase in assets. A separate temporary owner's equity account for the revenue (Professional Fees) is credited to show the indirect increase in equity produced by that revenue. This practice enables the owner to determine total revenue at any point in time without having to analyze the Capital account.

Transaction j

Professional services of $150 rendered on account.

	Accounts Receivable			Professional Fees	
(j)	+150		(i)	+1,500	
			(j)	+ 150	

Dr. Ford's assets have been increased as has the owner's equity. The increase in assets is recorded by debiting Accounts Receivable. The increase in owner's equity is recorded by crediting (increasing) the revenue account.

Transaction k

Payment of $500 rent.

	Cash				Rent Expense	
(a)	+5,000	(b)	−1,450	(k)	+500	
(f)	+1,000	(e)	− 150			
(i)	+1,500	(h)	− 500			
		(k)	− 500			

The decrease in the asset is offset by a decrease in the owner's equity. A separate temporary owner's equity account, Rent Expense, is debited (increased) to show the indirect decrease in owner's equity. Cash is credited to record the reduction in assets. When a separate account is kept for each expense, the total amount of expenses incurred can be determined without having to analyze the capital account.

Transaction l

Purchase of office supplies worth $150 on account from Hollis Supply Company.

	Accounts Payable				Office Supplies Expense	
(e)	−150	(c)	+450	(l)	+150	
		(l)	+150			

Liabilities have been increased, and owner's equity has been decreased. The reduction in owner's equity results from the incurrence of an expense. Accounts Payable is credited to record the increase to liabilities.

The decrease to owner's equity (expense increase) is recorded by debiting the expense account.

Throughout the process of recording these transactions, the equality of the accounting equation has been maintained as has the equality of the debits and credits.

The Recording Process

Most businesses need more information than T accounts can provide. They also need a more orderly, detailed way to account for their operations during a certain period of time. To accomplish this, certain procedures are performed in sequence during each time period. This sequence is called the **accounting cycle.** The accounting cycle is divided into several steps, but in this chapter only the recording process is discussed. The recording process includes (1) analyzing transactions, (2) recording transactions, and (3) posting transactions.

Source Documents

Up to this point, limited information has been provided about business transactions, and few details have been given about the proper recording process. In actual practice, specific data is provided for each transaction and a formal recording procedure is followed.

Data about each transaction is first recorded on a printed or written business form or paper. Such materials are called **source documents.** They serve to describe each transaction in detail. For instance, sales tickets provide the facts about sales of goods on credit. Bank deposit slips give information about amounts of money deposited in a firm's bank account. Time cards, check stubs, cash register tapes, and invoices are all forms of source documents.

Source documents are usually paper forms with the data written or printed on them, but with the increasing use of data processing, source documents may also appear as computer punched cards or paper tapes. The computer age has also introduced such devices as magnetic tapes and magnetic ink characters that can function as source documents.

The Journal

Recording debit and credit entries directly into T accounts is not practical for a number of reasons.

1. Each account shows only one half of a transaction, either the debit or credit entry. In order to locate a specific transaction, it might be necessary to search through every account to find both the debit and credit entries.
2. There is a greater chance of error due to the usually large number of debit and credit entries in each T account.
3. Locating errors is difficult because the debit and credit for each transaction do not appear together.
4. No daily record of transactions is kept.

Figure 2.1 A two-column general journal.

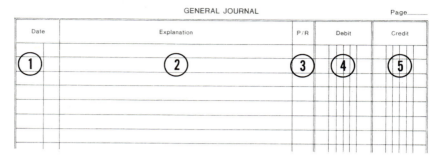

To avoid these problems, each transaction is first recorded in a book or a record known as a **journal** before being entered in the individual accounts. A journal contains a chronological record of all transactions. A journal is often thought of as a diary of a business. It is also referred to as a **book of original entry** because it contains the first formal recording of each transaction. The source document remains as the original record of a transaction, but it is not the first record in terms of double-entry accounting. The journal is recognized as the first step in double-entry accounting.

The process of entering transactions in a journal does not change the rules of debiting and crediting. Nor does it change the practice of recording transactions in accounts. It only changes the order in which these things are done.

Journals are available in many different forms. The particular form a company chooses depends upon the size of the firm and the nature of its operations. The simplest form is a two-column, all-purpose journal called the **general journal.** In contrast, a business may choose several multicolumn journals, each designed to handle a single type of transaction. These multicolumn journals are called **special journals.** In this chapter, only the general journal will be explained. Special journals will be discussed in chapter 7.

A two-column journal is shown in figure 2.1. The standard form consists of the following elements, which are keyed in figure 2.1:

1. A date column for recording the date of each transaction (the date the transaction occurs, not the date on which it is recorded)
2. An explanation or description column for recording the names of accounts affected by the transaction
3. A posting reference (PR) column for recording the account numbers to which amounts are transferred from the journal
4. A debit money column for recording debit amounts
5. A credit money column for recording credit amounts

A journal can be a bound book or a loose-leaf notebook. Entries can be made either by hand or by machine. Many businesses are currently switching to the use of machines.

Journalizing Transactions

A standard procedure, known as **journalizing,** is used for entering each transaction in a journal. The information to be journalized originates from a source document. The source document must be analyzed to determine the entry to be made in the journal. From this analysis, the accountant must determine—

1. what accounts are affected.
2. how they are affected (increased or decreased).
3. how the accounts are classified (asset, liability, owner's equity, revenue, or expense).
4. how increases or decreases to each of the accounts are recorded (by debiting or crediting).

Once these things have been determined, the transaction is entered in the journal in the manner described in figure 2.2.

The elements of the journal are keyed in the figure as follows:

1. Each page of the journal is numbered consecutively beginning with the number 1.
2. The date on which each transaction occurs is entered in the divided Date column. The year and month are written only once at the top of each page. They are not repeated on the page unless the year or month changes with a future entry on the page. The day is written for each transaction regardless of the number of transactions that occur on any one day.

Figure 2.2 Entries in a general journal.

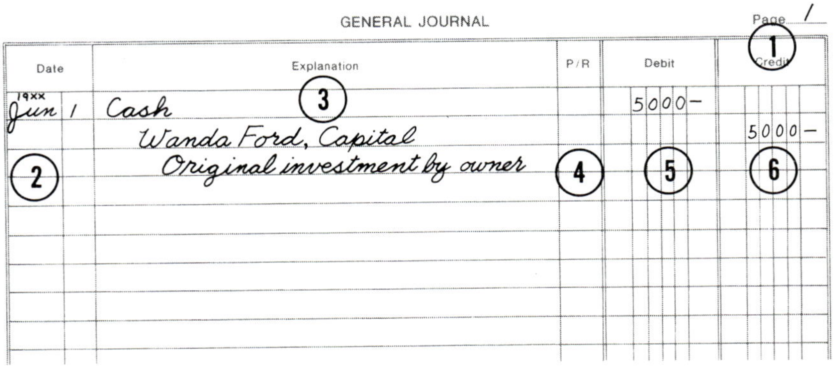

3. The titles of the accounts to be debited and credited, together with a brief explanation of the transaction, are entered in the Explanation column. The title of the account to be debited is written first along the left margin of the column on the same line as the date. The title of the account to be credited is written on the line below the debit entry. Credit entries are usually indented about one-half inch from the left margin. A brief explanation is written on the line below the credit entry. It too is indented slightly. Explanations should be concise, containing only pertinent information about the transaction. Occasionally, the explanation may be omitted if the nature of the transaction is obvious from the account titles.

4. Nothing is written in the Posting Reference column at the time the journal entry is made. This column is used when debit and credit amounts are transferred to the proper accounts. This procedure is explained later in this chapter.

5. The amount to be debited is written in the Debit column on the same line as the account title.

6. The amount to be credited is written in the Credit column on the same line as the account title.

The record of the transaction in the journal is called a **journal entry**. The business transactions of Dr. Wanda Ford provided in chapter 1 are again referred to in the examples in this chapter. Dates of the transactions have been added to facilitate the explanations. An entry should be journalized either at the time the transaction occurs or shortly thereafter.

The transactions for Dr. Wanda Ford are reviewed in the following list and journalized in figure 2.3.

19XX

June 1 Wanda Ford invested $5,000 cash to establish a medical practice.

12 Purchased medical equipment for $1,450 cash.

12 Bought $450 worth of office furniture on account from Hollis Supply Company

20 Purchased additional medical equipment by means of personal note of $500 to the Standard Equipment Company.

30 Paid Wilson Furniture Company $150 on account.

July 1 Made an additional investment of $1,000 cash.

1 Made additional investment of medical equipment worth $1,000.

Figure 2.3 Journalizing the transactions of Dr. Wanda Ford.

GENERAL JOURNAL   Page 1

Date	Explanation	P/R	Debit	Credit
19XX Jun 1	Cash		5000 —	
	Wanda Ford, Capital			5000 —
	Original investment by owner			
12	Medical Equipment		1450 —	
	Cash			1450 —
	Purchased medical equipment for cash			
12	Office Furniture		450 —	
	Accounts Payable			450 —
	Bought office furniture on account from Wilson Furniture Company			
20	Medical Equipment		500 —	
	Notes Payable			500 —
	Gave personal note to Standard Equipment Company for equipment			
30	Accounts Payable		150 —	
	Cash			150 —
	Paid Wilson Furniture Company on account			
Jul 1	Cash		1000 —	
	Wanda Ford, Capital			1000 —
	Additional investment by owner			
1	Medical Equipment		1000 —	
	Wanda Ford, Capital			1000 —
	Additional investment of medical		9550 —	9550 —
	equipment by owner			

5   Withdrew $500 for personal use.

10   Cash receipts of $1,500 for professional services for one week.

10   Performed services worth $150 on a charge basis.

31   Paid $500 rent for one month.

31   Purchased office supplies for $150 on account from Hollis Supply Company.

Figure 2.3—*Continued*

Date		Explanation	P/R	Debit	Credit
19XX Jul	5	Wanda Ford, Drawing		500—	
		Cash			500—
		Withdrawal of cash by owner			
	10	Cash		1500—	
		Professional Fees			1500—
		Cash receipts for professional services			
	10	Accounts Receivable		150—	
		Professional Fees			150—
		Professional services on account			
	31	Rent Expense		500—	
		Cash			500—
		Paid rent for one month			
	31	Office Supplies Expense		150—	
		Accounts Payable			150—
		Purchased office supplies on account		2800—	2800—
		from Hollis Supply Company			

Some points to be remembered when recording in the general journal are as follows:

1. Journal pages are numbered consecutively beginning with the number 1.
2. For each transaction, the total debits must equal the total credits.
3. The PR column is left blank at the time the entries are recorded. This column is used later when the amounts for the entries are transferred to the proper accounts.
4. Each entry should contain at least one debit amount, one credit amount, and an explanation. List first the account(s) to be debited, followed by the account(s) to be credited.
5. The complete entry should appear on one page. If there is not room to record the entire transaction on a page, begin the transaction on the following page.
6. Leave a blank line between each entry for ease in identifying each transaction.

Figure 2.4 A compound journal entry.

Aug	3	Medical Equipment	600	—		
		Cash			200	—
		Accounts Payable			400	—
		Purchased medical equipment for				
		cash ($200); remainder on account ($400)				

In some journal entries, more than two accounts are involved. An entry affecting more than two accounts is called a **compound journal entry.** A compound entry can involve more than one debit or more than one credit or both. Regardless of the number of accounts included in a compound entry, total debits must always equal total credits.

To illustrate how a compound entry is recorded, assume that Dr. Ford purchased additional medical equipment worth $600 on August 3. She paid $200 cash and charged the remaining $400. The journal entry for this transaction appears in figure 2.4.

An increase in one asset (Medical Equipment) is offset by a combined decrease in an asset (Cash) and an increase in the liability (Accounts Payable). The debit of $600 is offset by credits of $200 to Cash and $400 to Accounts Payable, and the debits and credits remain equal.

Proving the Journal

Since total debits must always equal total credits, the accuracy of the entries in the journal should be checked before transferring any amounts to individual accounts. The process of checking the accuracy of the debits and credits is known as **proving the journal.** This is done by totaling the amount columns. If the totals of the two columns are the same, the journal has been proved. However, it should be noted that those totals are proof only that the debit amounts equal the credit amounts. The procedure for proving the journal does not indicate whether other types of errors exist in the journal.

The total of each column is written on the last line of each filled page of the journal. On a partially filled page, the totals are written under the last entry on the page.

If the totals of the amount columns do not equal, the error or errors must be found and corrected. Errors are corrected by drawing a single line through the incorrect amount (fig. 2.5). The correction is then entered directly above the canceled amount. The person making the correction may

Figure 2.5   Correcting a journal error.

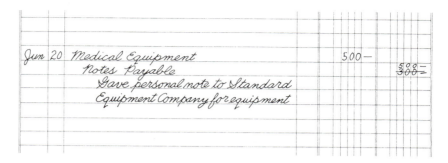

be required to initial the correction in the event questions arise later. Errors are not usually erased since that would completely remove the original entry. Furthermore, the practice of erasing could allow someone to alter accounting records with little difficulty. Such changes would also be hard to detect in a routine examination of the records.

This same procedure is followed in correcting any type of error found in the journal, whether it be an error in an amount, a date, a title, or an explanation.

The General Ledger

A journal provides a chronological listing of the daily transactions of a business. But a journal by itself is an incomplete means of keeping records. It does not provide information about all the changes for a specific account in one place. To find all the changes that have occurred in an account, it is necessary to check all the journal entries. Therefore, in order to be useful, the information recorded in a journal must be transferred to the proper accounts.

A separate account is kept for each asset, liability, owner's equity, revenue, and expense account. All of these accounts are grouped together in a book called the **general ledger,** or simply the **ledger.** The ledger serves as the second (or final) book of entry.

Generally, a separate page is used for each account, but more than one page may be used for an account that contains a large number of entries. These accounts may be kept on sheets of paper, computer cards, or plastic tape. They may be stored in bound books, in looseleaf binders, on cards in trays, or on tapes that yield computer printouts. Regardless of how they are kept, all the accounts are referred to as the general ledger.

In actual practice, a T account is not used since most businesses need more information than it provides. Instead, an expanded version of the T account, called the **standard two-column account,** and a four-column form, called the **balance form,** are commonly used. Another form, the **three-column balance form,** is illustrated and explained in chapter 8.

Figure 2.6 Standard two-column account form.

ACCOUNT _____ Account No._____

Date	Item	P/R	Debit	Date	Item	P/R	Credit

The standard two-column form shown in figure 2.6 provides two identically ruled sides for recording debit and credit amounts. The Date and PR columns provide a means of tracing an entry back to the journal or other source. The Item column, although seldom used, is included to record additional information about a transaction when necessary. Space for writing the account name and number is provided across the top of the form.

The four-column account form is preferred by many firms since the current balance of an account is always available. This account form contains four money columns instead of two. The first two money columns are used to record the amounts of the entries, and the last two are used to record the account balance. The column headings indicate where debit and credit amounts and balances are to be recorded. The Date, Item, and PR columns serve the same functions as in the two-column form. The four-column form is illustrated in figure 2.7.

Figure 2.7 Four-column balance form.

ACCOUNT _____ Account No._____

Date	Item	P/R	Debit	Credit	Balance	
					Debit	Credit

Figure 2.8 Chart of accounts.

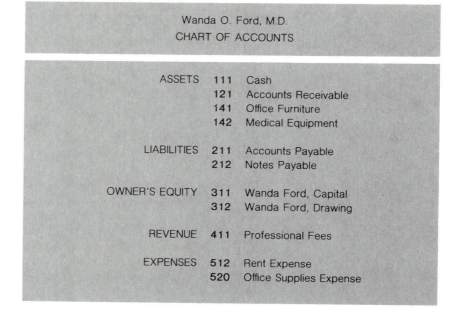

Wanda O. Ford, M.D.
CHART OF ACCOUNTS

ASSETS	111	Cash
	121	Accounts Receivable
	141	Office Furniture
	142	Medical Equipment
LIABILITIES	211	Accounts Payable
	212	Notes Payable
OWNER'S EQUITY	311	Wanda Ford, Capital
	312	Wanda Ford, Drawing
REVENUE	411	Professional Fees
EXPENSES	512	Rent Expense
	520	Office Supplies Expense

The Chart
of Accounts

Accounts are grouped in the ledger according to their classification. The standard order of accounts in the ledger is (1) assets, (2) liabilities, (3) owner's equity, (4) revenue, and (5) expenses. Not only does this grouping make the recording process easier, but also it aids in the preparation of financial statements.

As stated earlier, the number of accounts a firm uses depends on its size and the nature of its business. The extent of detailed information needed for financial reports must also be considered. The titles assigned to the various accounts depend on these same factors. One of the first tasks in setting up the accounting records of a firm is to decide upon the accounts that are necessary in the operation of the firm.

Each account is assigned a number, and the accounts are arranged in the ledger in numerical order. The numbering system is based on the five classifications of accounts. Accounts beginning with 1 represent assets; 2, liabilities; 3, owner's equity; 4, revenue; and 5, expenses. The first digit in any account number identifies the group in which the account belongs. The other digits indicate the position of the specific account within the general account grouping.

A list of all the accounts in the general ledger by name and number must first be prepared. This list is known as a **chart of accounts.** Accounts are arranged in the ledger in the same order as they are listed in the chart of accounts. A chart of accounts for Dr. Wanda Ford is shown in figure 2.8.

Observe that within each classification the numbers are not consecutive. The gaps in the numbering are intentional so that new accounts may be inserted in proper sequence. This way the insertion of new accounts can be made without disturbing other account numbers.

A three-digit numbering system is used in figure 2.8. This represents only one of the many different systems that can be used. Whatever numbering system is used, the chart of accounts makes it possible to locate an account quickly and easily.

Posting

After transactions have been journalized, the next step in the recording process is to transfer the debit and credit amounts in each journal entry to the proper general ledger accounts. The process of transferring information contained in the journal entries to the ledger is called **posting.**

Posting data to the proper ledger accounts makes it possible to summarize the changes taking place in the accounts. These summaries aid in the preparation of financial statements. Until posting has been completed, the information contained in a journal is in a relatively cumbersome form.

In posting, each amount listed in the Debit column of the journal is transferred to the debit column of the specific account named in the entry. Likewise, each amount entered in the Credit column of the journal is transferred to the credit column of the specific account named in the entry.

The following figures and explanations illustrate the posting procedure. The debit portion of the journal entry in figure 2.2 is posted as shown in figure 2.9.

Figure 2.9   Posting the debit portion of a journal entry.

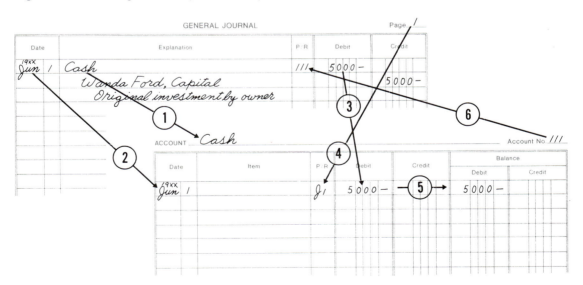

The posting procedure for the debit portion is performed in the following manner:

1. Find the account to be debited in the ledger.
2. Write the date of the transaction (not the date of the posting) in the Date column.
3. Write the amount in the Debit column.
4. Write the journal posting reference in the PR column. The reference J1 indicates that the amount is posted from page 1 of the general journal. The number in the PR column always tells where the entire entry (not just the debit or credit portion) can be found.
5. Enter the amount representing the balance of the account in the proper Balance (debit or credit) column.
6. Write the ledger posting reference (account number) in the PR column of the general journal.

The same procedure is followed when posting the credit portion of the journal entry (fig. 2.10).

Figure 2.10 Posting the credit portion of a journal entry.

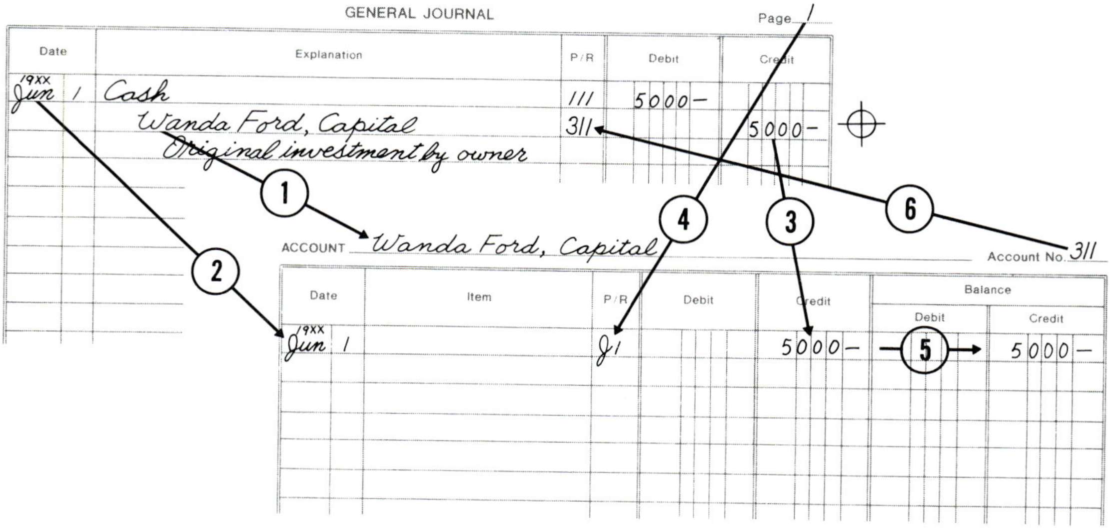

The complete ledger of Wanda Ford is shown in figure 2.11. All items have been properly posted from the journal entries in figure 2.3. Note the following features in the posting:

1. The year has been entered at the top of the Date column and the month is written only once even though there are several entries in some accounts during the same month.

Figure 2.11a   General journal of Dr. Ford's transactions.

GENERAL JOURNAL   Page 1

Date	Explanation	P/R	Debit	Credit
19XX				
Jun 1	Cash	111	5000 —	
	Wanda Ford, Capital	311		5000 —
	Original investment by owner			
12	Medical Equipment	142	1450 —	
	Cash	111		1450 —
	Purchased medical equipment for cash			
12	Office Furniture	141	450 —	
	Accounts Payable	211		450 —
	Bought office furniture on account from Wilson Furniture Company			
20	Medical Equipment	142	500 —	
	Notes Payable	212		500 —
	Gave personal note to Standard Equipment Company for equipment			
30	Accounts Payable	211	150 —	
	Cash	111		150 —
	Paid Wilson Furniture Company on account			
Jul 1	Cash	111	1000 —	
	Wanda Ford, Capital	311		1000 —
	Additional investment by owner			
1	Medical Equipment	142	1000 —	
	Wanda Ford, Capital	311		1000 —
	Additional investment of medical equipment by owner		9550 —	9550 —

Figure 2.11a—*Continued*

GENERAL JOURNAL   Page 2

Date	Explanation	P/R	Debit	Credit
19XX Jul 5	Wanda Ford, Drawing	312	500 —	
	Cash	111		500 —
	Withdrawal of cash by owner			
10	Cash	111	1500 —	
	Professional Fees	411		1500 —
	Cash receipts for professional services			
10	Accounts Receivable	121	150 —	
	Professional Fees	411		150 —
	Professional services on account			
31	Rent Expense	512	500 —	
	Cash	111		500 —
	Paid rent for one month			
31	Office Supplies Expense	520	150 —	
	Accounts Payable	211		150 —
	Purchased office supplies on account		2800 —	2800 —
	from Hollis Supply Company			

2. The Item column is not used (fig. 2.11 *b*). Rarely is anything written in this column since it is usually not necessary to repeat the explanation from the journal.

3. Cross-referencing in the PR column makes it easy to trace any entry from the journal to the ledger or from the ledger back to the journal.

4. After posting is completed, both the journal and the ledger contain the same information.

5. Journal entries are posted line by line. The posting of *both* debit and credit entries for each transaction is completed before the posting of the next transaction is begun.

   As previously indicated, if posting errors are found, the method of correcting them depends upon the type of error. If a wrong amount has been entered, simply draw a line through the wrong amount and write the correct amount above it. When a debit amount is posted as a credit, or vice versa, draw a line through the posting in the incorrect column. Then write

Figure 2.11b General ledger accounts.

ACCOUNT _Cash_   Account No. _111_

Date		Item	P/R	Debit	Credit	Balance Debit	Balance Credit
19XX Jun	1		J1	5000 —		5000 —	
	12		J1		1450 —	3550 —	
	30		J1		150 —	3400 —	
Jul	1		J1	1000 —		4400 —	
	5		J2		500 —	3900 —	
	10		J2	1500 —		5400 —	
	31		J2		500 —	4900 —	

ACCOUNT _Accounts Receivable_   Account No. _121_

Date		Item	P/R	Debit	Credit	Balance Debit	Balance Credit
19XX Jul	10		J2	150 —		150 —	

ACCOUNT _Office Furniture_   Account No. _141_

Date		Item	P/R	Debit	Credit	Balance Debit	Balance Credit
19XX Jun	12		J1	450 —		450 —	

ACCOUNT _Medical Equipment_   Account No. _142_

Date		Item	P/R	Debit	Credit	Balance Debit	Balance Credit
19XX Jun	12		J1	1450 —		1450 —	
	20		J1	500 —		1950 —	
Jul	1		J1	1000 —		2950 —	

ACCOUNT _Accounts Payable_   Account No. _211_

Date		Item	P/R	Debit	Credit	Balance Debit	Balance Credit
19XX Jun	12		J1		450 —		450 —
	30		J1	150 —			300 —
Jul	31		J2		150 —		450 —

Figure 2.11*b*—*Continued*

ACCOUNT _Notes Payable_   Account No. _212_

Date	Item	P/R	Debit	Credit	Balance Debit	Balance Credit
19XX Jun 20		J1		500—		500—

ACCOUNT _Wanda Ford, Capital_   Account No. _311_

Date	Item	P/R	Debit	Credit	Balance Debit	Balance Credit
19XX Jun 1		J1		5000—		5000—
Jul 1		J1		1000—		6000—
1		J1		1000—		7000—

ACCOUNT _Wanda Ford, Drawing_   Account No. _312_

Date	Item	P/R	Debit	Credit	Balance Debit	Balance Credit
19XX Jul 5		J2	500—		500—	

ACCOUNT _Professional Fees_   Account No. _411_

Date	Item	P/R	Debit	Credit	Balance Debit	Balance Credit
19XX Jul 10		J2		1500—		1500—
10		J2		150—		1650—

ACCOUNT _Rent Expense_   Account No. _512_

Date	Item	P/R	Debit	Credit	Balance Debit	Balance Credit
19XX Jul 31		J2	500—		500—	

ACCOUNT _Office Supplies Expense_   Account No. _520_

Date	Item	P/R	Debit	Credit	Balance Debit	Balance Credit
19XX Jul 31		J2	150—		150—	

the correct information in the proper column of the account. If an amount has been posted to the wrong account, the correction should be made through a journal entry, transferring the amount to the proper account.

Transactions should be journalized as soon as possible after the transaction occurs to lessen the risk of forgetting or losing important information. On the other hand, posting can be done on a less rigid schedule. If it is convenient, the posting can be done immediately after the transaction is journalized. However, posting is an activity that is often left to be done when other more pressing tasks have been completed. In some firms, the accountant waits until a large number of journal entries have been made and then posts all the entries at the same time. In other firms, posting is done after each journal page is filled or at the end of a day, week, or month. The needs of the business dictate the frequency with which the posting is done. Regardless of how often journal entries are posted, the information in the accounts should be kept up to date.

Posting completes the recording process of the accounting cycle. The flow of data through the recording process is summarized in figure 2.12.

Figure 2.12   Flow of data through the recording process.

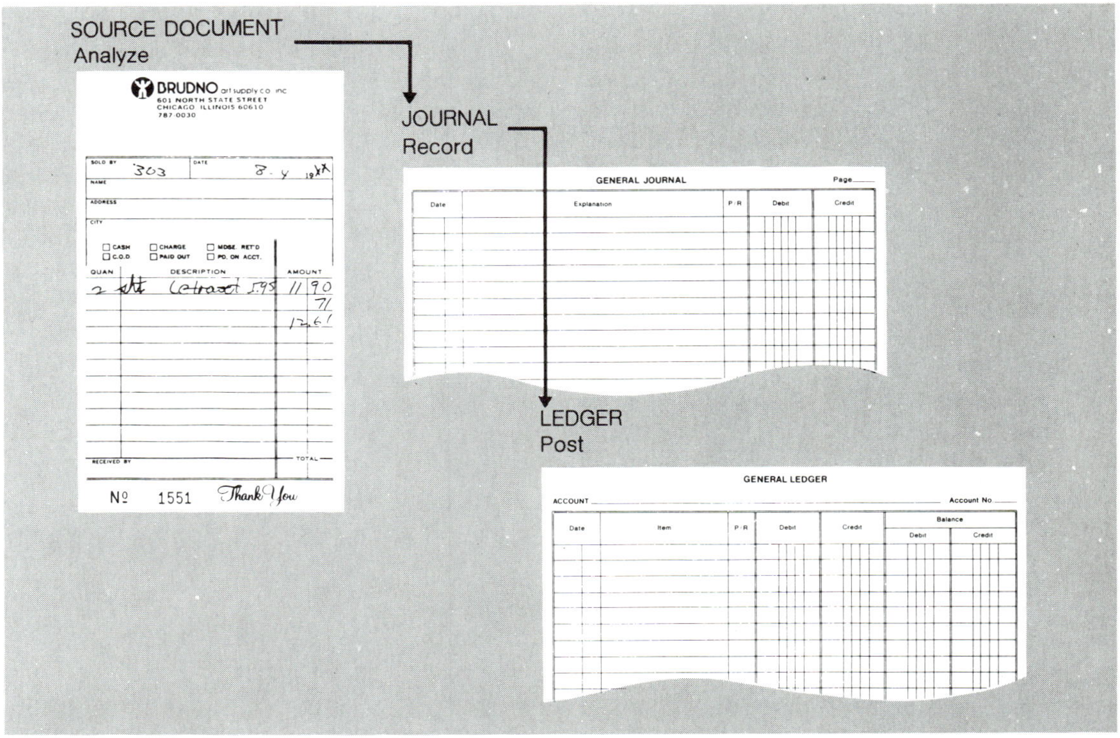

Summary

A separate account is maintained for each asset, liability, owner's equity, revenue, and expense account. Each account has a debit and credit column for recording increases or decreases. For every debit recorded, there must be a corresponding credit, and after each transaction has been recorded, debits must equal credits (pp. 20–21).

The recording process of the accounting cycle includes three steps: (1) analyzing, (2) recording, and (3) posting transactions (p. 25). The first evidence of business transactions comes from forms called source documents, which contain the facts about the transactions (p. 25). After these documents are analyzed, the transactions are entered in chronological order in a book called a journal. The journal is considered to be a book of original entry since it contains the first formal record of each transaction (pp. 25–27). The procedure for entering transactions in a journal is called journalizing (p. 27), and, in all journal entries, total debits must equal total credits.

The separate account sheets for each asset, liability, owner's equity, revenue, and expense are kept together in a book called the general ledger (pp. 32–33). These separate ledger accounts provide information about all the changes for a specific account in one place and make it easy to summarize information needed in the preparation of financial reports. Each account is given a number, and all accounts are grouped in the ledger in numerical order according to the five classifications. The name and number of all accounts in the ledger are listed in proper numerical order in a chart of accounts (pp. 34–35).

Debit and credit amounts for each journal entry are transferred, or posted, to the proper accounts in the ledger (pp. 35–41). Once journal entries have been posted, the recording process is complete. The flow of accounting data through the recording process is illustrated as follows:

Analyze   *Record*   *Post*

Source Documents ⟶ Journal ⟶ Ledger

Key Terms

account Device used to individually record and summarize changes in asset, liability, owner's equity, revenue, and expenses.

accounting cycle A sequence of procedures for handling the financial records of a company; the steps followed for each accounting period.

chart of accounts A list showing the arrangement of the accounts in the general ledger by name and number.

compound journal entry A journal entry that involves more than two accounts or more than one debit or credit.

credit The right side of an account.

debit The left side of an account.

general journal A book in which a chronological record of all business transactions is kept; book of original entry.

general ledger A book containing all of a firm's accounts; book of final entry.

journal entry The formal record of a transaction in a journal.

journalizing The process of recording a transaction in a journal.

posting The process of transferring information contained in a journal entry to the general ledger accounts.

proving the journal The process of checking the accuracy of the debit and credit columns on a page of a journal.

source document A printed or written form that contains the facts about a business transaction.

Objectives

Upon completion of this chapter, you should be able to:

1. Prepare a trial balance.
2. Prepare an income statement.
3. Prepare a balance sheet in account form.

3 The Accounting Cycle
The Reporting Process

---

4. Define the following accounting terms:

account balance	income statement
accounting period	normal balance
balance sheet	statement of owner's equity
calendar year	trial balance
fiscal year	

The first steps in the accounting cycle were discussed in chapter 2. These steps—analyzing, recording, and posting—make it easier for the accountant to trace a firm's daily transactions. The next steps in the cycle include adjusting, closing, and reporting activities. However, this chapter will deal only with the reporting process.

Periodic summaries of a firm's business activities are prepared as a standard practice. The specific period of time for which these summaries are prepared is called the **accounting period**. This period of time may vary; it can be a month, three months (a quarter), six months, or a year. An accounting period that covers a full year and ends on December 31 is called a **calendar year**. An accounting period that covers a full year and ends in a month other than December is called a **fiscal year**.

Summaries of the firm's operations are presented in two major reports called **financial statements**. One of these statements, the **income statement**, presents the results of operations *during the accounting period*. The other, the **balance sheet**, relates information about the financial status of the business *as of a given date*. Prior to the preparation of these statements, an informal report called a **trial balance** is prepared.

The Trial Balance

Because debits must equal credits in double-entry accounting, each journal entry should be carefully checked to ensure an accurate balance. Additional proof that debits equal credits in journal entries is yielded by simply totaling the two amount columns on each page of a journal. If the totals are equal, the equality of debits and credits in the journal is proven. Once posting to the general ledger accounts has been completed, the debit balances of the accounts must also equal the credit balances. A periodic check should also be made to verify the accuracy of the posting to ledger accounts. This accuracy check is accomplished by means of a statement called a **trial balance**, which is a listing of the ledger accounts and their debit or credit balances. The trial balance is not actually a formal statement since only the accountant sees it. It is more of a working paper used primarily to prove the equality of the debit and credit balances. In addition, it is used to locate errors and to provide data needed to prepare the financial statements. A trial balance may be prepared at any time, but it is usually prepared at the end of each accounting period.

Balancing
the Accounts

The first step in preparing a trial balance is to determine the balance of each ledger account. An **account balance** is the difference between the total debits and total credits in an account. The **normal balance** of any account occurs on the side where increases are recorded. This concept is based on the premise that increases in an account are usually greater than or equal to decreases. Therefore, normal balances are regarded as positive. Asset

Figure 3.1 Two-column account form balancing.

ACCOUNT _Cash_   Account No. _111_

Date	Item	P/R	Debit	Date	Item	P/R	Credit
19XX Jun 1		J1	5 0 0 0 —	19XX Jun 12		J1	1 4 5 0 —
Jul 1		J1	1 0 0 0 —	30		J1	1 5 0 —
10		J2	1 5 0 0 —	Jul 5		J2	5 0 0 —
	4,900–		7 5 0 0 –	31		J2	5 0 0 —
	③ ④	①				②	2 6 0 0 –

and expense accounts normally have debit balances, while liability, owner's equity, and revenue accounts normally have credit balances.

When a two-column account form is used, the balances of each ledger account must be determined at the time the trial balance is being prepared. The process for obtaining the balances is as follows:

1. Total the amounts in the debit column and record the total in *small* figures directly under the last debit amount. This total is written in pencil and is called a **footing**.
2. Total the amounts in the credit column and again record the total (footing) in small figures directly under the last amount.
3. Subtract the smaller total from the larger total to determine the account balance.
4. Record the balance in the Item column in small pencil figures on the side that has the larger total. If the total of the debit side is larger, the account is said to have a **debit balance**. If the total of the credit side is larger, the account is said to have a **credit balance**.
5. If an account has only one entry, it is not necessary to compute the footing since that one entry is the balance of the account.
6. If an account has several entries but they are all on one side, the footing of the column represents the account balance.
7. If the footings of an account are equal, the account is said to be in balance.

This process, referred to as **balancing the accounts**, is illustrated in figure 3.1. The steps in the balancing process are keyed in the figure.

If the four-column balance form of account is used, none of these steps are necessary since a current balance is always shown for each account. The ledger accounts of Dr. Wanda Ford, showing balances for the period ending July 31, 19XX, are reproduced in figure 3.2.

Figure 3.2 Balancing of four-column form.

ACCOUNT _Cash_   Account No. _111_

Date		Item	P/R	Debit	Credit	Balance	
						Debit	Credit
19XX Jun	1		J1	5000 —		5000 —	
	12		J1		1450 —	3550 —	
	30		J1		150 —	3400 —	
Jul	1		J1	1000 —		4400 —	
	5		J2		500 —	3900 —	
	10		J2	1500 —		5400 —	
	31		J2		500 —	4900 —	

ACCOUNT _Accounts Receivable_   Account No _121_

Date		Item	P/R	Debit	Credit	Balance	
						Debit	Credit
19XX Jul	10		J2	150 —		150 —	

ACCOUNT _Office Furniture_   Account No. _141_

Date		Item	P/R	Debit	Credit	Balance	
						Debit	Credit
19XX Jun	12		J1	450 —		450 —	

ACCOUNT _Medical Equipment_   Account No _142_

Date		Item	P/R	Debit	Credit	Balance	
						Debit	Credit
19XX Jun	12		J1	1450 —		1450 —	
	20		J1	500 —		1950 —	
Jul	1		J1	1000 —		2950 —	

ACCOUNT _Accounts Payable_   Account No. _211_

Date		Item	P/R	Debit	Credit	Balance	
						Debit	Credit
19XX Jun	12		J1		450 —		450 —
	30		J1	150 —			300 —
Jul	31		J2		150 —		450 —

Figure 3.2— *Continued*

ACCOUNT __Notes Payable__ Account No. 212

Date	Item	P/R	Debit	Credit	Balance Debit	Balance Credit
19XX Jun 20		J1		500 —		500 —

ACCOUNT __Wanda Ford, Capital__ Account No. 311

Date	Item	P/R	Debit	Credit	Balance Debit	Balance Credit
19XX Jun 1		J1		5000 —		5000 —
Jul 1		J1		1000 —		6000 —
1		J1		1000 —		7000 —

ACCOUNT __Wanda Ford, Drawing__ Account No. 312

Date	Item	P/R	Debit	Credit	Balance Debit	Balance Credit
19XX Jul 5		J2	500 —		500 —	

ACCOUNT __Professional Fees__ Account No. 411

Date	Item	P/R	Debit	Credit	Balance Debit	Balance Credit
19XX Jul 10		J2		1500 —		1500 —
10		J2		150 —		1650 —

ACCOUNT __Rent Expense__ Account No. 512

Date	Item	P/R	Debit	Credit	Balance Debit	Balance Credit
19XX Jul 31		J2	500 —		500 —	

ACCOUNT __Office Supplies Expense__ Account No. 520

Date	Item	P/R	Debit	Credit	Balance Debit	Balance Credit
19XX Jul 31		J2	150 —		150 —	

Figure 3.3 Debit and credit account balances.

Wanda O. Ford, M.D.
Trial Balance
July 31, 19XX

Account Name	Debit	Credit
Cash	4900 —	
Accounts Receivable	150 —	
Office Furniture	450 —	
Medical Equipment	2950 —	
Accounts Payable		450 —
Notes Payable		500 —
Wanda Ford, Capital		7000 —
Wanda Ford, Drawing	500 —	
Professional Fees		1650 —
Rent Expense	500 —	
Office Supplies Expense	150 —	
	9600 —	9600 —

After the balance has been determined for each account, the information is then reported in the format shown in figure 3.3.

The three-line heading is centered at the top of the report as shown in figure 3.3. The heading includes information about *who* (the company name), *what* (the name of the report), and *when* (the date on which the report is prepared).

Also note in figure 3.3 that the accounts are listed in the first column in the order in which they appear in the ledger. Sometimes, a column is also provided for the account numbers. The balance of each account is recorded in the proper debit or credit column. Generally only those accounts with balances are shown in the trial balance, although some accountants list all accounts whether or not they have a balance.

After all account balances have been listed, the amount columns are totaled using small pencil footings. If the totals of the two columns are equal, the amounts are written in large figures and the columns are double-ruled under the totals. In accounting, double rules indicate that the information shown above the rules is complete.

Discovery and Solution of Errors

If the column totals of the trial balance do not agree, one or more of the following errors could be responsible for the difference:

1. One of the columns of the trial balance was incorrectly added.
2. An incorrect amount of an account balance was recorded.

3. An account balance was recorded in the wrong column or omitted entirely.
4. An error was made in computing an account balance.
5. Only half of a journal entry was posted or both halves of an entry were posted on the same side of an account (two debits rather than a debit and a credit).

The fact that the debit and credit columns are equal does not always provide complete proof of the accuracy of the records kept for the accounting period. The equality of these columns merely proves that, *as recorded*, the debits equal the credits. Some types of errors that are not revealed by the trial balance are—

1. Failing to record a transaction.
2. Posting a part of a transaction in the wrong account. For example, a debit to the Cash account could be posted as a debit to the Medical Equipment account.
3. Posting the same transaction more than once.
4. Posting the same incorrect amount for both the debit and credit entries of a transaction.
5. Making offsetting arithmetic errors.

A specific procedure for locating errors in the trial balance does not exist; however, the first step in locating errors is to determine the amount of the difference between the two column totals. In many cases, this difference provides a clue to the type or location of the error. For example, the difference could be attributed to the omission of a debit or credit balance. On the other hand, if the difference is divisible by two, the error can most likely be attributed to the recording of a debit as a credit or vice versa. This type of error results in the trial balance being off by twice the amount involved.

Probably the most common errors are mistakes in addition. If the difference in the totals is a multiple of ten, in all likelihood, the error can be attributed to incorrect addition.

The transposition of numbers is another cause of errors in a trial balance. Transposing numbers involves altering the sequence of the numbers—recording $526 as $256 or $562. If this type of error occurs, the difference in the totals is evenly divisible by 9. Another type of error that can be detected in this same manner is known as a **slide**. A slide results when a decimal is shifted from its proper position, such as writing $526 as $52.60 or $5,260.

If the error cannot be detected by using one of these procedures, it is generally advisable to work back step-by-step until the error is found. The following sequence for retracing the recording procedure is suggested:

1. Readd the columns.
2. Check that all account titles together with their correct balances have been listed.
3. Recheck the balances for each account.
4. Check the transactions against the accounts to see that each entry is correctly posted.

Usually, it is not necessary to go through all these steps before detecting the error. Also, a trial balance that does not balance pinpoints the period in which an error has been made. Therefore, there is no need to check for errors beyond the date of the last correct trial balance.

The Income Statement

As noted earlier, one of the two major financial statements prepared periodically is the income statement. The income statement is a statement showing the revenue, expenses, and net income or net loss for a certain period of time. This statement shows the results of a firm's operations for the period and relates how successful a firm has been at maximizing its profit. It is sometimes referred to as a **profit and loss statement** or a **statement of operations**. The time period covered by the statement can vary but is rarely longer than one year.

A certain format is used in preparing the income statement. Revenue items are presented first, followed by the expense items. Total expenses are subtracted from total revenue to arrive at the net income for the period. When expenses exceed revenue, the difference represents a net loss.

The income statement may be either typed or handwritten. If it is handwritten, two-column, ruled paper is used. The columns are for entering amounts of money only and are not designated as debit or credit columns.

The income statement for Dr. Wanda Ford for the two months ending July 31, 19XX, is reproduced in figure 3.4. The following paragraphs represent the steps in the preparation of an income statement.

The centered three-line heading at the top of the statement contains information regarding who, what, and when. The company name (who) is entered on the first line, the name of the statement (what) on the second line, and the period of time (when) on the third. The income statement is concerned with the financial transactions during a certain period of time rather than the financial status on a specific date. For example, if the period of time is one month, the date line reads For the Month Ended July 31, 19XX. If the period of time is one year, the date line reads For the Year Ended December 31, 19XX.

Figure 3.4   Income statement.

Wanda O. Ford, M.D.			
Income Statement			
For the Two Months Ended July 31, 19XX			
Revenue:			
Professional Fees			1650 —
Expenses:			
Rent Expense		500 —	
Office Supplies Expense		150 —	
Total Expenses			650 —
Net Income			1000 —

The section heading Revenue is written on the first line along the left margin. The title of the revenue account is written on the second line and indented about one-half inch. If there are several revenue accounts, each one is listed on a separate line and aligned along the same indent. When there is only one revenue account, the amount is written in the second money column. If there are several revenue accounts, each amount is listed in the first money column. The total of these amounts is then written in the second money column. If there are several revenue accounts, the words *Total Revenue* are indented and written on the same line as the total figure in the second money column. If there is only one revenue account, it is not necessary to write Total Revenue.

The heading Expenses is written along the left margin under the last revenue entry. The titles of each expense account are listed and indented. The amount of each expense is written in the first money column. If there is only one expense, the amount is entered in the second money column. The words *Total Expenses* are indented and written beneath the last expense item, and the total amount of the expenses is written on the same line in the second money column.

A single rule is drawn under the last item in the second money column. Total expenses are subtracted from the total revenue. The difference is written under the single-ruled line. That difference is identified as Net Income or Net Loss. Double rules are then drawn under that figure. The double rules indicate that the report is complete and assumed to be correct.

The income statement in figure 3.4 is a simple one. However, as information becomes more detailed and complex, such a simple format may not be suitable. Variations in this form are illustrated in later chapters.

The Balance Sheet

Along with the information provided by the income statement, a firm needs information about its financial status. This information is provided by a statement called a balance sheet or a **statement of financial position**. The balance sheet is a report showing a firm's assets, liabilities, and owner's equity as of a given date. The balance sheet is, in effect, summarizing the information presented in the basic accounting equation. As a major financial statement, it lists the balances of the asset, liability, and owner's equity accounts and shows that the sum of the assets is equal to the sum of the liabilities and the owner's equity.

A balance sheet is originally prepared by a firm on the day it begins operations. This beginning balance sheet shows the value of the assets, liabilities, and owner's equity at the time the firm comes into existence. After that, the common practice is to prepare the balance sheet only at the end of an accounting period.

Account Form

One form that is used in preparing a balance sheet is called an **account form**, so named because of its resemblance to a standard account form. This form also bears a resemblance to the basic accounting equation. Assets are listed on the left side of the form. Liabilities and owner's equity are listed on the right. The columns on either side of the form are for entering amounts of money; they are not thought of as debit or credit columns in this instance.

The balance sheet for Dr. Wanda Ford shown in figure 3.5 uses the account form. Some guidelines for preparing a balance sheet using the account form are discussed here.

A three-line heading showing who, what, and when is centered at the top of the balance sheet. The date recorded is the day on which the statement is prepared.

The heading Assets is centered on the first line on the left side of the balance sheet. Each asset is listed along the left margin, and the amount of each asset is written on the same line in the first money column. In later chapters, it will be seen that assets are usually listed in the order in which they are expected to be exchanged for cash or used. Cash is always listed first because it is the most "liquid" asset. The totals of both sides of the balance sheet are written on the same line. Therefore, the words *Total Assets* and the amount of the total are not written until the right-hand side of the balance sheet is completed.

The heading Liabilities is centered on the first line on the right side of the balance sheet. Each liability is listed along the margin. The amount of each liability is written on the same line in the first money column. The liabilities in this example are listed in the order in which they appear in the trial balance. Usually, though, liabilities are listed in the order in which they must be paid. The ones with the earliest due dates are listed first. The

Figure 3.5 Balance sheet, account form.

Wanda O. Ford, M.D.
Balance Sheet
July 31, 19XX

ASSETS			LIABILITIES		
Cash	4900 —		Accounts Payable	450 —	
Accounts Receivable	150 —		Notes Payable	500 —	
Office Furniture	450 —		Total Liabilities		950 —
Medical Equipment	2950 —				
			OWNER'S EQUITY		
			Wanda Ford		
			Capital, June 1, 19XX	7000 —	
			Net Income $1000 —		
			less Withdrawals 500 —		
			Net Increase	500 —	
			Capital, July 31, 19XX		7500 —
Total Assets		8450 —	Total Liabilities and Owner's Equity		8450 —

words *Total Liabilities* and the amount of the total are written as shown in figure 3.5.

Skip a line and center the heading Owner's Equity under the liabilities section. Then the owner's name is written on a line by itself at the margin. Capital and the date of the beginning of the accounting period is written next and indented as shown. The amount is entered in the first money column. Net Income Less Withdrawals is written in the manner illustrated. The difference represents the net increase or decrease in the equity. That amount is entered in the first money column. On the following line is written Capital and the date on which the balance sheet is being prepared. The amount entered in the second money column is the total of the beginning capital plus the increase (or minus a decrease) in equity. A single line is drawn under the last amount in the second money column on the right-hand side and on the same line of the second money column on the left-hand side. Total the assets on the left-hand side. Enter the amount in the second money column below the single line, and write the words *Total Assets* on the same line. On the right-hand side, add the liabilities and owner's equity. Enter the total under the single ruled line. On the same line write the words *Total Liabilities and Owner's Equity*. The two totals should agree. Place a double rule under the totals to indicate that the balance sheet is complete and in balance.

Another way of handling the owner's equity section is to prepare a **statement of owner's equity** (fig. 3.6) as a separate report. This way only the figure representing the owner's equity need be shown in that section of the balance sheet.

An alternative form of the balance sheet, called the **report form**, is also frequently used. The report form is particularly well suited for recording more detailed and complex accounting information. In the report form, the liabilities and owner's equity are listed below the assets instead of to the right of them. The report form of the balance sheet is shown in figure 3.7.

Figure 3.6 Statement of owner's equity.

Wanda O. Ford, M.D.
STATEMENT OF OWNER'S EQUITY
July 31, 19XX

Wanda Ford, Capital, June 1, 19XX		$7,000
Net Income	$1,000	
less Withdrawals	500	
Net Increase		500
Wanda Ford, Capital, July 31, 19XX		$7,500

Figure 3.7 Balance sheet, report form.

Wanda O. Ford, M.D.
BALANCE SHEET
July 31, 19XX

ASSETS

Cash	$4,900	
Accounts Receivable	150	
Office Furniture	450	
Medical Equipment	2,950	
Total Assets		$8,450

LIABILITIES AND OWNER'S EQUITY

Liabilities		
Accounts Payable	$ 450	
Notes Payable	500	
Total Liabilities		$ 950
Owner's Equity		
Wanda Ford, Capital, June 1, 19XX		7,000
Net Income	$1,000	
less Withdrawals	500	
Net Increase		500
Wanda Ford, Capital, July 31, 19XX		7,500
Total Liabilities and Owner's Equity		$8,450

Figure 3.8   Relationship of the income statement and the balance sheet.

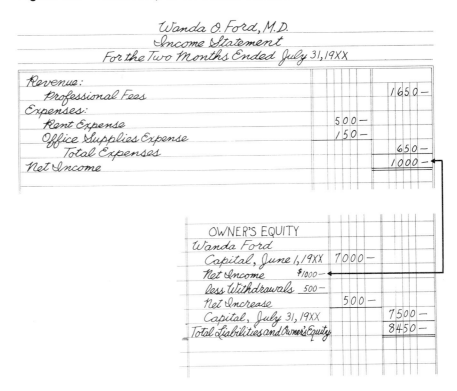

Wanda O. Ford, M.D.
Income Statement
For the Two Months Ended July 31, 19XX

Revenue:		
Professional Fees		1650 —
Expenses:		
Rent Expense	500 —	
Office Supplies Expense	150 —	
Total Expenses		650 —
Net Income		1000 —

OWNER'S EQUITY			
Wanda Ford			
Capital, June 1, 19XX	7000 —		
Net Income	$1000 —		
less Withdrawals	500 —		
Net Increase		500 —	
Capital, July 31, 19XX			7500 —
Total Liabilities and Owner's Equity			8450 —

In preparing a balance sheet, the amounts for each asset and liability are derived from the trial balance. In the owner's equity section, the amount of the owner's beginning capital is also taken from the trial balance. The net income (or net loss) is determined from the income statement. The withdrawal amount is indicated in the trial balance.

The relationship between the income statement and the balance sheet is reflected in the owner's equity section of the balance sheet (fig. 3.8). The net income figure from the income statement is the link between the two statements. The owner's equity section of the balance sheet shows how changes in the owner's equity occur whether they result from business operations or from actions by the owner. When a net income is shown on the income statement, that increase shows up as an increase in the owner's equity on the balance sheet. When a net loss results, that loss shows up as a decrease in the owner's equity on the balance sheet. Likewise, when assets have been withdrawn by an owner, that withdrawal is shown on the balance sheet as a decrease in the owner's equity. For illustration purposes, assume that Dr. Ford has a net loss of $1,000. This loss is shown in the owner's equity section of the balance sheet in figure 3.9.

Figure 3.9 A net loss in the owner's equity section of the balance sheet.

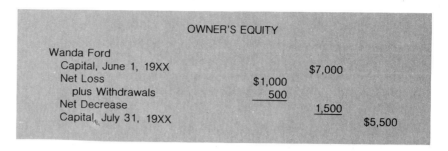

OWNER'S EQUITY		
Wanda Ford		
Capital, June 1, 19XX		$7,000
Net Loss	$1,000	
plus Withdrawals	500	
Net Decrease		1,500
Capital, July 31, 19XX		$5,500

Both the balance sheet and the income statement may be handwritten or typewritten. Handwritten statements are prepared on ruled accounting paper; in which case, dollar signs, decimals, and commas are used only with amounts *not* written in a money column. As a general rule, dollar signs are used ony when the financial statements are prepared for use by someone outside the firm. In that situation, dollar signs are placed in front of the first amount listed in a column and in front of the final total.

Summary

The reporting process includes the preparation of reports that give information about a firm's financial condition and the results of operations over a certain period of time. The specific period of time covered by these reports is called the accounting period (p. 46). The reports themselves are known as financial statements (p. 46).

After the transactions for a period have been journalized and posted, it is customary to prepare an informal report called a trial balance. A trial balance lists the ledger accounts and their debit and credit balances (pp. 46–50). It is used primarily as a means of verifying the accuracy of the posting to the general ledger and to assure that debit balances equal credit balances. It also provides the data needed to prepare the financial statements.

The first of these financial statements is the income statement. The income statement shows the results of a firm's operations for a certain period of time. It shows the revenue, expense, and net income or net loss for that period. Sometimes referred to as a profit and loss statement, it relates how successful a firm has been in maximizing its profit (pp. 52–53).

Information in the trial balance is also used in preparing a second important financial statement—the balance sheet. The balance sheet shows the firm's assets, liabilities, and owner's equity as of a given date and is often referred to as a statement of financial position (pp. 54–56).

There is a relationship between the financial statements that is reflected in the owner's equity section of the balance sheet. In that section, the statements are linked together by the net income or loss figure from the income statement. Changes that occur in the owner's equity due to actions of the owner and to business operations are detailed in that section of the balance sheet (pp. 57–58).

Key Terms

account balance The difference between the total debits and total credits in an account.

accounting period A period of time for which summaries of a firm's operations are prepared.

balance sheet A statement showing a firm's financial condition as of a specific date; often called a statement of financial position; lists the firm's assets, liabilities, and owner's equity.

calendar year An accounting period that covers one full year and ends on December 31.

fiscal year An accounting period that covers one full year and ends in a month other than December.

income statement A statement showing the results of operations for a period of time; often called a profit and loss statement; lists revenue, expenses, and net income or net loss.

normal balance The side of an account on which increases are recorded.

statement of owner's equity A statement showing the owner's net income (or net loss) and the withdrawals during an accounting period.

trial balance A listing of ledger accounts and their debit or credit balances; a means of proving the equality of debits and credits in the ledger.

Upon completion of this chapter, you should be able to:

1. Record transactions for a professional service enterprise in a combined journal.
2. Post transactions from a combined journal to general ledger accounts.

4 Accounting for a Personal Service Enterprise

3. Define the following accounting terms:

cash system of accounting   depreciation

combined journal   personal service enterprise

contra account   summary posting

Accountants are responsible for keeping records for two basic types of enterprises: (1) merchandising and (2) personal service. The preceding chapters have relied heavily on the example of Dr. Wanda Ford, who is engaged in a personal service enterprise, to illustrate some basic accounting procedures. In this chapter, the accounting procedures used by a personal service enterprise will be explained more fully. A discussion of the accounting procedures for a merchandising firm is presented in chapter 8.

Any firm that derives the major portion of its revenue from services performed for customers is classified as a **personal service enterprise.** Unlike merchandising or manufacturing businesses, which make or sell goods or products, the activities of a personal service enterprise seldom involve buying and selling. Occasionally, a service firm may sell some items in addition to the service it provides; however, the main source of revenue is still from providing a service. For example, a carpet cleaning service might sell rug shampoo or other cleaning products, but that does not provide the major source of revenue.

Personal service enterprises are classified into two types: (1) **professional enterprises,** which include doctors, dentists, lawyers, public accountants, engineers, and architects; and (2) **business enterprises,** which include businesses engaged in insurance, real estate, entertainment, advertising, transportation, storage, and consulting. In both classifications, the main source of revenue is the sale of services.

There are two basic systems of accounting for revenue currently in use: (1) the **accrual system**, which is used by merchandising and manufacturing firms (see chapters 8 and 9); and (2) the **cash system,** which is used mainly by service enterprises.

Cash System of Accounting

In the cash system of accounting, revenues are not considered earned until they are collected in cash. This means that revenue is not recorded until the cash has been received. It is possible that a service could be performed in one period, but the revenue not accounted for until a succeeding period. For example, a dentist could perform services for a patient in 1981 for which payment would not be made until 1982. The revenue would be recorded in 1982 when the cash was actually received.

The same principle is applied in accounting for expenses on a cash basis. Expenses are recorded only when cash has actually been paid out. Expenses are charged to the period in which the cash is actually disbursed, even though the expenses may have been incurred during an earlier period.

The cash system of accounting is preferred by most service enterprises because it is simple and convenient to use. However, a strictly cash basis of accounting for revenue and expenses is almost impossible. According to certain federal and state tax laws, some types of income must be accounted for in the period earned, whether or not the cash has been collected. Also, certain types of expenses must be recorded in the period in which they are incurred even though no cash has been paid out.

Exceptions to the cash system of accounting for expenses are usually made in connection with long-lived assets, advance payments of insurance premiums, and the purchase of large amounts of supplies. It is not practical to charge the cost of a long-lived asset as an expense of the period in which it is purchased. Such a practice distorts the financial statements for that period. Since long-lived assets are expected to serve for a number of years, their cost must be allocated over the estimated years of use. For instance, if machinery expected to serve a useful life of ten years is purchased for cash, a portion of the total cost of that machinery is charged as an expense to each of the expected years of service. It is unrealistic to charge the total cost in the month or year of purchase and nothing thereafter.

The portion of the cost assigned to each period is recorded as **depreciation expense.** A simple means of determining depreciation expense is to divide the depreciable cost (gross cost less salvage value) by the expected years of use. Precise methods for figuring depreciation expense are explained in chapter 10.

Another exception to the cash basis of accounting for expenses involves advance payments for insurance premiums. When the insurance coverage exceeds a period of one year, the total cost must be prorated over the life of the insurance contract.

The purchase of large amounts of supplies for cash is another common exception. If a large quantity of the supplies remains unused at the end of the period, the entire amount should not be treated as an expense of that period. Only the cost of those supplies actually used should be charged as an expense of the period. However, if the amount of supplies purchased is small, their cost is usually charged directly as an expense at the time of purchase.

Since these exceptions make it impossible to account for revenue and expenses on a strictly cash basis, a modified cash system of accounting is actually being used. The modified cash system requires some adjustments for depreciation, expired insurance, and supplies used at the end of the accounting period. The manner of handling these adjustments is explained in chapter 5.

Records Kept by a Doctor

The modified cash system of accounting typically used by a doctor is described in the following pages. The records for the private practice of Dr. Wanda O. Ford are again used as examples.

The accounting procedures and forms used in most doctors' offices are somewhat similar. Dr. Ford uses a patient service record (PSR) form (fig. 4.1) for recording such information as diagnoses, charges, and payments. This form is especially designed to simplify the billing and insurance reporting process.

Figure 4.1   Patient service record form.

ACCOUNT NUMBER			INSURED'S NAME _____		PSR NUMBER
MONTH	DAY	YEAR	ADDRESS _____		

CITY & STATE _____

TELEPHONE _____

PATIENT'S RELATIONSHIP TO INSURED
SELF   SPOUSE   CHILD   OTHER

PATIENT NAME   FIRST NAME   LAST NAME

DATE OF BIRTH ___ / ___ / ___

FOR SERVICES RELATED TO HOSPITALIZATION
GIVE HOSPITALIZATION DATES
ADMITTED   DISCHARGED
HOSPITAL:

Insurance Co. _____   Address _____   City & State _____   Zip _____

Policy # _____   Blue Cross Cert. # _____   Group # _____

OTHER HEALTH INSURANCE COVERAGE - Enter
Name of Policyholder and Plan Name and Address
and Policy or Medical Assistance Number.

SERVICES AND PROCEDURES

PLACE OF SERVICE   ☐ OV   ☐ IH   ☐ OH   ☐ ER

DIAGNOSIS

VAGINITIS
CERVICITIS
VULVITIS
UPPER TRACT INFECTION
URINARY TRACT INFECTION
PREGNANCY
ABDOMINAL PAIN
ABNORMAL UTERINE
    BLEEDING
OVARIAN CYST
POST-MENOPAUSAL
    BLEEDING
DYSMENORRHEA
INCOMPLETE ABORTION
INABILITY TO TOLERATE
    CONTRACEPTIVES
INFERTILITY
SYMPTOMATIC PELVIC
    RELAXATION
ABNORMAL PAP SMEAR
BREAST MASS
FIBROIDS
BARTHOLIN CYST
ENDOMETRIOSIS
OTHER:

Wanda O. Ford, M.D. / OB-GYN
Branch Medical Center
642 Mesa Vista, NE
Albuquerque, NM 87131
Phone (505) 292-0545

RVS #	DESCRIPTION	CODE	FEES
	EXAMINATIONS		
90060	GYN EXAM & EVALUATION	001	
90050	OFFICE VISIT	086	
90015	NEW PATIENT	214	
	POST OP CARE	160	
	OFFICE PROCEDURES		
58300	IUD INSERTION	228	
59862	THERAPEUTIC ABORTION	189	
	OBSTETRICAL CARE		
59400	NEW OB CARE	216	
	OB VISIT	059	
	LABORATORY		
88150	PAP SMEAR	150	
81000	URINALYSIS	535	
85034	HEMALOG	537	
86006	PREGNANCY TEST	226	
89007	PRENATAL LAB	212	
87210	WET PREP	542	
	SURGICAL		
58120	D & C	234	
58982	TUBAL LIGATION	078	
OTHER			

TOTAL FEE ▶

PATIENT'S OR AUTHORIZED PERSON'S SIGNATURE.
I Authorize the Release of any Medical Information Necessary to Process this Claim.

SIGNED _____   DATE _____

I AUTHORIZE PAYMENT OF MEDICAL BENEFITS TO ABOVE PHYSICIAN
FOR SERVICE DESCRIBED.

SIGNED (Insured or Authorized Person) _____

APPOINTMENT					CODE	AMOUNT	CODE	AMOUNT
TIME	MO.	DAY	YR.					
				PAYMENTS				

Figure 4.2 Statement of patient transactions.

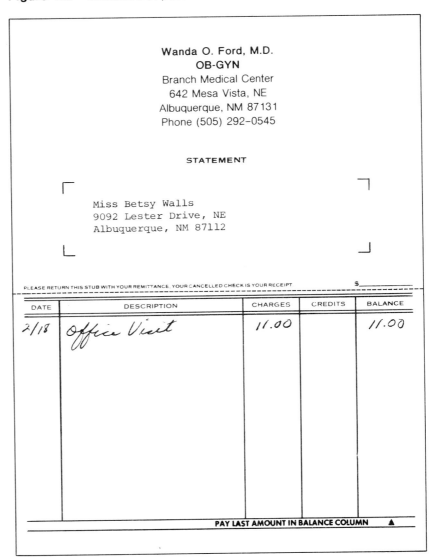

At the end of each billing period, statements showing the charges, payments, and current balance (fig. 4.2) are prepared from the PSR forms. Then when payment is received, it is recorded as revenue. If payment is made at the time of the office visit, the PSR form is marked *Paid* and the amount of payment is entered on the books as revenue. No statement is sent to the patient. Cash or any major bank credit card is an acceptable

Figure 4.3 Medicare request form.

REQUEST FOR MEDICARE PAYMENT

MEDICAL INSURANCE BENEFITS—SOCIAL SECURITY ACT (See Instructions on Back—**Type or Print Information**)

No Part B Medicare benefits may be paid unless this form is received as required by existing law and regulations (20 CFR 422.510)

NOTICE—Anyone who misrepresents or falsifies essential information requested by this form may upon conviction be subject to fine and imprisonment under Federal Law.

Form Approved
OMB No. 066-R-0012

PART I—PATIENT TO FILL IN ITEMS 1 THROUGH 6 ONLY

Copy from YOUR OWN HEALTH INSURANCE CARD *(See example on back)*

1 Name of patient (First name, Middle initial, Last name)

2 Health insurance claim number *(Include all letters)*   ☐ Male   ☐ Female

3 Patient's complete mailing address (including Apt. no.)   City, State, ZIP Code   Telephone Number

4 Describe the illness or injury for which you received treatment *(Always fill in this item if your doctor does not complete Part II below)*   Was your illness or injury connected with your employment? ☐ Yes ☐ No

5 If any of your medical expenses will be or could be paid by another insurance organization or government agency, show below

Name and address of organization or agency   Policy or Identification Number

Note: If you **Do Not** want information about this Medicare claim released to the above upon its request, check (X) the following block ☐

6 I authorize any holder of medical or other information about me to release to the Social Security Administration and Health Care Financing Administration or its intermediaries or carriers any information needed for this or a related Medicare claim. I permit a copy of this authorization to be used in place of the original, and request payment of medical insurance benefits either to myself or to the party who accepts assignment below.

SIGN HERE ▶   Signature of patient *(See instructions on reverse where patient is unable to sign)*   Date signed

PART II—PHYSICIAN OR SUPPLIER TO FILL IN 7 THROUGH 14

7 A. Date of each service	B. Place of service (*See Codes below)	C. Fully describe surgical or medical procedures and other services or supplies furnished for each date given (if lab service, indicate if automated) Procedure Code	D. Nature of illness or injury requiring services or supplies	E. Charges (If related to unusual circumstances explain in 7C)	Leave Blank
				$	

8 Name and address of physician or supplier *(Number and street, city, State, ZIP code)*   Telephone No.

Physician or supplier code

9 Total charges $

10 Amount paid $

11 Any unpaid balance due $

12 Assignment of patient's bill   ☐ I accept assignment *(See reverse)*   ☐ I do not accept assignment.

13 Name and address of person or facility where services were furnished *(if other than your own office or patient's residence).*

14 Signature of physician or supplier *(A physician's signature certifies that a physician's services were personally rendered by the physician or under the physician's personal direction).*   Date Signed

*O—Doctor's Office   H—Patient's Home *(if portable X-ray services, identify the supplier)*   SNF—Skilled Nursing Facility   OL—Other Locations
IL—Independent Laboratory   IH—Inpatient Hospital   OH—Outpatient Hospital   NH—Nursing Home

FORM **HCFA-1490 (2)** (7-77) (FORMERLY SSA-1490 (2))   Department of Health, Education, and Welfare—Health Care Financing Administration

form of payment; or a patient may assign charges to an insurance company or Medicare (fig. 4.3).

Today it is common practice for many professional service enterprises to contract computer services firms to handle their billing and collection records. If a computer service is used, copies of each PSR form, or a facsimile, are sent to the computer service. Records of payments received are also transmitted to the computer service. The computer service holds all the information until the end of the billing period. Then each patient is mailed a statement similar to the one in figure 4.4, which shows charges, payments, and the current balance. The accountant in the doctor's office also receives a copy of the statement and keeps that on file as a memorandum record for each patient.

Figure 4.4 Patient account statement.

STATEMENT OF ACCOUNT

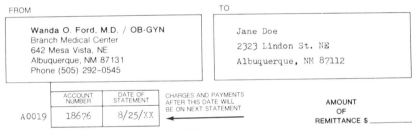

FROM	TO
Wanda O. Ford, M.D. / OB-GYN Branch Medical Center 642 Mesa Vista, NE Albuquerque, NM 87131 Phone (505) 292-0545	Jane Doe 2323 Lindon St. NE Albuquerque, NM 87112

	ACCOUNT NUMBER	DATE OF STATEMENT	CHARGES AND PAYMENTS AFTER THIS DATE WILL BE ON NEXT STATEMENT	AMOUNT OF REMITTANCE $ _____
A0019	18676	8/25/XX		

PLEASE RETURN TOP PORTION OF STATEMENT WITH PAYMENT

Date	Patient	Description	Amount
7/25	JANE DOE	90050-OFFICE VISIT	14.00
7/25		PAYMENT-CHECK	14.00CR
7/28	JANE DOE	90050-OFFICE VISIT	14.00
7/28	JANE DOE	81000-URINALYSIS	5.25
7/28	JANE DOE	G C SMEAR & CULT	9.00
7/28		PAYMENT-CHECK	20.00CR
		CHARGES INCLUDE APPLICABLE TAXES	

ANNUAL PERCENTAGE RATE	MONTHLY PERCENTAGE RATE	COMPUTED ON BALANCE OF	COMPUTED ON BALANCE OVER	MINIMUM PAYMENT	BALANCE
					8.25

CURRENT	AGE OF PAST DUE BALANCES			PAY EITHER ▲ AMOUNT ▲ SEE REVERSE SIDE
	31-60 DAYS	61-90 DAYS	OVER 90 DAYS	
8.25				PAYMENTS EXPECTED FROM INSURANCE ARE NOT REFLECTED UNTIL RECEIVED

If you have questions about your bill, please call ___123-4567___
If you have insurance claim questions, please call ___123-4556___

A partial chart of accounts for Dr. Ford is reproduced in figure 4.5. Notice that there are some accounts that begin with 0. The 0-numbered accounts are called **contra accounts.** A contra account is one that is directly related to another account and is used to record reductions in the balance of the related account. These reductions are shown on the balance sheet. The balance of the contra account is subtracted from the balance of its

Figure 4.5   Dr. Ford's chart of accounts.

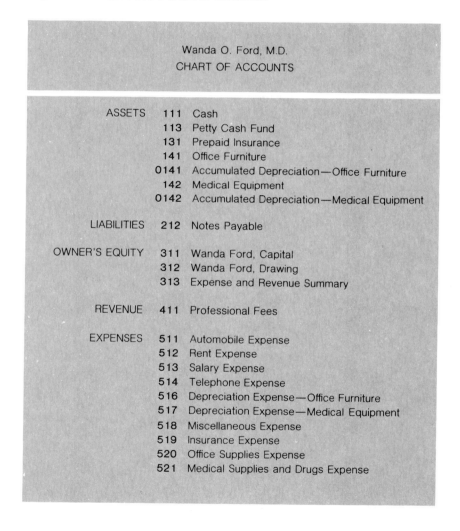

Wanda O. Ford, M.D.
CHART OF ACCOUNTS

ASSETS	111	Cash
	113	Petty Cash Fund
	131	Prepaid Insurance
	141	Office Furniture
	0141	Accumulated Depreciation—Office Furniture
	142	Medical Equipment
	0142	Accumulated Depreciation—Medical Equipment
LIABILITIES	212	Notes Payable
OWNER'S EQUITY	311	Wanda Ford, Capital
	312	Wanda Ford, Drawing
	313	Expense and Revenue Summary
REVENUE	411	Professional Fees
EXPENSES	511	Automobile Expense
	512	Rent Expense
	513	Salary Expense
	514	Telephone Expense
	516	Depreciation Expense—Office Furniture
	517	Depreciation Expense—Medical Equipment
	518	Miscellaneous Expense
	519	Insurance Expense
	520	Office Supplies Expense
	521	Medical Supplies and Drugs Expense

related account. The amount remaining is the actual value that is reported on the balance sheet. A contra account has a balance that is the opposite of the balance of its related account and is therefore referred to as an offsetting account. Each contra account is listed immediately following its related account.

The Combined Journal

Dr. Ford uses several books of account; however, only two are discussed in this chapter, the combined journal and the general ledger. She also keeps other detailed records, such as payroll and petty cash. These records will be discussed in later chapters.

In chapter 2 the use of the general journal was illustrated. Several of the transactions entered in the journal involved the same account or accounts. Cash figured in seven of the twelve transactions. Journalizing and posting the transactions involved much repetition. Repetition is costly and time-consuming; therefore, the accountant looks for ways to simplify the process. One way to do so is to use a special journal called a **combined journal.** A combined journal is a multicolumn journal that provides special columns for those accounts that have a large number of transactions. For example, a large number of transactions generally involve a debit to Cash; therefore, a special column in the journal might be Cash Debit. A combined journal can be designed to meet the specific needs of a firm by providing special debit and/or credit columns for frequently used accounts. In addition, General columns are provided for debits and credits to accounts for which there are no special columns. Since most of these combined journals include special amount columns for the Cash account, they are sometimes referred to as *combined cash journals.*

A combined journal saves both time and space. Most transactions can be recorded on one line. The use of special column headings eliminates the need to write the title for each account affected by the transaction. Explanations are usually not needed since most transactions are self-explanatory. Explanations can still be added in the Account Title column if the account titles do not provide adequate information about a transaction.

Additional time is saved in posting. It is not necessary to post each entry in a combined journal. The totals of special columns are posted only once—at the end of the month. The only individual posting necessary is for those amounts entered in the General column.

An example of the combined journal used by Dr. Ford is shown in figure 4.6. Special columns have been provided for Cash Dr. and Cr., General Dr. and Cr., Professional Fees Cr., and Medical Supplies and Drugs Expense Dr. The following representative transactions for December are shown in the journal:

19XX

December 1 Paid $950 office rent for the month. Check No. 72.

1 Received checks for $1,965 from patients for office visits.

4 Paid telephone bill of $94. Check No. 73.

4 Issued Check No. 74 to Moffitt Insurance Company for premiums for coverage for office furniture and equipment for three years, $375.

7 Purchased medical supplies and drugs from the Pitcher Drug Company, $197. Check No. 75.

8 Received checks from patients and insurance companies for $2,292.

8 Performed the end-of-the-week work.

11 Issued Check No. 76 to Dailey Service Station for gasoline and other automobile expenses charged during November, $65.

11 Dr. Ford withdrew $250 for personal use. Check No. 77.

14 Issued Check No. 78 to Lyons Office Supply Company for office supplies charged during November, $159.

14 Bought medical supplies and drugs from Crandall Medical Supply, $86. Check No. 79.

15 Paid office salaries for the period December 1 to December 15, $1,034. Check No. 80.

15 Cash receipts from patients totaled $2,076 for the week.

15 Performed the end-of-the-week work.

19 Received $796 from insurance companies for patients' accounts.

Figure 4.6 Combined journal.

For the month of *December*, 19XX — COMBINED JOURNAL — Page 25

Cash Deposits DR	Cash Checks CR	Ck. No.	Date	Explanation or Account	P/R	General DR	General CR	Professional Fees CR	Med. Supp. & Drugs Exp. DR
				Cash balance 10,564—					
	950—	72	19XX Dec 1	Rent Expense	512	950—			
1965—			1	Professional Fees	√			1965—	
	94—	73	4	Telephone Expense	514	94—			
	375—	74	4	Prepaid Insurance	131	375—			
	197—	75	7	Pitcher Drug Company	√				197—
2292—			8	Professional Fees	√			2292—	
4257—								4257—	197—
	65—	76	11	Automobile Expense 13,205—	511	1419— 65—			
	250—	77	11	Wanda Ford, Drawing	312	250—			
	159—	78	14	Office Supplies Expense	520	159—			
	86—	79	14	Crandall Medical Supply	√				86—
	1034—	80	15	Salary Expense	513	1034—			
2076—			15	Professional Fees	√			2076—	
6333—	3210—		19	Professional Fees 13,687—	√	2927—		6333—	283—
796—								796—	
	137—	81	21	Crandall Medical Supply	√				137—
3073—			22	Professional Fees	√			3073—	
10202—	3347—		27	Miscellaneous Expense 77,419—	518	2927— 250—		10202—	420—
	157—	83	27	Pitcher Drug Company	√				157—
2297—			28	Professional Fees	√			2297—	
	1034—	84	29	Salary Expense	513	1034—			
				78,275—		4211—			
12499—	4788—							12499—	577—
(111)	(111)					(√)		(411)	(521)

21 Purchased medical supplies and drugs from Crandall Medical Supply, $137. Check No. 81.

22 Cash receipts for the week totaled $3,073.

22 Performed the end-of-the-week work.

27 Issued Check No. 82 for charitable contribution, $250.

27 Purchased medical supplies from Pitcher Drug Company, $157. Check No. 83.

28 Received checks from patients and insurance companies totaling $2,297.

29 Paid office salaries for the period December 16 to December 31, $1,034. Check No. 84.

29 Performed the end-of-the-week work.

The following activities are usually performed at the end of each week:

1. The journal is proved. Each column is totaled using small pencil footings. The sum of the footings of the debit columns should equal the sum of the footings of the credit columns.
2. The bank balance is proved. Add the total of the Cash Dr. column to date to the beginning cash balance; subtract the total of the Cash Cr. Column to date. Enter the new balance in the Account Title column.
3. Entries in the General Dr. and Cr. columns are posted individually to the proper ledger accounts.

At the end of each month, the journal and the bank balance are proved and the remaining entries in the General Dr. and Cr. columns are posted individually. Special column totals are posted as described on page 73.

The recording process is greatly simplified by the use of the combined journal. The column headings aid in the selection of the debits and credits. Notice that most of the transactions have been recorded on one line; however, as many lines as necessary should be used in order to make the entry complete and clear. The Account Title column is used to record the account title for which there is no special column. If special columns are provided for each account affected by the transaction, the Account Title column may be used for a brief explanation.

Posting from the
Combined Journal

Posting is simplified when a combined journal is used since much repetitive posting is avoided by the use of the special columns. The procedure for posting from a combined journal is as follows (refer again to fig. 4.6):

1. The items in the General columns are posted individually. Individual posting is usually done on a daily or weekly basis; however, the accountant usually decides on a schedule that fits the needs of the office. As each entry is posted, the ledger account number is recorded in the PR column of the combined journal. In the individual ledger account, the notation CJ25 (combined journal, page 25) is entered in the PR Column.

2. For each transaction that is recorded completely in the special columns of the journal, no individual posting is necessary. A check mark is placed in the PR column to indicate that individual posting is not required. Some accountants prefer to use an NP (not posted) reference in such cases. If NP is used, the check mark can be used exclusively for posting to subsidiary ledgers. (Subsidiary ledgers are explained in chapter 8.)

3. The total of each special column is posted to the proper ledger account. This process is often called **summary posting.** As each total is posted, the ledger account number is written in parentheses under the column total, and the page number of the combined journal is entered in the PR column of the ledger account. A check mark is placed under the General Dr. and Cr. columns to show that these totals are not to be posted.

Once the posting has been completed, the accounts in the general ledger are then balanced. When the standard two-column form is used, balancing the accounts is done in the manner described in chapter 3. If, however, the four-column balance account form is used, a current balance is readily available so the necessity for balancing each account is eliminated. The four-column form is used for the ledger accounts shown in figure 4.7.

Figure 4.7 Dr. Ford's ledger accounts.

ACCOUNT _Cash_   Account No. _111_

Date		Item	P/R	Debit	Credit	Balance	
						Debit	Credit
Dec	1	Balance	✓			10564 —	
	29		CJ25	12499 —		23063 —	
	29		CJ25		4788 —	18275 —	

ACCOUNT _Petty Cash_   Account No. _113_

Date		Item	P/R	Debit	Credit	Balance	
						Debit	Credit
Dec	1	Balance	✓			150 —	

ACCOUNT _Prepaid Insurance_   Account No. _131_

Date		Item	P/R	Debit	Credit	Balance	
						Debit	Credit
Dec	4		CJ25	375 —		375 —	

ACCOUNT _Office Furniture_   Account No. _141_

Date		Item	P/R	Debit	Credit	Balance	
						Debit	Credit
Dec	1	Balance	✓			5300 —	

Figure 4.7 — *Continued*

ACCOUNT _Accumulated Depreciation — Office Furniture_   Account No. _0141_

Date	Item	P/R	Debit	Credit	Balance Debit	Balance Credit
Dec 19XX 1	Balance	✓				1060 —

ACCOUNT _Medical Equipment_   Account No. _142_

Date	Item	P/R	Debit	Credit	Balance Debit	Balance Credit
Dec 19XX 1	Balance	✓			14560 —	

ACCOUNT _Accumulated Depreciation — Medical Equipment_   Account No. _0142_

Date	Item	P/R	Debit	Credit	Balance Debit	Balance Credit
Dec 19XX 1	Balance	✓				2912 —

ACCOUNT _Notes Payable_   Account No. _212_

Date	Item	P/R	Debit	Credit	Balance Debit	Balance Credit
Dec 19XX 1	Balance	✓				1000 —

ACCOUNT _Wanda Ford, Capital_   Account No. _311_

Date	Item	P/R	Debit	Credit	Balance Debit	Balance Credit
Dec 19XX 1	Balance	✓				25602 —

ACCOUNT _Wanda Ford, Drawing_   Account No. _312_

Date	Item	P/R	Debit	Credit	Balance Debit	Balance Credit
Dec 19XX 11		CJ25	250 —		250 —	

Figure 4.7—*Continued*

ACCOUNT _Professional Fees_   Account No. _411_

Date	Item	P/R	Debit	Credit	Balance Debit	Balance Credit
19XX Dec 29		CJ 25		12499 —		12499 —

ACCOUNT _Automobile Expense_   Account No. _511_

Date	Item	P/R	Debit	Credit	Balance Debit	Balance Credit
19XX Dec 11		CJ 25	65 —		65 —	

ACCOUNT _Rent Expense_   Account No. _512_

Date	Item	P/R	Debit	Credit	Balance Debit	Balance Credit
19XX Dec 1		CJ 25	950 —		950 —	

ACCOUNT _Salary Expense_   Account No. _513_

Date	Item	P/R	Debit	Credit	Balance Debit	Balance Credit
19XX Dec 15		CJ 25	1034 —		1034 —	
29		CJ 25	1034 —		2068 —	

ACCOUNT _Telephone Expense_   Account No. _514_

Date	Item	P/R	Debit	Credit	Balance Debit	Balance Credit
19XX Dec 4		CJ 25	94 —		94 —	

ACCOUNT _Miscellaneous Expense_   Account No. _518_

Date	Item	P/R	Debit	Credit	Balance Debit	Balance Credit
19XX Dec 27		CJ 25	250 —		250 —	

Figure 4.7 — *Continued*

ACCOUNT _____ *Office Supplies Expense* _____ Account No. *520*

Date	Item	P/R	Debit	Credit	Balance Debit	Balance Credit
19XX Dec 14		CP14	159 —		159 —	

ACCOUNT _____ *Medical Supplies and Drugs Expense* _____ Account No. *521*

Date	Item	P/R	Debit	Credit	Balance Debit	Balance Credit
19XX Dec 31		CP14	577 —		577 —	

Figure 4.8 Trial balance.

Wanda O. Ford, M.D.
Trial Balance
December 31, 19XX

Account Name	Debit	Credit
Cash	18275 —	
Petty Cash	150 —	
Prepaid Insurance	375 —	
Office Furniture	5300 —	
Accumulated Depreciation – Office Furniture		1060 —
Medical Equipment	14560 —	
Accumulated Depreciation – Medical Equipment		2912 —
Notes Payable		1000 —
Wanda Ford, Capital		25602 —
Wanda Ford, Drawing	250 —	
Professional Fees		12499 —
Automobile Expense	65 —	
Rent Expense	950 —	
Salary Expense	2068 —	
Telephone Expense	94 —	
Miscellaneous Expense	250 —	
Office Supplies Expense	159 —	
Medical Supplies and Drugs Expense	577 —	
	43073 —	43073 —

When the accounts have been balanced, a trial balance is prepared and the books are ready for the final steps in the accounting cycle. The trial balance for Dr. Ford is shown in figure 4.8.

Accounting for Other Personal Service Enterprises

The modified cash system of accounting is most often used by personal service enterprises. In general, many personal service enterprises or professions use a modified cash system of accounting similar to that employed by Dr. Ford. The records kept by Dr. Ford could easily be adapted to the needs of almost any service-type business or professional office. Most service enterprises use a combined journal much like the one shown in figure 4.6. Similar petty cash and payroll records are also used. The source documents may differ, but the analyzing process is the same. Also, the basic principles of recording transactions in the journal and preparing financial statements remain the same with only slight modifications necessary to fit the needs of a particular enterprise.

Lawyers, dentists, and architects use patient or client record cards similar to the patient record cards to serve as memorandum records of charges and payments. These records are actually serving the same purpose as Accounts Receivable.

Many of the same asset and expense accounts can be used, with a few variations. For example, a lawyer would probably have an asset account for Law Library. Several different expense accounts might be needed, such as Law Library Expense, Legal Supplies Expense, and Dues and Subscriptions Expense.

One of the advantages of the cash system of accounting is its simplicity. The system is easy to set up, and once such a system has been installed, an office secretary or receptionist can do much of the routine accounting work.

Summary

Accountants are responsible for keeping records for two basic types of enterprises: merchandising and personal service. A personal service enterprise is one that derives the major portion of its revenue from services performed for customers (p. 62). Most of these service-type businesses use a cash system of accounting for revenue and expenses. Under the cash system of accounting, revenues are recorded only when cash has been received, and expenses are recorded only when cash has been paid out (p. 62).

A strictly cash basis of accounting is usually not feasible. Some federal and state tax laws require that certain types of revenue must be recorded at the time it becomes available to the owner regardless of when it is converted to cash. Likewise, the cost of certain long-lived assets must be allocated over the estimated years of service rather than as one lump sum at the time of purchase. Therefore, a modified cash system of accounting is most frequently used (p. 63).

A special combined journal is generally used for recording transactions. A combined journal provides special columns for accounts that are affected by a large number of transactions. This journal format saves considerable time in both recording and posting transactions (pp. 69–72).

Most personal service enterprises use a modified cash system of accounting because of its simplicity. Such a system is easy to install and use. It can also be easily modified to fit the particular needs of any professional office or service business.

Key Terms

cash system of accounting A system of accounting for revenue and expenses on a cash basis. Revenue is recorded only when cash is received, and expenses are recorded only when cash is paid out.

combined journal A multicolumn journal that provides special columns for those accounts that are often affected in the same way by a number of transactions.

contra account An account that is directly related to another account but that has an opposite or offsetting balance.

depreciation The allocation of the cost of a long-lived asset over the estimated years of service; a portion of the cost that is charged as an expense of each period of the asset's useful life.

personal service enterprise A firm that derives the major portion of its revenue from services performed for customers.

summary posting The process of posting the total of each special column from a journal to a ledger account rather than posting each amount in the column individually.

Objectives   Upon completion of this chapter, you should be able to:

1. Prepare a worksheet.
2. Journalize and post adjusting and closing entries.
3. Balance and rule open and closed accounts.
4. Prepare a postclosing trial balance.

5 The Accounting Cycle The Adjusting and Closing Process

5. Define the following accounting terms:

accumulated depreciation

adjusting entries

book value

closing entries

expense and revenue summary

mixed accounts

nominal accounts

open accounts

postclosing trial balance

salvage value

worksheet

The various steps in the accounting cycle have been explained in the previous chapters. Chapter 2 dealt with the steps in the recording process:

1. Analyzing transactions
2. Journalizing transactions
3. Posting to the ledger accounts

Chapter 3 explained the steps in the reporting process:

1. Preparing a trial balance
2. Preparing an income statement
3. Preparing a balance sheet

In actual practice, however, these steps are not performed in the order listed. There are some additional steps in the cycle that are performed prior to the preparation of the financial statements. These steps, which are explained in this chapter, involve:

1. Determining necessary adjustments
2. Preparing an end-of-the-period worksheet

This chapter also includes a discussion of the final steps in the accounting cycle, known as the closing process. These steps are:

1. Journalizing and posting the adjusting entries
2. Journalizing and posting the closing entries
3. Ruling the closed accounts
4. Balancing and ruling the open accounts
5. Preparing a postclosing trial balance

Account Adjustments

The amounts in the trial balance represent a summary of the ledger accounts at the end of the accounting period. Normally, assuming no journalizing or posting errors have been made, these amounts represent an accurate picture of the external activities of the business and are acceptable for inclusion in the financial statements. However, some of the account balances may have changed during the period in ways that have not been recorded as a part of the regular journalizing process of the period. These changes come about as a result of the internal transactions of the business; that is, no outside party is involved so that no formal journal entry is required. Advance payments for insurance premiums and depreciation of long-lived assets are examples of these internal activities.

For instance, when insurance premiums are paid in advance, they represent an asset to the business. However, these premiums are expiring on a day-to-day basis. That portion of the premiums that is expiring represents an expense to the business. But no daily journal entries are made to record this growing expense.

The same type of thing can occur with regard to supplies. The beginning balance of the supplies account represents the cost of supplies on hand. Some of the supplies are consumed during the accounting period, again on a daily basis; but it is impractical and time-consuming for the accountant to record an entry every time a pencil or piece of stationery is used.

Since these reductions in assets are not recorded on a daily basis, some of the assets will be overstated and some of the expenses will be understated. Therefore, at the end of the accounting period, the accountant must record the internal changes to bring the books up to date.

Actually, until the changes in these accounts are recorded, the accounts will have mixed balances—part balance sheet amounts and part income statement amounts. For that reason, they are sometimes referred to as **mixed accounts**.

As an example, examine the Prepaid Insurance account on page 84. The Prepaid Insurance balance in the trial balance is actually composed of two elements: the total unexpired insurance premium for the period (asset) and the insurance expired during the period (expense). Before the financial statements can be prepared, it is necessary to determine what portion of the balance is an asset and what portion is an expense. The ledger accounts must be brought up to date so the correct balance is reflected on the financial statements. In other words, the accounts must be "adjusted."

Adjusting Entries

The journal entries that record the internal transactions that bring the accounts up to date are called **adjusting entries**. Adjusting entries must be made whenever financial statements are prepared. If monthly statements are prepared, monthly adjustments are required. If yearly statements are prepared, yearly adjustments are required. The adjustments are made after the trial balance has been completed.

While there are several types of adjusting entries, we will examine only two in this chapter, those for prepaid insurance and depreciation. Illustrations of the adjusting procedures are based again on the ledger accounts of Dr. Ford. Other types are discussed in chapter 11.

Look first at the adjustment to be made to the Prepaid Insurance account. On December 4, Dr. Ford purchased an insurance policy to cover office furniture and equipment for three years. A premium of $375 was paid in advance. The journal entry recording the transaction follows.

| December 4 | Prepaid Insurance | 375 | |
| | Cash | | 375 |

Since no other insurance was purchased, the balance of the Prepaid Insurance account on December 31 was $375.

When the insurance policy was purchased, an asset was created. By December 31, one month of insurance coverage has been used up. Therefore, a part of the asset has expired. The part that has expired now represents an expense.

The insurance policy is in force for three years, and the cost of the policy can be evenly divided among the thirty-six months of coverage. In this example, one month's premium equals $10.42 ($375 ÷ 36 = $10.416 or $10.42). The expired portion of the insurance must be transferred from the asset account to the proper expense account. That transfer, or adjustment, is made by the following entry:

December 31 Insurance Expense	10.42	
Prepaid Insurance		10.42

After posting, the ledger accounts reflect the adjustment as shown. The Prepaid Insurance balance of $364.58 appears correctly in the balance sheet, while the Insurance Expense balance of $10.42 appears correctly in the income statement.

Prepaid Insurance		Insurance Expense	
375	10.42	10.42	
364.58			

Generally, the adjustment for expired insurance is made at the end of the accounting period rather than at the end of each month. However, in this example, the insurance policy was purchased during the last month of the accounting period, and only one month's insurance coverage had expired by the end of the period.

The next example involves adjusting entries for the depreciation of long-lived assets. The concept of depreciation was introduced in chapter 4 and represents another example of how the value of a previously recorded asset can be decreased with the passage of time. As the asset loses its usefulness, or "depreciates," the value of the asset is reduced. During each accounting period, that portion of the cost of the asset that is used up is charged as an expense of the period and is known as Depreciation Expense.

Since the accountant does not know exactly how long an asset will last or what the salvage value will be, the calculation of depreciation is only an estimate. (*Salvage value* is the estimated amount for which an asset can be sold at the end of its useful life.) Although estimating the expected depreciation for each period is not always accurate, it is preferred to charging the total cost as an expense at the time of purchase or at the time of disposal of the asset.

In its simplest form, depreciation is calculated by dividing the cost (gross or net) of the asset by the estimated years of life. Assume that a typewriter costing $980 is expected to last ten years with no salvage value. The depreciation is calculated by dividing the depreciable cost ($980) by the estimated years of life (10). Thus, the annual depreciation is $98. **Depreciable cost** is the original (or gross) cost less the salvage value; in other words, the amount to be depreciated. If the typewriter in the example has a salvage value of $100 at the end of ten years, the depreciable cost is $880 ($980 − $100 = $880), and the annual depreciation is $88 ($880 ÷ 10).

In a similar procedure, a percentage of the cost for each period can be applied as depreciation. For example, if an asset is expected to last ten years, let ten years equal 100 percent. One year would equal 10 percent. Ten percent of the cost of the asset would be charged as an expense at the end of each accounting period.

Examine again the ledger accounts of Dr. Ford (p. 000). She has two accounts that are subject to depreciation, Office Furniture and Medical Equipment. The expected useful life of those assets is ten years with no salvage value. Two years of depreciation have already been charged off. In other words, the asset accounts have been adjusted at the end of each of the two previous periods.

The amount of depreciation reduces the value of the asset, but that amount is not credited directly to the asset account. Instead a contra (reduction) account is used to record the **accumulated depreciation**. The contra account, usually called Accumulated Depreciation (or sometimes Allowance for Depreciation), has a credit balance, which builds as each year's depreciation is added to it. The difference between the related asset debit balance and the contra account credit balance shows the undepreciated cost (or book value) of the equipment or furniture. The book value is readily available at any time.

To illustrate this, refer again to the typewriter example. The annual depreciation for the typewriter is $98. After recording the annual depreciation, the ledger accounts look like this:

Typewriter		Accumulated Depreciation—Typewriter	
980			98

The current book value of the typewriter is $882 ($980 − $98).

While the amount of depreciation could be recorded directly in the asset account, it is preferable to record it in a separate account. This practice is justified because the amount of depreciation recorded is only an estimate and it may not coincide with the deterioration or loss of value of the asset. By recording the depreciation in a separate account, the original cost of the asset is maintained until it is fully depreciated or salvaged. Thus, both the original cost of the asset and the amount that has accumulated for depreciation are readily available.

Usually a separate contra account is kept for each depreciating asset. It may be desirable to keep separate depreciation expense accounts also, but it is not absolutely necessary.

The adjusting entries needed to record the depreciation in Dr. Ford's long-lived asset accounts are as follows:

December 31 Depreciation Expense—Office
             Furniture   530
             Depreciation Expense—Medical
             Equipment   1,456
                Accumulated Depreciation—
                Office Furniture   530
                Accumulated Depreciation—
                Medical Equipment   1,456

After posting, the ledger accounts reflect these entries as shown in the following:

Office Furniture		Medical Equipment	
5,300		14,560	

Accumulated Depreciation— Office Furniture		Accumulated Depreciation— Medical Equipment	
	Bal 1,060		Bal 2,912
	Dec 31 530		Dec 31 1,456
	1,590		*4,368*

Depreciation Expense—Office Furniture		Depreciation Expense— Medical Equipment	
Dec 31 530		Dec 31 1,456	

The current book value of Office Furniture is $3,710 ($5,300–$1,590), and the current book value of the Medical Equipment is $10,192 ($14,560–$4,368).

The balances of these asset accounts and their related accumulated depreciation accounts appear on the balance sheet. The balances of the Depreciation Expense accounts appear on the income statement as an operating expense.

Normally, these and other adjusting entries are not formally recorded until after the financial statements have been prepared. However, they must be taken into consideration and included in the work performed prior to the preparation of the statements. The reason for the delay in recording adjusting entries is to reduce the time necessary to prepare the financial statements. Most firms want the statements as quickly as possible after the end of the accounting period to insure that the information presented in them is current. Therefore, the recording of adjusting entries is delayed until after the financial statements have been completed. After the completion of the financial statements, the adjusting entries are journalized and posted. The following illustrations and explanations show the manner and order in which adjustments are usually made.

The Worksheet

Financial statements should be prepared as soon as possible after the end of the accounting period. The figures included on the statements must match those in the various ledger accounts. We have seen, however, that certain account balances must be adjusted before the figures in the ledger and on the financial statements agree. To adjust the ledger through the normal procedures of journalizing and posting can be time-consuming. The use of these procedures can also delay the preparation of the statements. The accountant requires a means of quickly and accurately determining the effects of the adjustments without journalizing and posting, while still permitting the accurate preparation of the financial statements. In order to accomplish this, the accountant commonly uses a special form referred to as a **worksheet**. A worksheet is a form, which contains columns for recording account titles and numbers and dollar amounts, that permits the accountant to gather data quickly at the end of the accounting period (see fig. 5.1). It is an informal statement seen only by the accountant and is therefore usually prepared in pencil. Once the data has been collected on the worksheet, it is not necessary for the accountant to refer elsewhere for information needed to prepare the financial statements and to complete the other end-of-the-period activities.

The worksheet can take a variety of forms, and the number of columns usually varies in relation to the size and nature of the business. However, for practical purposes, an eight- or ten-column worksheet is generally used. There is little difference between the two forms. A ten-column worksheet contains an extra pair of amount columns for recording an adjusted trial balance. While the ten-column worksheet is most commonly used, some firms that have a small number of adjustments prefer to use the eight-column worksheet. The worksheet in figure 5.1 contains ten columns. It shows the ledger accounts of Dr. Ford as they appeared in chapter 4.

A worksheet has a three-line heading that tells the name of the business, the kind of statement, and the period of time for which the worksheet is prepared. Columns are provided at the left margin for entering the account titles and numbers.

A ten-column worksheet consists of five pairs of amount columns. The first pair of columns is headed Trial Balance. This section makes it possible to prepare the trial balance directly on the worksheet rather than as a separate statement. In chapter 4 the trial balance for Dr. Ford was prepared as a separate statement. In actual practice, however, it is prepared in the Trial Balance columns of the worksheet (fig. 5.2). After the trial balance information is recorded, the debit and credit columns are totaled and double-ruled. Of course, if the column amounts are not equal, the error must be found and corrected before the worksheet is completed.

The second pair of columns, Adjustments, is used for computing and recording the adjustments (fig. 5.3). Each part of an adjusting entry is identified by a letter or number in parentheses. The letter or number facilitates checking for errors and making journal entries at a later date.

Figure 5.1 Worksheet for Dr. Wanda Ford.

Wanda O. Ford, M.D.
Worksheet
For the Year Ended December 31, 19XX

Account Name	Acct. No.	Trial Balance Debit	Trial Balance Credit	Adjustments Debit	Adjustments Credit	Adjusted Trial Balance Debit	Adjusted Trial Balance Credit
Cash	111	18275—				18275—	
Petty Cash	113	150—				150—	
Prepaid Insurance	131	375—			(a) 10 42	364 58	
Office Furniture	141	5300—				5300—	
Acc. Depr.-Office Furniture	0141		1060—		(b) 530—		1590—
Medical Equipment	142	14560—				14560—	
Acc. Depr.-Medical Eqpt.	0142		2912—		(c) 1456—		4368—
Notes Payable	212		1000—				1000—
Wanda Ford, Capital	311		25602—				25602—
Wanda Ford, Drawing	312	250—				250—	
Professional Fees	411		12499—				12499—
Automobile Expense	511	65—				65—	
Rent Expense	512	950—				950—	
Salary Expense	513	2068—				2068—	
Telephone Expense	514	94—				94—	
Miscellaneous Expense	518	250—				250—	
Office Supplies Expense	520	159—				159—	
Med. Supp. & Drugs Expense	521	577—				577—	
		43073—	43073—				
Depreciation Exp.-Off. Furn.	516			(b) 530—		530—	
Depreciation Exp.-Med Eqpt.	517			(c) 1456—		1456—	
Insurance Expense	519			(a) 10 42		10 42	
				1996 42	1996 42	45059—	45059—
Net Income							

Debits must equal credits for each entry. After all adjustment data has been recorded, the columns are totaled and double-ruled. The column totals must be equal before proceeding with the rest of the worksheet.

As previously stated, the adjustments are usually entered directly on the worksheet and later journalized and posted to the ledger accounts to save time and to aid in the preparation of the financial statements.

The third pair of columns is used to record the Adjusted Trial Balance (fig. 5.4). Amounts in this section show the effects of the adjustments. If there is no adjustment for an account, the original balance is transferred

| Income Statement | | Balance Sheet | |
Debit	Credit	Debit	Credit
		18275 —	
		150 —	
		36458	
		5300 —	
			1590 —
		14560 —	
			4368 —
			1000 —
			25602 —
		250 —	
	12499 —		
65 —			
950 —			
2068 —			
94 —			
250 —			
159 —			
577 —			
530 —			
1456 —			
1042			
6159 42	12499 —	38899 58	32560 —
6339 58			6339 58
12499 —	12499 —	38899 58	38899 58

directly to the proper column in the Adjusted Trial Balance section. If adjustments have been made to an account, the information from the Trial Balance and Adjustments columns is combined to arrive at a new balance. The balance appearing in the Trial Balance is increased or decreased by the adjustment. The net result is entered in the proper Adjusted Trial Balance column. The columns are totaled, and if total debits equal total credits, the columns are double-ruled. Under no circumstances should the accountant proceed from one section of the worksheet to another until each set of columns is in balance.

Figure 5.2
Trial Balance columns
of the worksheet.

Figure 5.3
Adjustments columns.

Figure 5.4
Adjusted Trial Balance columns.

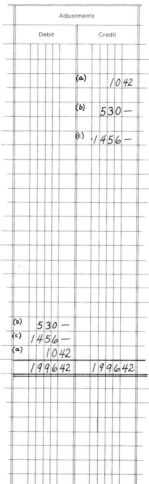

Figure 5.2 — Trial Balance

Acct. No.	Debit	Credit
	18275 —	
	150 —	
	375 —	
	5300 —	
		1060 —
	14560 —	
		2912 —
		1000 —
		25602 —
	250 —	
		12499 —
	65 —	
	950 —	
	2068 —	
	94 —	
	250 —	
	159 —	
	577 —	
	43073 —	43073 —

Figure 5.3 — Adjustments

	Debit	Credit
(a)		1042
(b)		530 —
(c)		1456 —
(b)	530 —	
(c)	1456 —	
(a)	1042	
	199642	199642

Figure 5.4 — Adjusted Trial Balance

Debit	Credit
18275 —	
150 —	
36458	
5300 —	
	1590 —
14560 —	
	4368 —
	1000 —
	25602 —
250 —	
	12499 —
65 —	
950 —	
2068 —	
94 —	
250 —	
159 —	
577 —	
530 —	
1456 —	
1042	
45059 —	45059 —

The last four columns on the worksheet directly aid in the preparation of the financial statements (figs. 5.5 and 5.6). After the equality of the Adjusted Trial Balance columns has been confirmed, the figures in that section are extended to one of the four remaining columns. Revenue and expense amounts are extended to the proper Income Statement columns (fig. 5.5). Assets, liabilities, and owner's equity amounts are extended to the proper Balance Sheet columns (fig. 5.6).

The debit and credit columns for the Income Statement section are totaled. These totals are usually not equal. The difference represents the

Figure 5.5
Income statement columns.

Figure 5.6
Balance sheet columns.

Income Statement	
Debit	Credit
	12499 —
65 —	
950 —	
2068 —	
94 —	
250 —	
159 —	
577 —	
530 —	
1456 —	
10 42	
615942	12499 —
633958	
12499 —	12499 —

Balance Sheet	
Debit	Credit
18275 —	
150 —	
36458	
5300 —	
	1590 —
14560 —	
	4368 —
	1000 —
	25602 —
250 —	
3889958	32560 —
	633958
3889958	3889958

Net Income or Net Loss. If the credit column total (revenue exceeds expenses) is larger, a net income results. If the debit column total (expenses exceed revenue) is larger, a net loss results. The difference is then added to the smaller total to make the columns balance. The words *Net Income* or *Net Loss* are written in the Account Name column on the same line as the difference. The example in figure 5.5 shows a Net Income.

Next, the debit and credit columns of the Balance Sheet section are totaled. These column totals are usually not equal. The difference between the two should be the same as the difference between the debit and credit columns in the Income Statement section. The difference is added to the smaller total to make the columns balance. If there is a net income, the difference is added to the Balance Sheet Cr. column. If there is a net loss, the difference is added to the Dr. column. The addition of the net income to the credit side of the Balance Sheet section represents an increase to owner's equity. The addition of a net loss to the debit side of the Balance sheet section represents a decrease to owner's equity. The Balance Sheet section of the worksheet illustrated in figure 5.6 shows a Net Income.

Preparing the Financial Statements

With the totaling and ruling of the last four columns, the worksheet is complete. All the information needed to prepare the financial statements is readily available. The formal financial statements can now be prepared directly from the worksheet. The income statement (fig. 5.7) and the balance sheet (fig. 5.8) have been prepared from the worksheet of Dr. Wanda Ford. Note on the balance sheet that accumulated depreciation is subtracted from the proper related asset accounts to show the actual book value of those assets at the time of the report.

Figure 5.7   Income statement for Dr. Wanda Ford.

Wanda O. Ford, M.D.
Income Statement
For the Year Ended December 31, 19XX

Revenue:		
Professional Fees		12499 —
Expenses:		
Automobile Expense	65 —	
Rent Expense	950 —	
Salary Expense	2068 —	
Telephone Expense	94 —	
Depreciation Expense—Office Furniture	530 —	
Depreciation Expense—Medical Equipment	1456 —	
Miscellaneous Expense	250 —	
Insurance Expense	1042	
Office Supplies Expense	159 —	
Medical Supplies and Drugs Expense	577 —	
Total Expenses		6159 42
Net Income		6339 58

Figure 5.8 Balance sheet for Dr. Wanda Ford.

Wanda O. Ford, M.D.
Balance Sheet
December 31, 19XX

ASSETS			LIABILITIES		
Cash	18275 —		Notes Payable	1000 —	
Petty Cash	150 —		Total Liabilities		1000 —
Prepaid Insurance	364 58				
Office Furniture 5,300 —			OWNER'S EQUITY		
less Acc.Depr.-Off.Furn. 1,590 —	3710 —		Wanda Ford		
Medical Equipment 14,560 —			Capital, Jan. 1, 19XX	25602 —	
less Acc.Depr.-Med.Eqpt. 4,368 —	10192 —		Net Income 6,339.58		
			less Withdrawals 250 —		
			Net Increase	6089 58	
			Capital, Dec. 31, 19XX		31691 58
Total Assets		32691 58	Total Liabilities and Owner's Equity		32691 58

The income statement is usually prepared first. Then the Net Income (or Net Loss) figure from the income statement is recorded in the owner's equity section of the balance sheet. This figure provides the link between the two statements.

Journalizing and Posting the Adjusting Entries

The end-of-the-period adjustments are first computed and recorded on the worksheet to provide the correct balances for the financial statements. After the financial statements have been prepared, the ledger accounts must contain the same information that is reported on the statements. Up to this point, the adjustments appear only in the Adjustments section of the worksheet, so the figures in the ledger accounts do not agree with the figures on the financial statements. It is necessary, therefore, to journalize and post the adjustments that have been recorded on the worksheet.

The data for the adjusting entries is copied directly from the worksheet into a combined journal or a general journal. If the entries are made in a combined journal, only the General Dr. and Cr. columns are used. An identifying heading, Adjusting Entries, precedes the journal entries. This heading eliminates the need for a separate explanation for each entry, though some accountants prefer to write an explanation for each adjusted item. Once these entries have been posted, the amounts in the ledger ac-

Figure 5.9a Adjusting entries in the general journal.

GENERAL JOURNAL   Page 1

Date	Explanation	P/R	Debit	Credit
19XX	*Adjusting Entries*			
Dec 31	Insurance Expense	519	10 42	
	Prepaid Insurance	131		10 42
31	Depreciation Expense-Office Furniture	516	530 —	
	Acc. Depr.-Office Furniture	0141		530 —
31	Depreciation Expense-Medical Equipment	517	1456 —	
	Acc. Depr.-Medical Equipment	0142		1456 —

counts agree with the amounts on the financial statements. The adjusting entries for Dr. Ford and the ledger accounts as they appear after the posting are shown in figure 5.9a and 5.9b.

Journalizing and Posting the Closing Entries

One of the last things the accountant does at the end of the accounting period is to prepare the records for the accounting activities of the next period. This procedure is known as **closing the books**. It begins with the closing of the revenue and expense accounts.

Revenue and expense accounts, sometimes referred to as *nominal* accounts, are temporary owner's equity accounts. They are used to gather data for *one* accounting period only. Their use also makes it possible to keep revenue and expenses separate from the owner's investments and withdrawals. At the end of each accounting period, after the financial statements have been prepared, these accounts will have served their purpose. Their balances must now be brought to zero so that these accounts are ready for use in collecting data for the following accounting period. This is accomplished by a series of journal entries called **closing entries**, which transfer the balances of the temporary accounts to the permanent owner's equity account (the owner's Capital account). The Income Statement columns of the worksheet contain the information necessary for the closing entries.

The balances of the revenue and expense accounts are not usually transferred directly to the owner's Capital account. Such a procedure would

Figure 5.9*b*   Ledger accounts after posting the adjusting entries.

ACCOUNT _Prepaid Insurance_   Account No. _131_

Date		Item	P/R	Debit	Credit	Balance	
						Debit	Credit
Dec 19XX	20		CP 25	375 —		375 —	
	31		J 1		1 0 42	364 58	

ACCOUNT _Accumulated Depreciation—Office Furniture_   Account No. _0141_

Date		Item	P/R	Debit	Credit	Balance	
						Debit	Credit
Dec 19XX	1	Balance	✓				1060 —
	31		J 1		530 —		1590 —

ACCOUNT _Accumulated Depreciation—Medical Equipment_   Account No. _0142_

Date		Item	P/R	Debit	Credit	Balance	
						Debit	Credit
Dec 19XX	1	Balance	✓				2912 —
	31		J 1		1456 —		4368 —

ACCOUNT _Depreciation Expense—Office Furniture_   Account No. _516_

Date		Item	P/R	Debit	Credit	Balance	
						Debit	Credit
Dec 19XX	31		J 1	530 —		530 —	

ACCOUNT _Depreciation Expense—Medical Equipment_   Account No. _517_

Date		Item	P/R	Debit	Credit	Balance	
						Debit	Credit
Dec 19XX	31		J 1	1456 —		1456 —	

ACCOUNT _Insurance Expense_   Account No. _519_

Date		Item	P/R	Debit	Credit	Balance	
						Debit	Credit
Dec 19XX	31		J 1	1 0 42		1 0 42	

result in a confusing mass of figures in the account. It would be difficult to determine which amounts represent investments and withdrawals and which amounts represent revenue and expenses. To avoid this confusion, another temporary owner's equity account titled Expense and Revenue Summary is used. It is used only at the end of the accounting period and is strictly a summarizing device. This Expense and Revenue Summary account has a balance only during the closing process. Once it has served its purpose, the balance of the account is reduced to zero. Its balance, which in effect is a summary of the balances of the revenue and expense accounts, is transferred to the owner's Capital account.

Four journal entries, which are keyed in figure 5.10a, are required to close the temporary owner's equity accounts:

1. Each revenue account is closed to the Expense and Revenue Summary. Debit each revenue account for its balance to reduce it to zero. Credit the Expense and Revenue Summary account for the same amount.

2. Each expense account is closed to the Expense and Revenue Summary. Credit each expense account for its balance to reduce it to zero. Debit the Expense and Revenue Summary account for the same amount. This entry is usually made as one compound entry rather than as several separate entries.

3. The Expense and Revenue Summary account is closed to the owner's Capital account. If the Summary account has a credit balance, it will be debited and the Capital account will be credited. If a loss has occurred and the Summary account has a debit balance, it will be credited and the Capital account will be debited.

4. The owner's Drawing account (provided there have been withdrawals during the period) is closed to the owner's Capital account. Credit the Drawing account for its balance, and debit the Capital account for the same amount.

The closing entries for Dr. Ford are shown in figure 5.10a. The ledger accounts of Dr. Ford after the closing entries have been posted are presented in figure 5.10b.

Figure 5.10a Closing entries in the general journal.

GENERAL JOURNAL   Page 1

Date		Explanation	P/R	Debit	Credit
19XX		Closing Entries			
Dec	31	Professional Fees	411	12499 —	
(1)		Expense and Revenue Summary	313		12499 —
	31	Expense and Revenue Summary	313	615942	
		Automobile Expense	511		65 —
		Rent Expense	512		950 —
		Salary Expense	513		2068 —
		Telephone Expense	514		94 —
(2)		Depreciation Expense – Office Furniture	516		530 —
		Depreciation Expense – Medical Equipment	517		1456 —
		Miscellaneous Expense	518		250 —
		Insurance Expense	519		1042
		Office Supplies Expense	520		159 —
		Medical Supplies and Drugs Expense	521		577 —
	31	Expense and Revenue Summary	313	633958	
(3)		Wanda Ford, Capital	311		633958
	31	Wanda Ford, Capital	311	250 —	
(4)		Wanda Ford, Drawing	312		250 —

Figure 5.10b Ledger accounts after posting the closing entries.

ACCOUNT Wanda Ford, Capital   Account No. 311

Date		Item	P/R	Debit	Credit	Balance Debit	Balance Credit
19XX Dec	1	Balance	√				25602 —
	31		J1		633958		31941 58
	31		J1	250 —			31691 58

ACCOUNT Wanda Ford, Drawing   Account No. 312

Date		Item	P/R	Debit	Credit	Balance Debit	Balance Credit
19XX Dec	11		CJ25	250 —		250 —	
	31		J1		250 —	— 0 —	— 0 —

Figure 5.10b—Continued

ACCOUNT __Expense and Revenue Summary__   Account No. 313

Date		Item	P/R	Debit	Credit	Balance	
						Debit	Credit
19XX Dec	31		J1		12499 —		12499 —
	31		J1	615942			633958
	31		J1	633958		— 0 —	— 0 —

ACCOUNT __Professional Fees__   Account No. 411

Date		Item	P/R	Debit	Credit	Balance	
						Debit	Credit
19XX Dec	29		CJ25		12499 —		12499 —
	31		J1	12499 —		— 0 —	— 0 —

ACCOUNT __Automobile Expense__   Account No. 511

Date		Item	P/R	Debit	Credit	Balance	
						Debit	Credit
19XX Dec	11		CJ25	65 —		65 —	
	31		J1		65 —	— 0 —	— 0 —

ACCOUNT __Rent Expense__   Account No. 512

Date		Item	P/R	Debit	Credit	Balance	
						Debit	Credit
19XX Dec	1		CJ25	950 —		950 —	
	31		J1		950 —	— 0 —	— 0 —

ACCOUNT __Salary Expense__   Account No. 513

Date		Item	P/R	Debit	Credit	Balance	
						Debit	Credit
19XX Dec	15		CJ25	1034 —		1034 —	
	29		CJ25	1034 —		2068 —	
	31		J1		2068 —	— 0 —	— 0 —

ACCOUNT __Telephone Expense__   Account No. 514

Date		Item	P/R	Debit	Credit	Balance	
						Debit	Credit
19XX Dec	4		CJ25	94 —		94 —	
	31		J1		94 —	— 0 —	— 0 —

Figure 5.10b—*Continued*

ACCOUNT _Depreciation Expense–Office Furniture_   Account No. 516

Date		Item	P/R	Debit	Credit	Balance	
						Debit	Credit
19xx Dec	31		J1	530 —		530 —	
	31		J1		530 —	— 0 —	— 0 —

ACCOUNT _Depreciation Expense–Medical Equipment_   Account No. 517

Date		Item	P/R	Debit	Credit	Balance	
						Debit	Credit
19xx Dec	31		J1	1456 —		1456 —	
	31		J1		1456 —	— 0 —	— 0 —

ACCOUNT _Miscellaneous Expense_   Account No. 518

Date		Item	P/R	Debit	Credit	Balance	
						Debit	Credit
19xx Dec	27		CJ25	250 —		250 —	
	31		J1		250 —	— 0 —	— 0 —

ACCOUNT _Insurance Expense_   Account No. 519

Date		Item	P/R	Debit	Credit	Balance	
						Debit	Credit
19xx Dec	31		J1	1042		1042	
	31		J1		1042	— 0 —	— 0 —

ACCOUNT _Office Supplies Expense_   Account No. 520

Date		Item	P/R	Debit	Credit	Balance	
						Debit	Credit
19xx Dec	14		CJ25	159 —		159 —	
	31		J1		159 —	— 0 —	— 0 —

ACCOUNT _Medical Supplies and Drugs Expense_   Account No. 521

Date		Item	P/R	Debit	Credit	Balance	
						Debit	Credit
19xx Dec	29		CJ25	577 —		577 —	
	31		J1		577 —	— 0 —	— 0 —

Figure 5.11 The closing process.

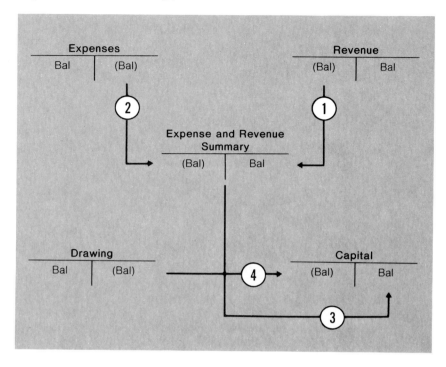

The closing process is summarized in figure 5.11. The following elements of the closing process are keyed in the figure:

1. The balance of the revenue account is moved to the credit side of the Expense and Revenue Summary account.
2. The balances of the expense accounts are moved to the debit side of the Expense and Revenue Summary account.
3. The balance of the Expense and Revenue Summary account is moved to the credit side of the owner's Capital account (that is, if a profit has been made as in figure 5.11). If a loss has occurred, the account has a debit balance. The debit balance is moved to the debit side of the owner's Capital account.
4. The balance of the Drawing account is moved to the debit side of the owner's Capital account.

The data for closing entries is taken from the Income Statement columns of the worksheet. The entries may be entered in either a combined journal or a general journal. An identifying heading, Closing Entries, precedes the journal entries.

Open and Closed Accounts

After the closing entries have been posted, the temporary accounts have zero balances. These accounts are generally ruled to indicate that they have been closed. If a balance form of account is being used, a double line is drawn under all columns except the Item column, as shown in figure 5.12. Some accountants prefer not to rule balance form accounts, which is also an acceptable practice.

If the standard two-column form of account is used, a slightly different procedure is required.

If only one entry has been posted to each side of the account, double lines are drawn under the entries across all columns except the Item column (fig. 5.13).

If two or more entries have been posted to one or both sides of the account, a single line is drawn under the lowest entry across both the Dr. and Cr. columns (fig. 5.14). The totals are written below this line. Double-rule below the totals across all columns except the Item column.

Figure 5.12   Balance form closed account.

Date		Item	P/R	Debit	Credit	Balance	
						Debit	Credit
19XX Dec	31		J1		12499—		12499—
	31		J1	615942			633958
	31		J1	633958			—0—

ACCOUNT *Expense and Revenue Summary*   Account No. *313*

Figure 5.13   Two-column closed account, one entry.

ACCOUNT *Rent Expense*   Account No. *512*

Date		Item	P/R	Debit	Date		Item	P/R	Credit
19XX Dec	1		CJ25	950—	*19XX* Dec	31		J1	950—

Figure 5.14   Two-column closed account, two entries.

ACCOUNT *Expense and Revenue Summary*   Account No. *313*

Date		Item	P/R	Debit	Date		Item	P/R	Credit
19XX Dec	31		J1	615942	*19XX* Dec	31		J1	12499—
	31		J1	633958					
				12499—					12499—

Figure 5.15 New accounting period entry on balance form.

ACCOUNT _Wanda Ford, Capital_   Account No. _311_

Date		Item	P/R	Debit	Credit	Balance Debit	Balance Credit
19XX Dec	1	Balance	✓				25602 —
	31		J1		6339 58		31941 58
	31		J1	250 —			31691 58
19XX Jan							

Figure 5.16 New accounting period entry on two-column form.

ACCOUNT _Cash_   Account No. _111_

Date		Item	P/R	Debit	Date		Item	P/R	Credit
19XX Dec	1	Balance	✓	10564 —	19XX Dec	29		CJ25	4788 —
	29		CJ25	12499 —		31	Balance	✓	18275 —
				23063 —					23063 —
19XX Jan	1	Balance	✓	18275 —					

The balances in the asset, liability, and owner's equity accounts are carried forward from one accounting period to the next. These accounts are called **open**, or **real**, accounts. If a balance form of account is used, no ruling is necessary. The date and amount of the next transaction is entered on the line below the last entry (fig. 5.15).

If the standard two-column form of account is used, a different procedure is followed. The balance of the account must be determined. Then the account is ruled in the manner shown in figure 5.16.

Accounts that have entries on only one side of the account are not ruled and balanced. If an account has more than one debit and no credits, or vice versa, simply foot the column. The footing represents the balance, and ruling and balancing are not necessary.

Postclosing Trial Balance

Before beginning any accounting activity for a new period, it is wise to verify that the ledger is in balance—that debit balances equal credit balances. This brings us to the final step in the accounting cycle, preparing a **postclosing trial balance**. A postclosing trial balance is prepared just like a regular trial balance. However, it lists only the balances of those accounts that have not been closed.

Figure 5.17 Postclosing trial balance.

Wanda O. Ford, M.D.
Postclosing Trial Balance
December 31, 19XX

Account Name	Debit	Credit
Cash	18275 —	
Petty Cash	150 —	
Prepaid Insurance	364 58	
Office Furniture	5300 —	
Accumulated Depreciation—Office Furniture		1590 —
Medical Equipment	14560 —	
Accumulated Depreciation—Medical Equipment		4368 —
Notes Payable		1000 —
Wanda Ford, Capital		31691 58
	38649 58	38649 58

The open accounts are balanced and ruled. Their titles and balances are listed in the postclosing trial balance. The columns are totaled and ruled. If the totals do not equal, the error(s) must be found and corrected before double-ruling the statement. The open accounts and their balances listed on the postclosing trial balance should agree exactly with the items on the Balance Sheet prepared at the end of the accounting period. A postclosing trial balance is shown in figure 5.17.

The entire accounting cycle has now been presented. The steps in the accounting cycle are listed as follows:

1. Analyze the transactions.
2. Journalize the transactions.
3. Post the transactions.
4. Prepare a trial balance.
5. Make the necessary adjustments.
6. Complete the worksheet.
7. Prepare the financial statements.
8. Journalize and post the adjusting and closing entries.
9. Rule the accounts.
10. Prepare a postclosing trial balance.

Summary

At the end of each accounting period, financial statements must be prepared and the books made ready for the beginning of the new period. To facilitate these activities, the accountant prepares an informal statement called a worksheet. The worksheet makes it possible to gather all the data needed for the end-of-the-period activities in one spot (pp. 87–91).

Worksheet columns are provided for preparing a regular trial balance, and the balances in these columns are then adjusted as necessary so that the correct figures are reported on the financial statements. Adjustments must be made in order to account for certain internal transactions that have not been recorded during the accounting period (pp. 82–85). By making the adjustments in the Adjustments columns of the worksheet, it is possible to prepare the financial statements directly from the worksheet. After the statements are prepared, the adjustments must be formally journalized and posted to bring the ledger accounts in line with the financial statements (pp. 93–94).

The ledger accounts must then be prepared for the new accounting period. At this point, temporary owner's equity accounts have served their purpose, so their balances are reduced to zero. The balances of these accounts are transferred to another temporary account, Expense and Revenue Summary. The balance of the Expense and Revenue Summary account, which reflects the Net Income or Net Loss for the period, is closed to the owner's Capital account. Withdrawals are also transferred to the Capital account. This closing process is accomplished by a series of journal entries called closing entries (pp. 94–100).

After closing entries are posted, the temporary accounts are ruled to show the end of one period and the beginning of another. Assets, liabilities, and owner's equity accounts have balances that are carried forward from one accounting period to the next (pp. 101–2). A postclosing trial balance is prepared to check the equality of the debit and credit balances of those open accounts before the beginning of the new period (pp. 102–3).

Key Terms

accumulated depreciation A contra account used to record periodic depreciation of long-lived assets.

adjusting entries Journal entries that record the internal transactions that bring the ledger accounts up to date; usually recorded first on a worksheet.

book value The cost of an asset less accumulated depreciation; often called *undepreciated cost.*

closing entries Journal entries made at the end of an accounting period that close the temporary owner's equity accounts and reduce their balances to zero; often referred to as closing the books.

expense and revenue summary A temporary owner's equity account used as a summarizing device; account to which all revenue and expense account balances are closed at the end of an accounting period.

mixed accounts Accounts whose balances are part balance sheet amounts and part income statement amounts.

nominal accounts Temporary owner's equity accounts whose balances are used for one accounting period only; these accounts are closed at the end of each accounting period.

open accounts Asset, liability, and owner's equity accounts whose balances are carried forward from one accounting period to the next; often referred to as real accounts.

postclosing trial balance A trial balance prepared after the temporary owner's equity accounts have been closed; lists only the balances of open accounts.

salvage value The estimated value of a long-lived asset at the end of its expected useful life.

worksheet An informal statement that facilitates the preparation of financial statements and other end-of-the-period activities.

Objectives Upon completion of this chapter, you should be able to:

1. Understand the basic principles of the internal control of cash.
2. Reconcile a bank statement.
3. Establish and use a petty cash fund.

6 Control of Cash

---

4. Define the following accounting terms:

ABA number	full endorsement
bank reconciliation	MICR number
bank statement	not sufficient funds
blank endorsement	outstanding check
canceled check	payee
check	petty cash disbursements record
deposit in transit	petty cash fund
deposit slip	petty cash voucher
dishonored check	restrictive endorsement
drawee	service charge
drawer	signature card

Inherent in any accounting system is the necessity to maintain adequate control over the assets of the firm. Most accounting systems are designed to provide some form of internal control over the assets.

Of all the assets, cash is the most difficult to control. It can be easily misappropriated since it can be concealed and has no special marks for ready identification. For this reason, a business needs to take special precautions to protect both cash receipts and disbursements from loss or theft. This chapter deals with the nature of controlling cash. Other forms of internal control over other assets will be dealt with at appropriate points in future chapters.

While there are a number of elements to be considered in the control of cash, two basic principles should be observed:

1. A separation of duties among personnel is necessary so that the persons who handle cash are not the same persons who keep the cash records. By dividing the duties between two or more persons, the chances for theft or embezzlement are greatly reduced. Also, the division of duties provides a check against innocent errors that might go undetected if only one person is designated to process and verify cash receipts.
2. All cash receipts should be deposited intact in the bank each day, and all cash payments should be made only by check or from controlled cash funds. This procedure provides an independent, external (the bank's) record of all receipts and disbursements of cash by the firm. The bank's record may be used as a check on the firm's own records. Such a practice also reduces the opportunities for employees to pocket cash.

Composition of Cash

Most of us think of cash as currency and coins. However, in accounting, the term *cash* refers to many other items as well. Cash in the accounting sense includes currency, coins, checks, money orders—any item that a bank will accept for deposit. It does not include postage stamps, postdated checks, or IOU's, even though these items are often handled like cash.

The name of the ledger account used to record cash transactions differs from company to company. The most common practice, however, is to title the ledger account with the name of the bank with whom the account is held. In addition, a separate ledger account is used for Petty Cash. A firm may have several accounts with one bank or accounts with several different banks. A separate ledger account should be maintained for each.

The Bank Account

As a means of cash control, most businesses deposit all cash receipts in a bank and make all payments by checks drawn against a bank account. The bank is then responsible for keeping its depositors accurately informed about all transactions involving their individual accounts.

To open a checking account, the bank requires that a signature card (fig. 6.1) be completed. This card bears the signature of each person authorized to sign checks. Signatures on the card must be written exactly as they will appear on the checks. The card is kept on file by the bank as a means of verifying the signature on the checks presented for payment. If the depositor is a corporation, the bank will also require a copy of a board of directors' resolution authorizing the named person to sign checks.

Funds are transferred from a depositor's account to another party by means of a **check.** A check is a written order for a bank to pay a specified sum of money to a designated party. There are three parties involved in the process of issuing a check: the **drawer,** the person who signs the check; the **drawee,** the bank on which the check is drawn; and the **payee,** the person (or firm) to whose order the check is drawn (fig. 6.2).

Checks are printed in a variety of sizes and colors. They may also be prenumbered. Prenumbered checks offer an added measure of control since no two checks written on a given account have the same number.

Most checks are attached to a check stub, which is used for duplicating the information that appears on the check as well as for keeping a

Figure 6.1 Signature card.

Acct.
Name

Time Deposit Savings ☐ Regular Checking ☐
Savings ☐ Special Checking ☐

Acct.
No. ______

TYPE OF ACCOUNT:
☐ INDIVIDUAL ☐ JOINT ☐ PARTNERSHIP ☐ SOLE OWNER ☐ TENANTS IN COMMON

The Bank is authorized to recognize the signatures subscribed below in the transaction of any banking business for this account. Depositor's signature constitutes assent to the terms and conditions of the Deposit Agreement contained herein.

Balance

Any ______ of the below signatures required. ______

1. Signature ______ SS or IRS Acct. No. ______

2. Signature ______ SS or IRS Acct. No. ______

3. Signature ______ SS or IRS Acct. No. ______

The Bank is authorized to mail check statements to address below ☐ Hold statement for pickup ☐

ADDRESS ______ PHONE ______

______ ZIP CODE ______

Opened by ______ Amt. ______ Original Opening Date ______

Closed

Where did you last bank? ______

Employed by ______ Phone ______

OPBR-1

Figure 6.2 Sample check.

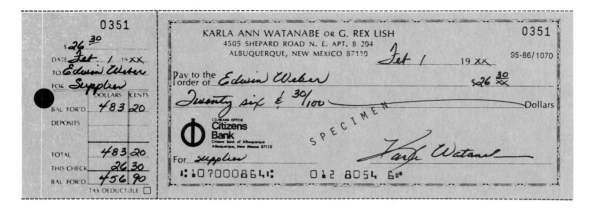

Figure 6.3 Check register.

NUMBER	DATE	DESCRIPTION OF TRANSACTION	PAYMENT/DEBIT (−)	√ T	FEE (IF ANY) (−)	DEPOSIT/CREDIT (+)	BALANCE
		RECORD ALL CHARGES OR CREDITS THAT AFFECT YOUR ACCOUNT					$ 602 26
56	11/2	Marshall Wilson	$ 56 12		$	$	546 14

running balance of the checking account. The information on the check stub is the basis for later journal entries. Stubs are usually attached to the checks along the side (fig. 6.2) or above the check. In some cases, the information usually recorded on the stub is contained in a separate booklet called a check register (fig.6.3).

A few basic rules to be observed in writing checks are:

1. The check stub should be filled in first.
2. The check should be written in ink or typewritten. A check-writing machine may also be used.

3. The amount in figures should be written as close to the dollar sign as possible.
4. The amount in words should be written at the extreme left of the line provided. Any blank space remaining should be filled in by drawing a line up to the word *dollars*. Some companies use a check-writing machine to print the amounts on the checks to prevent check alterations.
5. The name of the drawer should be written on the check in ink exactly as it appears on the signature card.

Funds deposited in a bank are listed on a printed form supplied by the bank called a **deposit slip** (fig. 6.4). The amount of currency and coins and an itemized list of all checks appear on the deposit slip.

Deposit slips may be prepared in duplicate. The duplicate is stamped or initialed by the bank teller and serves as a receipt for the money. The

Figure 6.4 Deposit slip.

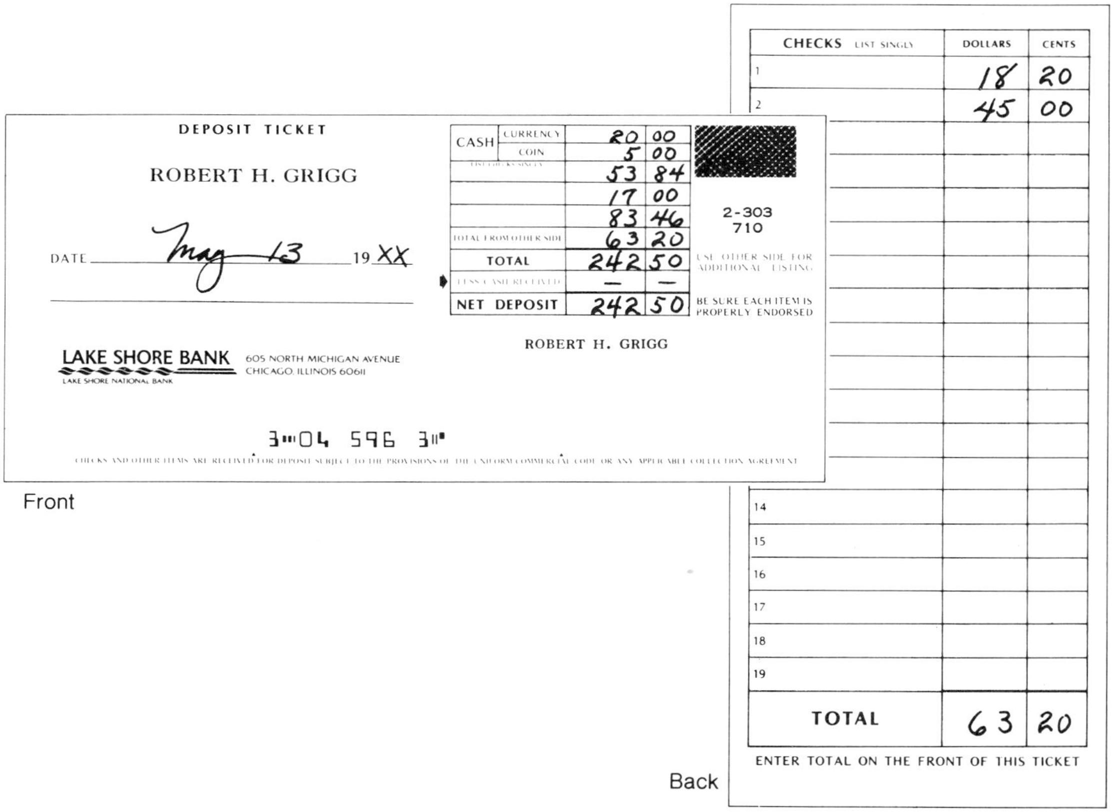

DEPOSIT TICKET

ROBERT H. GRIGG

DATE May 13 19 XX

LAKE SHORE BANK 605 NORTH MICHIGAN AVENUE CHICAGO, ILLINOIS 60611
LAKE SHORE NATIONAL BANK

CASH	CURRENCY	20	00
	COIN	5	00
LIST CHECKS SINGLY		53	84
		17	00
		83	46
TOTAL FROM OTHER SIDE		63	20
TOTAL		242	50
LESS CASH RECEIVED		—	—
NET DEPOSIT		242	50

2-303
710

USE OTHER SIDE FOR ADDITIONAL LISTING

BE SURE EACH ITEM IS PROPERLY ENDORSED

ROBERT H. GRIGG

3⑈04 596 3⑈

CHECKS AND OTHER ITEMS ARE RECEIVED FOR DEPOSIT SUBJECT TO THE PROVISIONS OF THE UNIFORM COMMERCIAL CODE OR ANY APPLICABLE COLLECTION AGREEMENT

Front

CHECKS LIST SINGLY	DOLLARS	CENTS
1	18	20
2	45	00
14		
15		
16		
17		
18		
19		
TOTAL	63	20

ENTER TOTAL ON THE FRONT OF THIS TICKET

Back

Figure 6.5 Machine-printed deposit receipt.

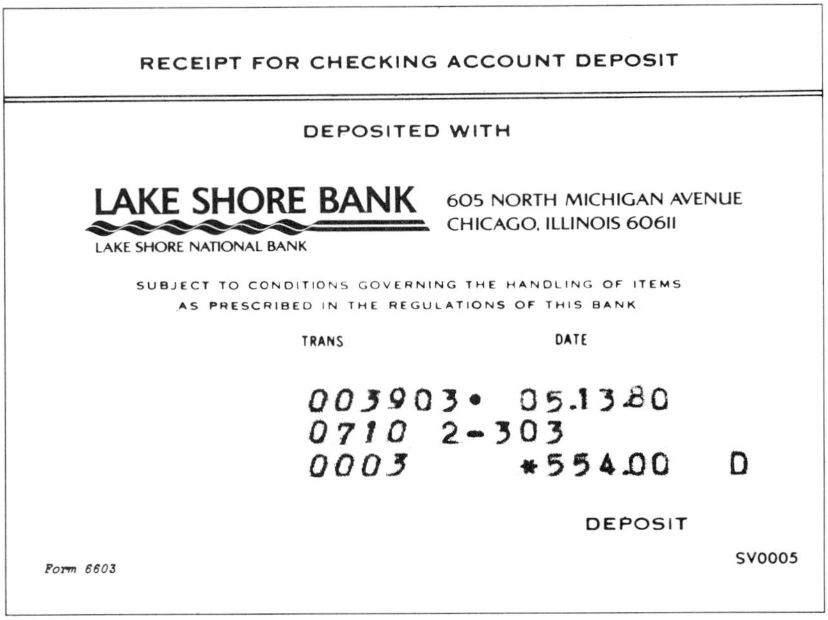

RECEIPT FOR CHECKING ACCOUNT DEPOSIT

DEPOSITED WITH

LAKE SHORE BANK 605 NORTH MICHIGAN AVENUE
CHICAGO, ILLINOIS 60611
LAKE SHORE NATIONAL BANK

SUBJECT TO CONDITIONS GOVERNING THE HANDLING OF ITEMS
AS PRESCRIBED IN THE REGULATIONS OF THIS BANK

TRANS	DATE

003903• 05.13 80
0710 2-303
0003 *554.00 D

DEPOSIT

Form 6603   SV0005

original may be returned to the depositor with the monthly bank statement. If a duplicate ticket is not prepared, the depositor is sometimes given a machine-printed receipt (fig. 6.5) at the time of the deposit. In some banks the original is later returned with the monthly statement.

Currency is prepared for deposit by arranging the bills in the order of the denominations. The smaller denominations are placed on top. If large quantities of coins are being deposited, they should be wrapped in coin wrappers provided by the bank. The name and account number of the depositor should be written on the outside of each coin wrapper.

Checks are listed separately on the deposit slip and identified by the **American Bankers Association (ABA) number** that appears in the upper-right-hand corner of each check (fig 6.6). The number identifies the bank holding the account on which the check is drawn and the Federal Reserve district in which the bank is located.

Another means of identifying a check is the **magnetic ink character recognition (MICR) number** that appears in the lower-left-hand corner of the check (fig. 6.7). The first part of the number is a routing and identifying code that gives the same information as the ABA number, except in a different form. The second part of the number is the individual account number of the person or firm writing the check. The MICR number is also used for automatic sorting by the bank.

Figure 6.6   American Bankers Association number.

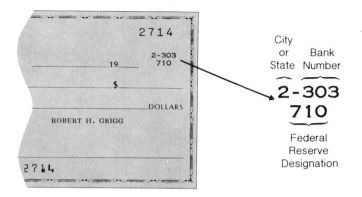

Figure 6.7   Magnetic ink character recognition number.

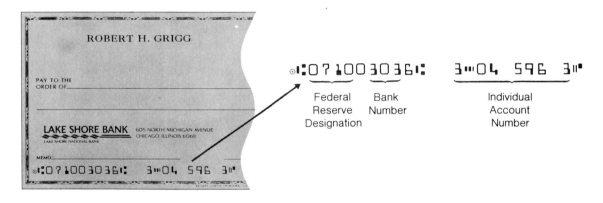

Checks must be endorsed before the bank accepts them for deposit. To endorse a check, the name of the check holder is written or stamped across the back of the check on the same end as the words *pay to the order of*. This endorsement transfers the ownership of the check.

Several types of endorsements are used. The simplest type is the **blank endorsement**. The holder of the check signs his or her name on the back of the check, thus making the check payable to whoever presents it for payment. This type of endorsement should be used only when a check is being presented for payment at the bank.

Another type of endorsement is a **full endorsement.** A full endorsement, sometimes called a *special endorsement,* includes the name of the

Figure 6.8 Check endorsements.

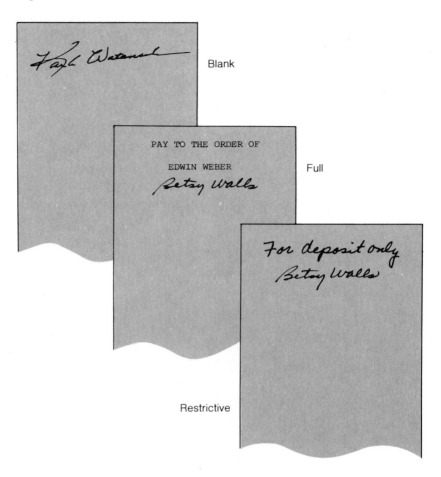

party to whom the check is being transferred. Usually the words *pay to the order of* precede the name of the person to whom the check is being transferred.

A **restrictive endorsement** may also be used. This type of endorsement specifies the purpose for which the money is to be used and restricts any further negotiation of the check. For example, an endorsement, *For Deposit Only,* indicates that the check can only be deposited in the account of the person or firm cashing the check. If the party endorsing the check has more than one account at the bank, the number of the account to which the check is being deposited should also be specified.

Examples of these endorsements are shown in figure 6.8.

Most banks provide a night depository service for those firms and individuals who are not able to make deposits during regular banking hours. Deposits are placed in bags and dropped through a chute into the bank vault. When deposits are made at night, a time lag usually occurs between the date the deposit is recorded in the checkbook and the date on which it is recorded in the bank account. This does not normally create any operational problems, although the deposit may be a factor in the reconciliation of the bank statement.

Another service provided by banks for those who cannot make deposits during regular hours is banking by mail. This means of making a deposit is recommended only if the entire deposit is made up of checks.

The Bank Statement

Banks periodically send each depositor a statement of account referred to as the **bank statement** (see fig. 6.8). The bank statement is a record of the transactions in the account for a certain period of time. The statement is usually sent once a month. While some banks send out all statements at the end of the month, it is more common for banks to send out a certain quantity of statements every day, thus avoiding the preparation and mailing of thousands of statements at the end of each month. According to this cyclic procedure, depositors receive their statements on the same day each month. These statements cover one month, even though it may not be a calendar month. A depositor should verify that the balance of the cash account in the general ledger agrees with the checkbook balance and the bank balance. If all cash receipts have been deposited and all cash payments have been made by check, the balance of the cash account should agree with the checkbook balance. When these two balances agree, the next step is to verify that the checkbook balance agrees with the balance on the bank statement.

The bank statement shows the beginning balance of the account. It also shows deposits and other amounts added to the account during the month, checks and other deductions from the account during the month, and the ending balance. Along with the bank statement, the bank sends deposit slips, the checks paid by the bank during the month, and notices or memos of bank charges or credits. The checks paid by the bank during the month and returned to the depositor are called **canceled checks.** They are perforated or stamped "Paid" and arranged in the order of payment by the bank.

One example of a bank statement is shown in figure 6.9. Notice that there is a special letter code used to designate charges and credits other than ordinary checks and deposits. The key to the code is printed on the statement for easy reference.

Figure 6.9 Bank statement.

LAKE SHORE BANK
LAKE SHORE NATIONAL BANK
605 NORTH MICHIGAN AVENUE
CHICAGO, ILLINOIS 60611
(312) 787-1900

STATEMENT OF ACCOUNT

MR ROBERT H GRIGG
43 E OHIO STREET
CHICAGO, ILLINOIS   60611

ACCOUNT NUMBER
20   304-596-3
STATEMENT DATE
07/31/**XX**

PREVIOUS STATEMENT BALANCE	CHECKS — DEBITS		DEPOSITS — CREDITS		SERVICE CHARGE	BALANCE
	NO	AMOUNT	NO	AMOUNT		
318.79	15	1,059.50	3	1,815.00	.00	1,074.29

07/01	400.00DP		
07/02	35.00CK		
07/07	105.00CK		
07/09	808.00DP		
07/10	6.62CK	15.00CK	154.37CK
07/11	231.06CK		
07/16	8.36DM		
07/17	12.68CK		
07/18	50.00CK		
07/21	7.99CK		
07/22	307.35CK		
07/23	14.49CK		
07/25	50.00CK		
07/28	50.00CK		
07/29	11.53CK		
07/31	607.00DP		
		BALANCE	1,074.29
15			

SAFEGUARD VALUABLES
RENT A LOW COST SAFE DEPOSIT BOX FROM LAKE SHORE

CK CHECK
DP DEPOSIT
EC ERROR CORRECTION CREDIT
ED ERROR CORRECTION DEBIT
TD AUTOMATIC DEPOSIT FROM SAVINGS
DM DEBIT MEMO
CM CREDIT MEMO
IF INSUFFICIENT FUND CHG
LS TOTAL OF SEVERAL CHECKS
CC CERTIFIED CHECK
OD ACCOUNT OVERDRAWN
SC SERVICE CHARGE
RT RETURNED CHECK

Each depositor insured to $40,000
FDIC
FEDERAL DEPOSIT INSURANCE CORPORATION

NOTICE
THIS STATEMENT OF ACCOUNT AND ENCLOSURES SHALL BE CONSIDERED CORRECT FOR ALL PURPOSES AND THE BANK SHALL NOT BE LIABLE FOR CHARGES MADE TO YOUR ACCOUNT UNLESS YOU NOTIFY THE BANK IN WRITING OF ANY FORGERIES OR OTHER APPARENT DISCREPANCIES WITHIN 30 DAYS OF DELIVERY OR MAILING OF THIS STATEMENT

The Bank Reconciliation

When the bank statement is received, it is important that the balance on the statement be compared with the depositor's cash records (the checkbook balance). Rarely will the two amounts agree. The difference is usually caused by one or more of the following factors:

1. Checks that have been issued by the depositor but that have not been presented to the bank for payment are called **outstanding checks.** There are usually some checks outstanding at the time the bank statement is received.

2. Deposits that have been entered on the depositor's books and sent to the bank but that have not been received by the bank are called **deposits in transit.** They are recorded with the next month's transactions and are shown as deposits on the next month's statement.

3. Fees charged by banks for the services they provide are called **service charges.** Service charges are usually deducted directly from the depositor's account. These charges are deducted from the bank statement balance but are usually not deducted from the books of the depositor until the bank statement is received. Notice of these charges appears as a code (SC for service charge) on the bank statement and/or through debit memoranda included with the bank statement. Examples of these charges include customary charges for handling the depositor's account, charges for collecting notes or drafts, and charges for stopping payment on a check.

4. A check that is not paid when presented for payment is referred to as a **dishonored check.** The most common reason for dishonoring a check is **not sufficient funds** (**NSF**) to cover the check. A depositor guarantees all items that he or she deposits. When the person writing the check does not have enough funds in his or her bank account to cover the amount of the check, the bank refuses to pay the holder of the check. The dishonored check is returned to the depositor, and the amount of the check is subtracted from the depositor's bank balance. The bank statement reflects the deduction, but the depositor's books do not. The depositor should deduct the amount of the dishonored check from the balance shown on the checkbook stub. It is then the responsibility of the depositor to try to collect the amount of the dishonored check from the drawer.

5. Occasionally the bank acts as a collection agent for the depositor. The bank adds the amount collected to the depositor's account and sends a notice—a credit memorandum—with the bank statement. The amount collected is added to the depositor's cash balance.

6. There is always the possibility that either the bank or the depositor may make mistakes in recording entries. Such mistakes can cause misstatements in either balance.

The process of checking the bank statement against the depositor's records is known as *reconciling the bank statement*. The statement that is prepared to report the results of the reconciling is called a **bank reconciliation**. A bank reconciliation, which is prepared monthly, accounts for, or explains, the difference between the bank's and the depositor's figures.

The procedure for preparing a bank reconciliation is as follows:

1. Compare the amounts on the deposit slips, canceled checks, and any memoranda accompanying the bank statement with the amounts on the statement. A check mark is placed by each item as a means of verifying that no errors have been made by the bank.
2. Compare the deposit amounts on the bank statement with those listed on the check stubs.
3. Sort the canceled checks into numerical order according to the check numbers. Compare them first with the list of outstanding checks on the previous month's reconciliation. Then compare the checks with those listed on the check stubs. Place a check mark beside those checks that have been paid by the bank.
4. Note any additions or deductions made on the bank statement, such as service charges or collection items.
5. Prepare the bank reconciliation.

A bank reconciliation contains two sections—one that shows adjustments to the bank statement balance and one that shows adjustments to a checkbook balance. The section showing adjustments to the bank statement balance is usually prepared first in the following manner:

1. Write down the balance as shown on the bank statement.
2. List any deposits in transit as well as any other adjustments of the bank's balance due to bank errors.
3. Add the listed amounts to the bank statement balance.
4. List the outstanding checks by check number and amount, and subtract the total from the subtotal obtained in step 3. The balance is the adjusted bank statement balance and represents the actual current balance of the account.

The section showing adjustments to the checkbook balance is then prepared in the following manner:

1. Write down the current checkbook balance.
2. List any corrections for errors and/or collections made by the bank that increase the checkbook balance and add them to the current balance. For example, if you have written a check for $10.00 and have shown the amount as $10.50 on the check stub, the difference between the two amounts ($.50) is added to the checkbook balance.

3. List any charges that are shown on the bank statement but that are not recorded in the checkbook. Subtract the total of these charges from the subtotal obtained in step 2. The difference is the adjusted checkbook balance and represents the actual current balance of the account.

The amount of the adjusted checkbook balance must agree with the amount of the adjusted bank statement balance. When the two balances are in agreement, double rules are drawn under each balance. The double rules show that the balances are the same and that the statement is completed.

A sample form used to prepare a bank reconciliation is shown in figure 6.10. The reconciliation may be typewritten or handwritten on forms printed on the back of most bank statements. Additional copies may be photocopied or duplicated in some other acceptable manner.

Figure 6.10 illustrates a simple bank reconciliation that has no unusual transactions to account for. Figure 6.11 illustrates a more complicated reconciliation with several different kinds of transactions to be accounted for.

After the bank reconciliation has been completed, journal entries must be made to record any items appearing on the bank statement that are not recorded in the depositor's books and to correct any errors that have been found in the depositor's books. No entries need be made to correct bank errors; however, the bank should be notified of any errors it has made so that its books can be corrected.

Figure 6.10 Simple bank reconciliation.

```
                       BANK RECONCILIATION
                          April 30, 19XX

Bank Statement Balance, April 30, 19XX                      $5,694.15
    Add: Deposit in Transit                                    305.00
                                                             5,999.15


    Less: Checks Outstanding
             No. 15                            $100.90
             No. 21                              54.60         155.50
Adjusted Bank Statement Balance, April 30, 19XX             $5,843.65


Checkbook Balance, April 30, 19XX                           $5,846.15
    Less: Bank Service Charge                                    2.50
Adjusted Checkbook Balance, April 30, 19XX                  $5,843.65
```

Figure 6.11   More involved bank reconciliation.

BANK RECONCILIATION
February 28, 19XX

Bank Statement Balance, February 28, 19XX		$1,349.72
Add: Deposit in Transit		206.69
		1,556.41
Less: Checks Outstanding		
No. 29	$ 56.73	
No. 36	9.18	
No. 39	193.46	259.37
Adjusted Bank Statement Balance, February 28, 19XX		$1,297.04
Checkbook Balance, February 28, 19XX		$ 795.04
Add: Note Collected by Bank	$500.00	
Interest Collected	5.00	
Error on stub for Check No. 35	.50	505.50
		1,300.54
Less: Bank Service Charge	1.50	
Collection Charge	2.00	3.50
Adjusted Checkbook Balance, February 28, 19XX		$1,297.04

After completion of the bank reconciliation in figure 6.10, one journal entry must be made to record the bank service charges on the depositor's books.

April 30	Miscellaneous Expense	2.50	
	Cash		2.50
	To record April bank service charge		

The bank reconciliation in figure 6.11 requires journal entries to record the collections and service charges as well as the error found on Check No. 35. Two journal entries are made.

February 28	Cash	505.50	
	Notes Receivable		500.00
	Interest Income		5.00
	Miscellaneous Expense		.50
	To record note collected by the bank and an error found in Check No. 35.		
February 28	Miscellaneous Expense	3.50	
	Cash		3.50
	To record bank charges for February		

Miscellaneous Expense has been used to record the bank charges and the correction of the check error. Some firms use a separate expense account, Bank Service Charge Expense, for bank charges. Also, when check errors are corrected, some firms credit (or debit) the account for which the check was written, especially if the error involves a large amount. For example, if Check No. 35 was originally written to pay a utility bill, the $.50 error would be credited to Utilities Expense.

Once the journal entries for the items appearing on the bank reconciliation have been recorded and posted, the balance of the Cash account in the general ledger should agree with the adjusted balance of the bank statement as shown on the reconciliation.

The Petty Cash Fund

One of the basic principles of cash control is that all payments should be made by check. In most firms, however, there are a number of daily transactions requiring the payment of small amounts of money, such as delivery charges, postage, and small office supply items. It is time-consuming and expensive to write checks for such small amounts. Therefore, a small sum of money called a **petty cash fund** is set aside, and payments are made from this fund. The establishment of a petty cash fund permits small cash payments to be made without the inconvenience and expense of writing a check. At the same time, it is still possible to maintain adequate control over cash disbursements.

In establishing a petty cash fund, an estimate is made of the amount of cash needed for a short period, usually two to four weeks. A check for the estimated amount is cashed, and the money is given to the person who is responsible for making payments from the petty cash fund. The money is kept in a secure place—usually a cash box or locked drawer. At the time the fund is established, an entry is made in the combined journal debiting Petty Cash and crediting Cash.

As each disbursement is made, a **petty cash voucher** or receipt is completed showing the amount paid, the name of the person receiving the money, and the purpose of the payment (fig. 6.12). The voucher is usually signed by both the person receiving the money and the person approving the payment. The vouchers are kept in the cash box or drawer together with the money remaining in the fund. The amounts of the vouchers represent expenses or asset acquisitions and are later recorded in the proper expense or asset accounts.

At all times, the amount of money on hand together with the vouchers should equal the amount that was originally placed in the fund. The voucher system is the *imprest method* for handling petty cash and is the method most commonly used by business firms.

In order to exercise additional control over petty cash, some firms keep a formal record of all disbursements called a **petty cash disbursements**

record or **petty cash register.** The vouchers are entered in this record in chronological order. One such form of record is illustrated in figure 6.13.

The register provides a memorandum record of petty cash transactions and also helps to classify payments according to the expense or asset accounts affected by the transactions. It is an auxiliary record used to supplement the regular accounting records. No posting is done from this register.

When it becomes necessary to replenish the fund, a check is cashed for the total amount of the vouchers. The money is placed in the fund, restoring it to the original amount. The fund is replenished when the person

Figure 6.12 Petty cash voucher.

PETTY CASH VOUCHER

NO. 15 DATE January 6, 19XX

PAID TO Jim Holt AMOUNT

FOR Postage 2 | 70

CHARGE TO Miscellaneous Expense

PAYMENT RECEIVED:

Jim Holt APPROVED BY C McQueen

Figure 6.13 Petty cash disbursements record.

Page 1 PETTY CASH DISBURSEMENTS

Day	Description	Vou No.	Total Amount	517	518	522	523
	Amount forwarded 100.00						
5	Messenger fee	26	1 75	1 75			
5	Charitable contribution	27	10 —				10 —
11	Telegram	28	2 10		2 10		
15	Messenger fee	29	1 —	1 —			
19	Jesse Arnold, Drawing	30	15 —				
25	Advertising bulletin	31	3 40			3 40	
			33 25	2 75	2 10	3 40	10 —
31	Balance $66.75						
	Rec'd in fund 33.25						
	$100.00						

in charge thinks the cash on hand is getting low. It should also be replenished at the end of each accounting period.

The small daily payments that are made from the fund represent expenses or asset acquisitions and therefore must eventually be recorded in the proper expense or asset accounts. This is accomplished at the time the fund is replenished.

A statement of petty cash disbursements is prepared from the petty cash disbursements record. This statement lists the amounts to be recorded

Figure 6.14 Statement of petty cash disbursements and accompanying journal entry.

STATEMENT OF PETTY CASH DISBURSEMENTS
January 31, 19XX

Jesse Arnold, Drawing	311	$15.00
Miscellaneous Expense	517	2.75
Telephone and Telegraph Expense	518	2.10
Advertising Expense	522	3.40
Charitable Contributions Expense	523	10.00
Total Disbursements		$33.25

JOURNAL ENTRY

Jan. 31	Jesse Arnold, Drawing	15.00	
	Miscellaneous Expense	2.75	
	Telephone and Telegraph Expense	2.10	
	Advertising Expense	3.40	
	Charitable Contributions Expense	10.00	
	Cash		33.25
	To replenish petty cash fund		

For the month of _January, 19XX_

Distribution of Charges

		Account	Amount
		Jesse Arnold, Drawing	15 —
			15 —

in the appropriate accounts. It provides the information for the journal entry to determine the amount needed to replenish the petty cash fund. The journal entry is made in the combined journal and brings the expense and asset accounts up to date. A statement of petty cash disbursements, together with the journal entry that results from it, are shown in figure 6.14.

The balance of the Petty Cash account is not affected by the entry to replenish the fund. The petty cash fund is a revolving fund that does not change in amount unless the fund is increased or decreased. The only amount in the Petty Cash ledger account is the initial amount debited to set up the petty cash fund. This amount changes only if the fund is increased or decreased, which requires another journal entry. The fund is increased by debiting Petty Cash and crediting Cash for the amount of the increase. If the fund is to be decreased, Cash is debited and Petty Cash is credited for the amount of the decrease.

Since the fund is established by writing a check and replenishment is also accomplished by writing a check, the flow of cash is still controlled by check. Therefore, the petty cash fund represents an indirect application of the basic principle of cash control.

Cash Short and Over

It is not unusual for errors to occur in handling cash, which result in more or less cash than can be accounted for. Errors that are the result of mistakes in the cash records can be found and corrected. However, if no error can be found in the cash records, it is usually assumed that a mistake has occurred in making change. While the shortage or overage may be small in amount, businesses still need to record the discrepancy. A discrepancy of this kind cannot usually be traced to a specific error and corrected; but without a record of the difference, a proof of cash cannot be made. Therefore, an account called Cash Short and Over is used for the purpose of recording any discrepancies.

Shortages of cash represent an expense and are recorded by debiting Cash Short and Over.

May 15	Cash Short and Over	3.00	
	Cash		3.00
	To record cash shortage		

Overages represent revenue and are recorded by crediting the account.

May 26	Cash	5.00	
	Cash Short and Over		5.00
	To record cash overage		

If the account has a debit balance at the end of the accounting period, it is included on the income statement as Miscellaneous Expense. If there is a credit balance, it is included on the income statement as Other Income. At the end of the accounting period, assume that the account appears as shown in the following. The credit balance of $2 represents income and is shown on the income statement as Other Income. Regardless of whether the account has a debit or credit balance, it is a temporary owner's equity account and is therefore closed at the end of the accounting period.

Cash Short and Over			
15	3.00	26	5.00
			2.00

Summary

It is necessary to maintain adequate control over the assets of a firm. Because cash is the most difficult of all assets to control, special precautions must be taken to safeguard cash receipts and disbursements (p. 108).

Cash includes currency, coins, checks, drafts, money orders—all items that a bank will accept for deposit (p. 108). Cash transactions are usually posted in a ledger account titled with the name of the bank with whom the account is held. A separate ledger account is used for Petty Cash (p. 108)

Each month the bank sends a statement to the depositor showing transactions affecting the depositor's account during the month. Rarely will the ending balance on the bank statement agree with the balance in the firm's checkbook or cash account. The process of checking the statement with the books is known as reconciling the bank statement. A statement called a bank reconciliation is prepared to explain the difference between the balances (pp. 117–20).

After the bank reconciliation has been prepared, journal entries must be made to record the items appearing on the bank statement that are not recorded and to correct any errors that have been found in the depositor's books (p. 120).

In any business, there are small daily cash expenditures. A petty cash fund is established to handle these expenditures. At the time the fund is replenished, the proper expense or asset accounts, as shown on a statement of petty cash disbursements, are charged for the daily expenditures (pp. 121–24).

Errors often occur in the handling of cash, resulting in more or less cash than can be accounted for. The discrepancy must be recorded regardless of how small it may be (pp. 125–27).

Key Terms

ABA number The number assigned by the American Bankers Association to a particular bank; appears in the upper-right-hand corner of each check.

bank reconciliation A statement prepared each month that accounts for or explains the difference between the bank statement balance and the checkbook balance.

bank statement A statement of the transactions of a depositor's account for a certain period of time; usually sent once each month.

blank endorsement The simplest means of transferring ownership of a check; includes only the signature of the payee.

canceled check A check paid by the bank during the month and returned to the depositor with the bank statement.

check A written order for a bank to pay a specified sum of money to a designated party.

deposit in transit A deposit that has been entered on the depositor's books and sent to the bank but that has not been received by the bank at the time the bank statement is prepared.

deposit slip A printed form used by the depositor to list all items being deposited.

dishonored check A check that is not paid when presented for payment; usually for not sufficient funds (NSF) to cover the check.

drawee The bank on which a check is drawn.

drawer The person who signs a check.

full endorsement A means of transferring ownership of a check, which includes the name of the party to whom the check is being transferred.

MICR number (magnetic ink character recognition) An identification number printed on each check and used to aid the bank in automatic sorting of checks and deposit tickets.

not sufficient funds A situation that occurs when a person does not have enough funds in his or her bank account to cover a check that has been written.

outstanding check A check issued by the depositor but not presented to the bank for payment at the time the bank statement is mailed.

payee The person or firm to whose order a check or promissory note is drawn.

petty cash disbursements record An auxiliary record used to record petty cash transactions; classifies payments according to the expense or asset accounts to be charged.

petty cash fund A sum of money set aside to make small daily cash payments.

petty cash voucher A receipt showing the amount paid out of the petty cash fund, the name and signature of the person receiving the money, the purpose of the payment, and the signature of the person making the payment.

restrictive endorsement The safest means of transferring ownership of a check; specifies the purpose for which the check is to be used and restricts any further negotiation of the check.

service charge A fee charged by banks for the services they provide.

signature card A card bearing the signature of each person authorized to sign checks on a certain account; kept on file by the bank as a means of verifying signatures.

Upon completion of this chapter, you should be able to:

1. Understand the need for and advantages of using special journals.
2. Record transactions in a cash receipts journal and post from a cash receipts journal to a general ledger.
3. Record transactions in a cash payments journal and post from a cash payments journal to a general ledger.
4. Record transactions in a sales journal and post from a sales journal to a general ledger.
5. Record transactions in a purchases journal and post from a purchases journal to a general ledger.

7 Special Journals

6. Define the following accounting terms:

   cash payments journal   purchases journal
   cash receipts journal   sales journal

In chapter 2, it was shown how transactions are first recorded in a two-column general journal called a book of original entry. That journal provides a record of each transaction in a single place in chronological order. The use of a general journal makes it easy to locate the complete details of a transaction quickly; however, much time-consuming, repetitive work is involved. Since such repetition is impractical and costly, accountants are continually searching for ways to simplify the journalizing and posting process.

Chapter 4 presented one way in which this can be done. The two-column journal was expanded to a multicolumn journal called a combined journal. Additional amount columns were added to the basic two-column journal. Each column added was used to record transactions affecting one particular account in the same way. For example, the column Cash Dr. can be added to record only debits to the Cash account. The use of the special columns eliminates the need to write account titles for each transaction. Furthermore, much repetitive posting is also eliminated.

The combined journal is frequently used by small firms that require the services of only one accountant. However, as the number of transactions increases, the use of a single multicolumn journal is no longer feasible. A more efficient method of journalizing and posting must be devised. One approach is to replace or supplement the multicolumn journal with several special journals. Each special journal is designed to record a certain type of transaction.

The four special journals used most frequently are (1) a **cash receipts journal** to record all transactions involving the receipt of cash, (2) a **cash payments journal** to record all transactions in which cash is paid out, (3) a **sales journal** to record all transactions involving the sale of goods on account, and (4) a **purchases journal** to record all transactions involving purchases made on account. Some businesses have need for all of these special journals. Others find it practical to use a combined journal with only one or two special journals. Most firms use the combined journal (or a general journal) for those transactions that cannot be recorded in a special journal.

In this chapter, the functions of the cash receipts and cash payments journals are explained in detail. Examples of the sales and purchases journals are presented along with a brief explanation of their functions. Detailed explanations of these two journals will be presented in chapter 8.

Function of Special Journals

The basic function of a special journal is to reduce journalizing and posting time. While a multicolumn journal is an improvement over the two-column form, its use presents certain problems. If a large number of columns are used to obtain the maximum benefit from summary posting, the journalizing process can be slowed down considerably. This delay results because of the time required to locate the proper column in which to record each figure. Also, when all the transactions of a period are recorded in the same journal, several pages are required to handle the transactions. This practice results in further slowdown because columns must be added and totals carried forward for each page. Carrying forward the totals requires the copying of more figures and thus increases the possibility of errors.

Another function of a special journal is to allow for a division of labor. The larger the enterprise, the larger the number of accountants. It is difficult and impractical to divide the work of journalizing among several accountants when only one multicolumn journal is used. With special journals, several persons can work simultaneously on the accounting records.

Special journals are also used to facilitate control of assets. For instance, one of the principles of the control of cash specifies that the cash records should be kept by more than one person. When a single journal is being used, this means of control is almost impossible since only one accountant is normally responsible for recording such transactions. When two or more special journals are used, the work can be divided among several persons. An independent cross-check can then be performed to determine the accuracy of the journal accounts. Later we shall see how the use of special journals also facilitates control over accounts receivable and accounts payable.

Special journals are designed to meet the specific needs of a firm and are provided only for those types of transactions that occur frequently. The needs of firms vary. Not all firms need all of the special journals. However, there are some special journals that are commonly used by almost all kinds of businesses. Virtually all businesses engage in numerous transactions that involve the receipt or payment of cash. Therefore, it is a common practice to use special journals for cash receipts and cash payments.

Cash Receipts Journal

Every business has transactions that involve the receipt of cash. Personal service businesses, professional enterprises, merchandising firms, manufacturing concerns, financial institutions—none of these types of businesses can operate without the receipt of cash. The number of transactions and the amount of cash involved vary according to the type and size of the business.

The major sources of cash are (1) cash sales, (2) payments of customer accounts, (3) additional investments in the business, (4) collection of money for payment of a loan, and (5) borrowing of money from a bank. The cash receipts journal is used to record *all* receipts of cash. Any transaction that involves the receipt of cash *must* be recorded in this special journal.

The form of the cash receipts journal used varies from firm to firm. Some firms use a single-column cash receipts journal; however, a multicolumn journal is more commonly used. The number of special columns the journal contains depends upon the needs of the particular firm. The titles of these columns vary also. The column titles are determined by the sources of a firm's cash receipts or the frequency of certain types of transactions in which cash is received. Any account that is affected in the same way by frequently recurring transactions requires a special column. A column entitled Cash Dr. is always provided since all entries result in a debit (increase) to cash. A General Cr. column (sometimes labeled Miscellaneous Cr. or Sundry Cr.) is also provided for recording credits to any account for which there is no special column.

The following list contains some of the December transactions for Dr. Wanda Ford (from chapter 4) that involve the receipt of cash. Some other transactions have been included to provide additional examples of transactions that result in the receipt of cash.

19XX

December 1 Received $1,965 from patients for office visits.

8 Received checks from patients and insurance companies for $2,292.

11 Sold office furniture for cash, $150.

15 Cash receipts from patients totaled $2,076 for the week.

18 Received $500 from a bank; gave a promissory note (Notes Payable) in exchange for the cash.

19 Received $796 from insurance companies.

21 Dr. Ford invested an additional $1,000 cash in her medical practice.

22 Cash receipts for the week totaled $3,073.

28 Received checks from patients and insurance companies totaling $2,297.

One form of cash receipts journal used to record such transactions is shown in figure 7.1. The column headings in this form indicate that the major source of cash receipts is professional fees. This simple form is adaptable for use by professional or personal service enterprises using the cash basis of accounting.

Another form of cash receipts journal is illustrated in figure 7.2. The column headings indicate that the most frequent source of cash receipts is cash sales (Sales Cr.) and collections from customers on account (Accounts

Receivable Cr.). A sales tax is collected for each cash sale, so a special Sales Tax Payable Cr. column is also used. (Sales taxes are explained in detail in chapter 8.) This form of journal is appropriate for a merchandising firm.

The procedure for recording transactions in a combined journal has been previously explained. The same procedure is used to record transactions in a cash receipts journal. Most transactions can be entered on a single line, although a few will require more than one line. For instance, if payment of a note receivable plus interest is received, two lines are needed

Figure 7.1 Cash receipts journal for a professional enterprise.

CASH RECEIPTS JOURNAL   Page 16

Date		Account Name	P/R	Cash DR	Prof. Fees CR	General CR
19XX Dec	1	Professional Services	✓	1965 —	1965 —	
	8	Professional Services	✓	2292 —	2292 —	
	11	Office Furniture	141	150 —		150 —
	15	Professional Services	✓	2076 —	2076 —	
	18	Notes Payable	212	500 —		500 —
	19	Professional Services	✓	196 —	196 —	
	21	Wanda Ford, Capital	311	1000 —		1000 —
	22	Professional Services	✓	3073 —	3073 —	
	28	Professional Services	✓	2297 —	2297 —	
				14149 —	12499 —	1650 —
				(111)	(411)	(✓)

Figure 7.2 Cash receipts journal for a merchandising firm.

CASH RECEIPTS JOURNAL   Page____

Date		Account Name	P/R	Cash DR	Accounts Receivable CR	Sales CR	Sales Tax Payable CR	General CR

Figure 7.3 Transactions recorded in a cash receipts journal.

CASH RECEIPTS JOURNAL   Page 1

Date	Account Name	P/R	Cash DR	Accounts Receivable CR	Sales CR	Sales Tax Payable CR	General CR
19xx Dec 1	Notes Receivable		505 —				500 —
	Interest Income						5 —

to record the transaction (fig. 7.3). One General Cr. line is used to record the credit to Notes Receivable. Another line is used to record the credit to Interest Income. The amount of the cash debit is recorded on the same line as the Notes Receivable credit.

At the end of each month, the columns are totaled and the equality of debits and credits is proved. The journal is ruled, and posting to the ledger accounts is completed (fig. 7.1).

The same rules for posting from a combined journal apply for posting from a cash receipts journal. All column totals except the General Cr. column total are summary posted to the proper general ledger accounts. Amounts in the General Cr. column are posted individually to the proper ledger accounts at various times during the month, so it is not necessary to post the column total at the end of the month. Amounts in the Accounts Receivable Dr. column are also posted individually, but that procedure is explained in chapter 8. The posting reference in the general ledger accounts is CR followed by the journal page number. The account number of the general ledger account to which the column total has been posted is placed under the column total to indicate that posting has been completed (see fig. 7.1). The ledger accounts of Dr. Ford after the posting of the December cash receipts transactions are shown in figure 7.4.

Cash Payments Journal

In any firm, there are numerous transactions that involve the payment of cash. Cash is disbursed (1) to pay creditors, (2) to pay for operating expenses, (3) to purchase assets, and (4) to repay loans. Generally, cash payments are made by check, and a special cash payments journal is used to record these payments. *All* transactions in which cash is paid out by check must be entered in this special journal. Small daily expenditures made out of a petty cash fund do not need to be recorded in the cash payments journal.

The form of a cash payments journal also varies from firm to firm. The number of special columns as well as the column titles is determined

Figure 7.4 Dr. Ford's ledger accounts after posting of December cash receipts transactions.

ACCOUNT __Cash__   Account No. _111_

Date		Item	P/R	Debit	Credit	Balance	
						Debit	Credit
19XX Dec	1	Balance	✓			10564 —	
	31		CR16	14149 —		24713 —	

ACCOUNT __Office Furniture__   Account No. _141_

Date		Item	P/R	Debit	Credit	Balance	
						Debit	Credit
19XX Dec	1	Balance	✓			5300 —	
	11		CR16		150 —	5150 —	

ACCOUNT __Notes Payable__   Account No. _212_

Date		Item	P/R	Debit	Credit	Balance	
						Debit	Credit
19XX Dec	18		CR16		500 —		500 —

ACCOUNT __Wanda Ford, Capital__   Account No. _311_

Date		Item	P/R	Debit	Credit	Balance	
						Debit	Credit
19XX Dec	1	Balance	✓				25602 —
	21		CR16		1000 —		26602 —

ACCOUNT __Professional Fees__   Account No. _411_

Date		Item	P/R	Debit	Credit	Balance	
						Debit	Credit
19XX Dec	31		CR16		12499 —		12499 —

by the nature of the transactions and the frequency with which they occur. This journal always includes a column headed Cash Cr. since any entry results in a credit (decrease) to cash. A special column for recording the check number is also included. A General Dr. column (sometimes designated Miscellaneous Dr. or Sundry Dr.) is used to record debits to accounts for which there is no special column.

The following list includes the December transactions for Dr. Ford. An additional transaction is included to provide another example in which cash is paid out.

19XX

December 1 Paid office rent for the month, $950, Check No. 72.

4 Paid telephone bill, $94, Check No. 73.

4 Issued Check No. 74 to Moffitt Insurance Company for premiums for coverage for office furniture and equipment for three years, $375.

7 Purchased medical supplies and drugs from the Pitcher Drug Company, $197, Check No. 75.

11 Issued Check No. 76 to Dailey Service Station for gasoline and other automobile expenses charged during November, $65.

11 Dr. Ford withdrew $250 for personal use, Check No. 77.

14 Issued Check No. 78 to Lyons Office Supply Company for office supplies charged during November, $159.

14 Bought medical supplies and drugs from Crandall Medical Supply, $86, Check No. 79.

15 Paid office salaries for the period December 1 to December 15, $1,034, Check No. 80.

21 Purchased medical supplies and drugs from Crandall Medical Supply, $137, Check No. 81.

27 Issued Check No. 82 for charitable contributions, $250.

27 Purchased medical supplies from Pitcher Drug Company, $157, Check No. 83.

29 Paid office salaries for the period December 16 to December 31, $1,034, Check No. 84.

29 Purchased office desk for $300, Check No. 85.

These transactions are recorded in a cash payments journal illustrated in figure 7.5. Column headings have been chosen for the accounts affected most frequently. A professional or personal service enterprise is most likely to use this type of journal since their records are usually kept on a modified cash basis.

Figure 7.6 shows another form of cash payments journal. This form is appropriate for a merchandising business in which frequent payments are made to creditors (Accounts Payable Dr.). The special column for Purchases Dr. simplifies the recording of the cash purchases of goods for resale.

Figure 7.5 Cash payments journal for a professional enterprise.

CASH PAYMENTS JOURNAL   Page 14

Date	Ck. No.	Account Name	P/R	General DR	Salary Expense DR	Med. Supp. & Drugs Exp. DR	Cash CR
19XX Dec 1	72	Rent Expense	512	950 —			950 —
4	73	Telephone Expense	514	94 —			94 —
4	74	Prepaid Insurance	131	375 —			375 —
7	75	Pitcher Drug Company	✓			197 —	197 —
11	76	Automobile Expense	511	65 —			65 —
11	77	Wanda Ford, Drawing	312	250 —			250 —
14	78	Office Supplies Expense	520	159 —			159 —
14	79	Crandall Medical Supply	✓			86 —	86 —
15	80	Office Salaries	✓		1034 —		1034 —
21	81	Crandall Medical Supply	✓			137 —	137 —
27	82	Miscellaneous Expense	518	250 —			250 —
27	83	Pitcher Drug Company	✓			157 —	157 —
29	84	Office Salaries	✓		1034 —		1034 —
29	85	Office Furniture	141	300 —			300 —
				3443 —	2068 —	577 —	5088 —
				(✓)	(513)	(521)	(111)

Figure 7.6 Cash payments journal for a merchandising firm.

CASH PAYMENTS JOURNAL   Page_____

Date	Ck. No.	Account Name	P/R	General DR	Accounts Payable DR	Purchases DR	Cash CR

Recording transactions in the cash payments journal is similar to recording transactions in the cash receipts journal. Posting follows the same pattern also. Amounts in the General Dr. column are posted individually at intervals during the month. Amounts in the Accounts Payable Dr. column are also posted individually, but that procedure is explained in chapter 8. At the end of the month, the columns are totaled, the equality of debits and credits is proved, and the journal is ruled (fig. 7.5). All special column totals except the General Cr. column are summary posted to the proper general ledger accounts. It is not necessary to post the General Cr. total since the amounts in that column have been posted individually throughout the month. CP and the page number of the journal are used as the posting reference in the ledger accounts. The general ledger account numbers to which the column totals have been posted are used as the posting reference in the journal (see fig. 7.5). The ledger accounts of Dr. Ford after the December cash payments transactions have been posted are shown in figure 7.7.

Figure 7.7 Dr. Ford's ledger accounts after posting of December cash payments transactions.

ACCOUNT _Cash_ Account No. _111_

Date	Item	P/R	Debit	Credit	Balance Debit	Balance Credit
19XX Dec 1	Balance	✓			10564 —	
31		CR16	14149 —		24713 —	
31		CP14		5088 —	19625 —	

ACCOUNT _Prepaid Insurance_ Account No. _131_

Date	Item	P/R	Debit	Credit	Balance Debit	Balance Credit
19XX Dec 4		CP14	375 —		375 —	

ACCOUNT _Office Furniture_ Account No. _141_

Date	Item	P/R	Debit	Credit	Balance Debit	Balance Credit
19XX Dec 1	Balance	✓			5300 —	
11		CR16		150 —	5150 —	
29		CP14	300 —		5450 —	

Figure 7.7—*Continued*

ACCOUNT _Wanda Ford, Drawing_   Account No. 312

Date	Item	P/R	Debit	Credit	Balance Debit	Balance Credit
19XX Dec 11		CP14	250 —		250 —	

ACCOUNT _Automobile Expense_   Account No. 511

Date	Item	P/R	Debit	Credit	Balance Debit	Balance Credit
19XX Dec 11		CP14	65 —		65 —	

ACCOUNT _Rent Expense_   Account No. 512

Date	Item	P/R	Debit	Credit	Balance Debit	Balance Credit
19XX Dec 1		CP14	950 —		950 —	

ACCOUNT _Salary Expense_   Account No. 513

Date	Item	P/R	Debit	Credit	Balance Debit	Balance Credit
19XX Dec 31		CP14	2068 —		2068 —	

ACCOUNT _Telephone Expense_   Account No. 514

Date	Item	P/R	Debit	Credit	Balance Debit	Balance Credit
19XX Dec 4		CP14	94 —		94 —	

ACCOUNT _Miscellaneous Expense_   Account No. 518

Date	Item	P/R	Debit	Credit	Balance Debit	Balance Credit
19XX Dec 27		CP14	250 —		250 —	

Figure 7.7—*Continued*

ACCOUNT _Office Supplies Expense_ Account No. 520

Date	Item	P/R	Debit	Credit	Balance Debit	Balance Credit
Dec 9XX 14		CJ 25	159 —		159 —	

ACCOUNT _Medical Supplies and Drugs Expense_ Account No. 521

Date	Item	P/R	Debit	Credit	Balance Debit	Balance Credit
Dec 9XX 29		CJ 25	577 —		577 —	

Although no single-column cash receipts or cash payments journals have been presented, some small firms find single-column cash journals more practical than the multicolumn journals illustrated in this chapter.

Sales Journal

Up to this point, only the accounting procedures for personal service and professional enterprises have been explained. The accounting procedures for merchandising enterprises have been, for the most part, ignored. In this chapter, some aspects of the accounting procedures for merchandising firms, such as special journals for sales and purchases, have been briefly touched upon. Because this topic is detailed in later chapters, only those explanations necessary for illustrative purposes are included in this chapter.

We have seen how service and professional enterprises derive their revenue by performing services for customers. A merchandising firm, however, derives its revenue from the sale of merchandise. The revenue account for a merchandising business is usually titled Sales.

Sales are made for cash and on account (Accounts Receivable). Sales for cash are recorded in a special cash receipts journal. Another special journal, a sales journal, is used solely to record sales of merchandise on account. When goods are sold on account, Accounts Receivable is debited and Sales is credited. Because the amount of the debit to Accounts Receivable is the same as the amount credited to Sales, a single-column sales journal is often used (fig. 7.8). Columns for recording customer names and invoice numbers are also provided.

Each transaction is entered on a single line. The standard totaling and ruling procedure is used at the end of the month. The column total is posted as a debit to Accounts Receivable and a credit to Sales. The page number of the journal preceded by S is used to indicate that the entry in the general ledger account has been posted from the sales journal.

Up-to-date records are kept for each customer. The methods used for keeping accounts for individual customers are explained in chapter 8.

If a company is subject to a retail sales tax, a three-column sales journal is used (fig. 7.9). Special columns are provided for Sales Cr., Accounts Receivable Dr., and Sales Tax Payable Cr.

Figure 7.8 Single-column sales journal.

SALES JOURNAL Page____

Date	Inv. No.	Customer's Name	P/R	Accts. Rec. DR Sales CR

Figure 7.9 Three-column sales journal.

SALES JOURNAL Page____

Date	Inv. No.	Customer's Name	P/R	Accounts Receivable DR	Sales CR	Sales Tax Payable CR

Each entry is still recorded on a single line. The debit to Accounts Receivable (selling price of the goods plus the sales tax) is equal to the credits to Sales and Sales Tax Payable. The totaling, ruling, and posting procedures are the same as previously described.

Purchases Journal

A large number of the transactions of a merchandising firm involve the purchase of goods for resale to customers. Purchases of merchandise for resale are recorded in an expense account entitled Purchases. These purchases may be made for cash; however, the majority of them are made on account.

Purchases of goods for which cash is paid are recorded in a special cash payments journal. A special purchases journal is provided for those goods bought on account. Only the purchases of merchandise on account are recorded in this journal. The simplest form of purchases journal is the single-column form (fig. 7.10). Since the amount debited to Purchases is the same as the amount credited to Accounts Payable, a single column is sufficient. Additional columns can be provided for the invoice number and date and the terms of the purchase.

At the end of the month, the journal is totaled and ruled. The total is summary posted as a debit to the Purchases account and a credit to Accounts Payable. P and the page number of the journal is entered in the general ledger account to indicate that the posting source is the purchases journal.

Figure 7.10   Single-column purchases journal.

	PURCHASES JOURNAL						Page____

Date	Creditor's Name	Invoice No.	Invoice Date	Terms	P/R	Purchases DR Accts. Pay. CR

Figure 7.11 Multicolumn purchases journal.

PURCHASES JOURNAL   Page_____

Date	Purchased From	Terms	✓	Accts. Pay. CR	Merchandise Purchases DR	Miscellaneous Purchases		
						Amount DR	Acct. No.	Account

Records are also kept for each creditor. The methods used for keeping these individual accounts are also explained in chapter 8.

In addition to merchandise for resale, firms also purchase other items on account, such as supplies, furniture, equipment, and other assets. A multicolumn journal designed to record everything purchased on account often proves more practical. Such a journal is designed to fit the needs of the company using it. Figure 7.11 is an example of such a form. Any number of debit columns can be designated for those accounts most frequently affected.

The procedure for recording transactions, totaling and ruling, and posting are the same as for the other special journals described in this chapter.

Other Journals

There are some transactions that do not fit conveniently into one of the special journals described (e.g., a note given in exchange for merchandise). Such transactions can be entered in a general journal or in the General Dr. and Cr. columns of a combined journal. Even if no such transactions exist, a general journal can still be used to record the adjusting and closing entries.

The special journals approach can be modified in many ways to suit the needs of a particular firm. A combined journal is often used alone or in conjunction with any of the special journals. A combined journal in its most complete form is a combined sales, purchases, cash receipts, cash payments, and general journal. Another form of combined journal, often referred to as a combined cash journal, is frequently used. Both cash receipts and cash payments are recorded in it. It is possible to combine other special journals also. For instance, the sales and cash receipts journals are sometimes combined.

Careful thought should be given to combining journals. It should be remembered that one of the reasons for using special journals is to provide for a division of labor for internal control. Whenever journals are combined, fewer people are able to work with the data in the journals at the same time.

Advantages of Special Journals

There are several advantages obtained from the use of special journals.

1. Time is saved in journalizing. Only one line is used for most transactions, so the time it takes to record transactions is reduced.
2. Time is also saved in posting. Summary posting of column totals greatly reduces the time it takes to post data.
3. A division of labor is possible. Several persons can work simultaneously on the accounting records.
4. Internal control is facilitated. By dividing the work among several persons, independent cross-checks are provided.

In a large firm, it is usually necessary for several persons to work on the accounting records at the same time. The use of special journals makes this possible. One special journal can be assigned to one accountant. However, in a small firm with only one accountant or with very few transactions, it may be both unnecessary and inconvenient to use special journals. In the final analysis, the decision regarding the use of special journals should be made on the basis of whether or not their use will provide maximum efficiency in handling transactions.

Summary

Because the use of a general journal involves much time-consuming, repetitive work, accountants continually look for ways to simplify the journalizing and posting process. One way in which this can be done is to expand the two-column general journal to a multicolumn journal called a combined journal. Many small firms with only one accountant or with very few transactions use the combined journal. However, firms with a large volume of transactions find the use of a combined journal not feasible. Instead, large firms usually depend on several special journals, each designed to record a certain type of transaction (p. 130).

The most frequently used special journals are the cash receipts, cash payments, sales, and purchases journals. When special journals are used, a general journal may still be used to record those transactions that cannot be recorded in one of the special journals (p. 130).

The special journal approach can be modified to suit the needs of a particular firm. Different combinations of the four journals described can be used (i.e., sales and cash receipts, purchases and cash payments). Or a special journal can be designed by a firm that has a great many transactions particular to its own activities. The combining of journals should be done carefully, however, if an efficient division of labor is to be accomplished (p. 144).

The use of special journals provides several advantages. Time and effort are saved in journalizing and posting. A division of labor is possible since many persons can work simultaneously on the accounting records. Internal control is also facilitated (p. 144).

Special journals should be used only in the event and to the extent that they contribute to obtaining maximum efficiency in handling transactions.

Key Terms

cash payments journal A special journal used to record all transactions in which cash is paid out.

cash receipts journal A special journal used to record all transactions involving the receipt of cash.

purchases journal A special journal in which all purchases of merchandise for resale on account are recorded.

sales journal A special journal in which all sales of merchandise on account are recorded.

Upon completion of this chapter, you should be able to:

1. Use the accrual basis of accounting for the revenues and expenses of a period.
2. Understand the special accounts used for the sale and purchase of merchandise.
3. Journalize and post transactions involving the sale and purchase of merchandise.
4. Use subsidiary ledgers for keeping individual customer and creditor accounts.
5. Calculate the cost of goods sold for a period.

8 Accounting for a Merchandising Firm

6. Define the following accounting terms:

accrual system of accounting	purchase invoice
cash discount	purchase returns and allowances
control account	purchases
cost of goods sold	realized revenue
credit (debit) memorandum	retail sales tax
FOB destination	sales invoice (ticket)
FOB shipping point	sales returns and allowances
gross margin	schedule of accounts payable
merchandise inventory	schedule of accounts receivable
merchandising business	subsidiary accounts payable ledger
net purchases	subsidiary accounts receivable ledger
net sales	trade discount

In the preceding chapters, we have discussed accounting procedures for personal service and professional enterprises. These types of firms sell services and derive their revenue from the fees charged for the services performed. Their records are kept on a modified cash basis. In this chapter, accounting procedures are introduced for another type of business—merchandising businesses.

Merchandising businesses are those whose primary source of revenue is from the sale of merchandise. They may be classified as retail or wholesale businesses. A retailer sells goods directly to the public, while a wholesaler sells to retailers.

Accounting procedures for merchandising firms are based on the same general principles of double-entry accounting presented in previous chapters. However, merchandising firms have certain characteristics that make a cash system of accounting impractical and that require the use of some special accounts and procedures not applicable to a service-type enterprise. These characteristics are explained in this chapter.

Accrual System of Accounting

According to the cash basis of accounting, revenue and expenses are recorded according to the period in which they are received or incurred. The net income or loss for a period is determined by subtracting expenses from revenue. While this system is satisfactory for most service enterprises, it does not give a realistic measure of net income for a merchandising firm for a certain period.

Merchandising firms usually buy and sell goods on a charge basis. Payment is postponed for a time. If a cash basis of accounting were used by these firms, their financial position for a period would be distorted due to several factors.

Revenues related to charge sales would be ignored until cash was received, and expenses related to charge purchases would be ignored until cash was paid out. Also, cost and expense reductions related to the stock of goods on hand would not be considered. The matching of revenue and expenses would not show what had actually happened during the accounting period.

Consequently, merchandising firms generally use an **accrual system of accounting**. When an accrual system is used, revenue is assigned to the period in which it is *earned*, and expenses are assigned to the period in which they are *incurred*, regardless of whether cash has been collected or paid out. Revenue and expenses are matched, even though no consideration is given to when cash is received or paid out.

The goal of the accrual system of accounting is to match the realized revenue of a period against the expenses incurred to produce that revenue. **Realized revenue** includes cash or a claim to cash that is received in return for something of value given up.

Merchandise
Inventory

As stated previously, the primary source of revenue for a merchandising firm is the sale of goods. The goods held for resale are called *merchandise*. A merchandising firm must keep a stock of merchandise on hand to sell to its customers. The amount of merchandise on hand at the beginning of an accounting period plus purchases during the period represents goods available for sale. These goods are known as the **merchandise inventory**.

A general ledger account entitled Merchandise Inventory is kept to record the value of the merchandise on hand at the end of an accounting period. Although Merchandise Inventory is an asset account, it differs from other types of assets, such as equipment, furniture, and supplies, which are acquired for use in the business and are not for resale. Merchandise Inventory, however, is acquired strictly for resale to customers.

Two different systems of accrual accounting for merchandise inventory—perpetual and periodic—are commonly used. These inventory systems are discussed in detail in chapter 10.

Accounting for Sales and Purchases

In any firm whose primary function is to buy and sell merchandise, special accounts are used for recording transactions that involve the purchase and sale of its merchandise. Following is a discussion of some of those special accounts.

Sales

Because the principal source of revenue for merchandising firms is from sales of merchandise, the revenue account is usually titled Sales. It is similar to the Professional Fees account used by Dr. Ford. In some situations, it is desirable to use several revenue accounts. Some companies record sales on a departmental or divisional basis in order to have a better picture of the sources of their revenue. For example, a service station might have revenue accounts titled Sales—Gasoline, Sales—Oil, and Sales—Automobile Accessories.

The Sales account is a temporary owner's equity account. It is closed to the Expense and Revenue Summary account at the end of the accounting period in the same manner in which the Professional Fees account was closed in chapter 5.

When a sale is made, legal ownership of the goods is transferred from one party to another. Sales are made on a cash or credit basis. Retail businesses are typically engaged in numerous transactions that involve both cash and credit sales. A wholesale business, however, deals largely on a credit basis and has few, if any, cash sales. Each time a sale is made, the revenue account Sales is credited (increased). The offsetting debit depends on the nature of the sale. In a cash sale, Cash is the offsetting debit. In a charge sale, Accounts Receivable is the offsetting debit. Remember that an account receivable represents an asset since it can be converted to cash

Figure 8.1 A bank credit card.

later. Occasionally, a note may be taken in exchange for merchandise. In that case, Notes Receivable is debited.

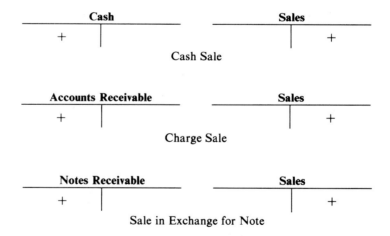

Many charge sales are also made by means of bank credit cards (fig. 8.1). These cards are issued by banks to persons who have established credit reliability. In effect, the banks issuing the cards are granting the credit, not the firms that accept the cards. Participating retail firms submit copies of the invoices or sales tickets to the bank (fig. 8.2). The bank handles the transaction in either of two ways: (1) The bank "buys" the tickets imme-

Figure 8.2 Bank credit card invoice.

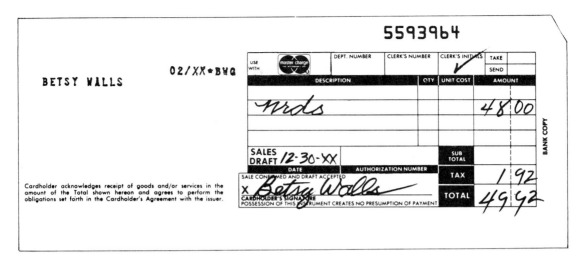

diately at a discount or (2) gives the retailer credit for the full amount of the tickets and, once a month, charges the retailer for the discount.

The retailer handles bank credit card sales in nearly the same manner as cash sales. The full amount of the sale is credited to Sales, and the amount received from the bank is debited to Cash. (A separate sales account can be kept for bank credit card sales, i.e., Sales—MasterCard.) The amount of the discount represents an expense and is usually debited to an account called Bank Credit Card Expense or something similar. Many firms prefer to use this form of credit because it lessens their risk of uncollectible accounts receivable; the bank bears the risk.

Only sales of merchandise are credited to the Sales account. A sale of an asset acquired for use in the business is credited to the proper asset account. For example, if a piece of office furniture previously used in the business is sold, the asset Office Furniture is credited.

The source document for sales takes several forms. Source documents for cash sales are usually in the form of cash register tapes or prenumbered sales slips (fig. 8.3). A duplicate of the tape or sales slip is given to the customer as a receipt for the sale.

When sales are made on account, the source document is a **sales ticket** invoice. In retail sales, the ticket is prepared by the salesperson at the time of the sale, usually in duplicate or triplicate (fig. 8.4). The original copy is forwarded to the accounting department where it is used as the basis for a journal entry. The second copy is given to the customer. If applicable, a third copy may be used for determining inventory control or computing commissions.

Figure 8.3 Cash register tape (left) and prenumbered sales slip (right).

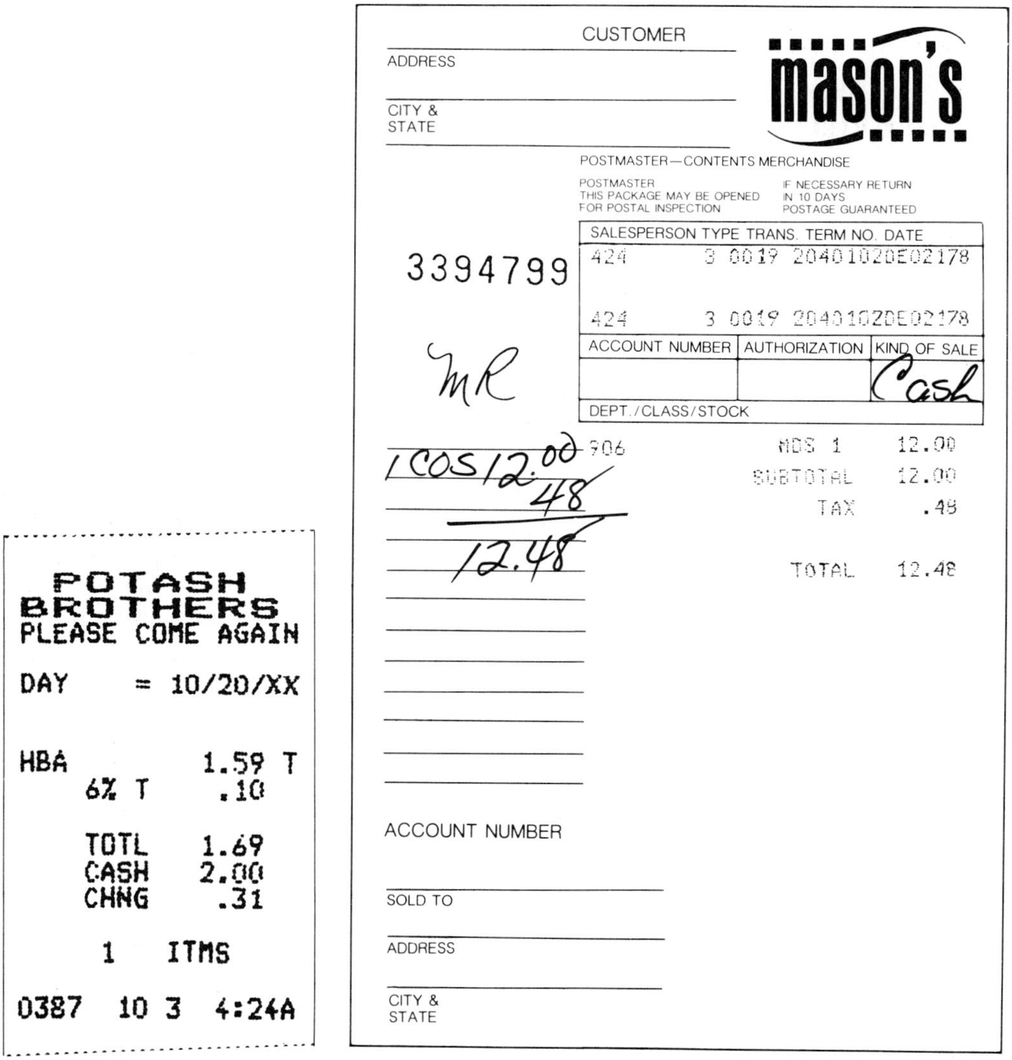

CUSTOMER					
ADDRESS					
CITY & STATE					

mason's

POSTMASTER—CONTENTS MERCHANDISE

POSTMASTER THIS PACKAGE MAY BE OPENED FOR POSTAL INSPECTION	IF NECESSARY RETURN IN 10 DAYS POSTAGE GUARANTEED

3394799

SALESPERSON	TYPE	TRANS.	TERM NO.	DATE
424	3	0019	20401020E02178	
424	3	0019	20401020E02178	

ACCOUNT NUMBER	AUTHORIZATION	KIND OF SALE
		Cash

DEPT./CLASS/STOCK

1 COS 12.00 706	MDS 1	12.00
12.48	SUBTOTAL	12.00
12.48	TAX	.48
	TOTAL	12.48

ACCOUNT NUMBER

SOLD TO

ADDRESS

CITY & STATE

```
  POTASH
 BROTHERS
PLEASE COME AGAIN

DAY    = 10/20/XX

HBA         1.59 T
   6% T      .10

   TOTL     1.69
   CASH     2.00
   CHNG      .31

   1   ITMS

0387  10 3  4:24A
```

In wholesale businesses, the source document is always referred to as a **sales invoice**. The invoice contains detailed information about the items sold, credit terms, and shipping arrangements. Figure 8.5 shows a typical sales invoice used by a wholesale firm. The invoice in the illustration is called a sales invoice by the seller, Tarrants, Inc. and a purchase invoice by the buyer, Signature B.

Figure 8.4 Sales ticket.

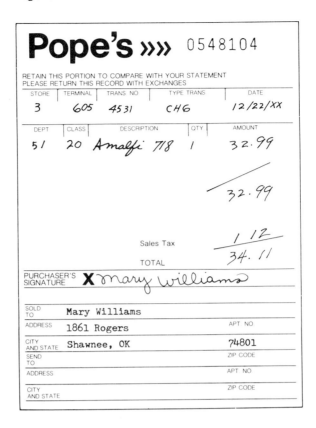

Pope's »»» 0548104

RETAIN THIS PORTION TO COMPARE WITH YOUR STATEMENT
PLEASE RETURN THIS RECORD WITH EXCHANGES

STORE	TERMINAL	TRANS NO	TYPE TRANS	DATE
3	605	4531	CHG	12/22/XX

DEPT	CLASS	DESCRIPTION	QTY	AMOUNT
51	20	Amalfi 718	1	32.99
				32.99

Sales Tax   1 12

TOTAL   34.11

PURCHASER'S SIGNATURE   X Mary Williams

SOLD TO	Mary Williams	
ADDRESS	1861 Rogers	APT. NO.
CITY AND STATE	Shawnee, OK	74801
SEND TO		ZIP CODE
ADDRESS		APT. NO.
CITY AND STATE		ZIP CODE

Figure 8.5 Sales invoice used by a wholesale firm.

INVOICE NO.   9A243   SOLD TO

salesperson Adair
cust. order no. 5706   Signature B
shipped via Fast-Way Freight   2212 Lester Drive
terms 2/15, n/30   Albuquerque, NM 87112
f.o.b. Destination   date October 26,19XX

quan.	item	style no.	unit price	amount
12	Blouses, Ladies, White Silk	B62	$12.00	$144.00
	less 5% discount			7.20
	Total Invoice			$136.80

TARRANTS, inc.   5672 Williams St., New York, NY 10012

Purchases

The **purchases** of a merchandising firm include supplies, assets for use in the business, and goods for resale to customers. The explanation that follows deals only with the purchase of goods for resale.

Purchases of merchandise for resale are made by cash or on account. However, the majority of such purchases are made on a credit basis. Since these purchases represent an expense to the business, they are recorded in an expense account usually titled Purchases. Generally only one account is used; however, if sales records are kept on a departmental or divisional basis, it is sometimes desirable to keep several Purchases accounts (e.g., Purchases—Oil, Purchases—Gasoline).

The Purchases account is a temporary owner's equity account that is closed to the Expense and Revenue Summary account at the end of the accounting period. The closing procedure is again the same as that described in chapter 5.

When a purchase of merchandise for resale is made, the Purchases account is debited (increased). The offsetting credit depends on the nature of the purchase. In a cash purchase, the credit is to Cash. In a charge purchase, the credit is to Accounts Payable. A purchase of supplies or assets for use in the business results in a debit to the proper asset account rather than to Purchases.

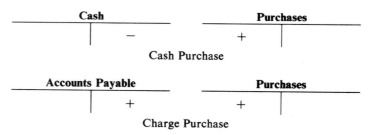

The procedures for purchasing differ somewhat from company to company. The size of a firm has a bearing on the manner in which the buying is done. In general, though, the basic activities are similar.

1. The purchasing procedure begins with a request for the merchandise. Usually the request is written on a form called a *purchase requisition.* This form is sent to a purchasing official or department for approval.

2. After the requisition has been approved, a *purchase order* is prepared and sent to a supplier. The number of copies prepared varies with the needs of the firm.

3. When the supplier (seller) receives the purchase order, a check is normally made on the buyer's credit rating. Once credit has been approved, the order is sent to the billing department where the order is filled and a **purchase invoice** is prepared. The purchase invoice contains information such as the buyer of the merchandise, the date

Figure 8.6 Invoice verification form.

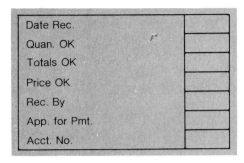

Date Rec.	
Quan. OK	
Totals OK	
Price OK	
Rec. By	
App. for Pmt.	
Acct. No.	

of purchase, credit terms, shipping arrangements, type and quantity of goods shipped, and total amount of the invoice. The invoice is usually sent with the merchandise.

4. Upon receipt of the merchandise, the buyer checks the quantity of goods received against the purchase invoice and verifies extensions and totals. A form may be printed on the face of the invoice for this verification (fig. 8.6). The invoice is then used as the source document for subsequent journal entries.

Discounts

Merchandise that is bought and sold on account requires an agreement between buyer and seller regarding payment arrangements. The payment arrangements agreed upon appear on each invoice and are called credit terms. For example, terms stated n/30 or net 30 mean that the invoice must be paid in full thirty days from the date of the invoice. Other commonly used credit terms are:

2/10, n/30: A reduction of 2 percent from the amount of the invoice is allowed if payment is made within ten days from the date of the invoice; otherwise, the full amount is due within thirty days.

3/10, EOM: A reduction of 3 percent from the amount of the invoice is allowed if the payment is made within ten days after the end of the month in which the purchase is made.

2/EOM, n/60: A 2 percent reduction in the amount of the invoice is allowed if payment is made by the end of the month in which the purchase is made. Otherwise, the full amount is due within sixty days from the date of the invoice.

These reductions in the amount of the invoice are called **cash discounts**. To illustrate how a cash discount is figured, assume than an invoice dated February 1 for $200 lists credit terms of 2/10, n/30. If the invoice is paid by February 11, the net amount to be paid is $196.

	$200	Amount of invoice	$200	
×	.02	Percent of discount	− 4	Amount of discount
	$4.00	Amount of discount	$196	Net amount to be paid

If the invoice is not paid by February 11, the total amount of $200 must be paid.

Any time merchandise is sold on account, problems can arise in collecting the amounts owed. To encourage prompt payment of amounts due, sellers frequently offer cash discounts. In the seller's records, the cash discount is known as a *sales discount*. Although retail firms do not usually offer sales discounts, it is common practice for wholesale firms to offer the discounts.

Sales discounts are ignored at the time of recording the sales invoice. If the customer takes advantage of the discount, it is recorded at the time payment is received.

The discount can be treated as an expense or as a reduction in sales. The latter treatment is preferred. While the discount can be debited (decreased) directly to the Sales account, a separate contra account called Sales Discounts is most frequently used. (The use of contra accounts was explained in chapter 4). This contra account is debited for the amount of the discount, and Cash is debited for the amount of cash actually received. For instance, assume that a sale for $500 is made under terms 2/10, n/30. The journal entry to record the sale is as follows:

Accounts Receivable	500	
Sales		500

If the customer takes advantage of the discount and pays $490 ($500 less 2%) within ten days, the journal entry is as follows:

Sales Discounts	10	
Cash	490	
Accounts Receivable		500

After the posting of these transactions, the ledger accounts look like this:

Cash		Accounts Receivable	
490		500	500

Sales Discounts		Sales	
10			500

Sales Discounts is a temporary owner's equity account. Its debit balance represents a reduction from the total amount recorded in the Sales account. The balance of the Sales Discounts account is shown on the income statement as a subtraction from Sales.

On the purchaser's books, cash discounts are referred to as *purchase discounts*. The purchase invoice is recorded at the gross invoice price. The purchase discount is ignored at the time the purchase is recorded. Then, if and when the discount is taken, it is recorded on the buyer's books. For example, assume that goods are purchased for $500 with credit terms of 3/10, n/30. At the time of purchase the journal entry is as follows:

Purchases	500	
Accounts Payable		500

Purchase discounts are considered as reductions in the amount of purchases. The amount of a purchase discount taken can be recorded as a direct credit (decrease) to the Purchases account. However, it is preferred to keep a separate contra account called Purchase Discounts. By keeping a separate account, management has information readily available about the total amount of cash discounts that are being taken. However, this does not provide management with information regarding the amount of cash discounts that are lost because invoices are not paid within the discount period.

When payment is made, Purchase Discounts is credited for the amount of the discount. Cash is credited only for the amount actually paid out. Accounts Payable is debited for the full amount of the invoice. If the foregoing invoice is paid with ten days, the purchaser pays only $485 ($500 less 3%). The journal entry to record this transaction is as follows:

Accounts Payable	500	
Cash		485
Purchase Discounts		15

After posting these transactions, the ledger accounts would look like this:

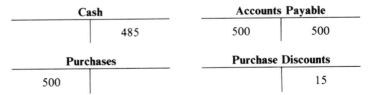

Purchase Discounts is a temporary owner's equity account that is reported in the income statement as a deduction from Purchases.

In addition to these cash discounts, retailers often give buyers other discounts from the catalog or list prices. These discounts are a convenient way of handling price fluctuations without continually reprinting catalogs.

They are called **trade discounts** and show up on the purchase invoice as deductions from the gross price. They may be single discounts (5%) or a series of discounts (5%, 10%, 15%). If a series of discounts is given, each discount is computed separately on the successive net amounts. For example, if trade discounts of 5, 10, and 5 percent are allowed on an invoice with a gross amount of $200, the net amount is computed as follows:

Gross amount of invoice	$200.00
less 5%	10.00
Balance	$190.00
less 10%	19.00
Balance	$171.00
less 5%	8.55
Net amount of invoice	$162.45

The net amount remaining after the trade discounts are figured represents the price the buyer records for the purchase.

The trade discount is not recorded on either the books of the buyer or the seller. For instance, if an item listed at $200 has trade discounts amounting to $20, the buyer's records would show Purchases debited for $180. On the seller's books, Sales would be credited for $180.

An invoice can be subject to both trade and cash discounts. The cash discount is taken on the net amount that remains after the trade discount has been subtracted. In the example in the preceding paragraph, a cash discount would be taken on the $180, not the $200.

Sales Tax

Most states and many cities levy a tax on retail sales. The tax, known as a **retail sales tax**, is generally levied as a certain percentage of the gross sales price. The tax is collected by the retailer from the customer at the time of the sale and remitted later to the proper taxing agency—city, county, or state government.

Sales tax amounts cannot be considered as revenue. They are considered as liabilities of the collector because they must be remitted to the taxing agency at a later time. A special liability account called Sales Tax Payable is used to record the amount of tax collected. At the time of a sale, the Sales account is credited only for the selling price of the goods. The amount of the tax is credited to Sales Tax Payable. The debit to Cash or Accounts Receivable is for the combined amounts (selling price plus sales tax). For example, a sale of $200 on account, subject to a tax of 2%, is recorded as follows:

Accounts Receivable		Sales		Sales Tax Payable	
204			200		4

The sales tax should be listed separately on a sales ticket.

Because some goods are exempt from sales tax, no taxes should be collected on those goods. Also, adjustments must be made in the taxes collected on any goods that are subsequently returned by the customer or on which an allowance is given.

Returns and Allowances

Occasionally merchandise is **returned** or a price adjustment requested. Merchandise is returned for a variety of reasons (i.e., wrong color or size or weight). A price adjustment, called an **allowance**, may be requested if the merchandise contains defects, has been damaged, or is of inferior quality. The return or allowance may be for a cash refund or a credit to an account.

For the seller, a return or an allowance represents a decrease in the firm's revenue (Sales) and likewise a decrease to the assets (Cash or Accounts Receivable). The returns and allowances can be recorded by debiting Sales and crediting the proper asset account. If this procedure is followed, the balance of the Sales account at the end of the accounting period would show only net sales. The volume of sales returns and allowances would not be shown. However, management needs information about sales returns and allowances to maintain effective control over merchandising operations. Therefore, it is preferable to use a separate contra account called Sales Returns and Allowances. This account is debited for the amount of a return or an allowance. The offsetting credit is to Cash or Accounts Receivable, depending on the nature of the original sale.

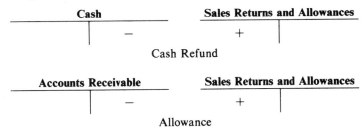

When the return or allowance refers to a charge sale, the seller issues the customer a **credit memorandum** (fig. 8.7). (Assets are reduced by crediting, hence the term *credit memorandum*.) The memorandum shows the amount and the reason for which the customer is given credit. When a credit memorandum is given, the balance of the customer's account is reduced by the amount of the memorandum.

Sales Returns and Allowances, a temporary owner's equity account, normally has a debit balance. On the income statement its balance is deducted from the balance of the Sales account to determine net sales.

To the buyer, a return or an allowance represents a decrease in expenses (Purchases). It also represents either an increase in assets (Cash) or a decrease in liabilities (Accounts Payable), depending upon the nature of the original purchase. The amount of the allowance or refund can be

Figure 8.7 Credit memorandum.

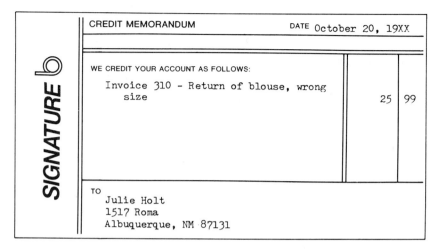

credited directly to the Purchases account. Usually though, a separate contra account called Purchase Returns and Allowances is credited. Cash is debited if a cash refund is given, and Accounts Payable is debited if an allowance is given.

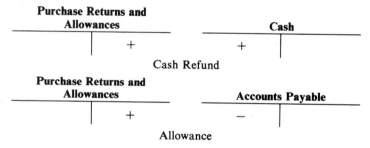

When the return or allowance refers to a charge purchase, the memorandum given to the buyer is called a **debit memorandum** (fig. 8.8). It shows the amount of the allowance and the reason for making the allowance. The balance of what is owed the seller is reduced by the amount of the memorandum. (Liabilities are reduced by debiting, hence the term *debit memorandum.*)

When a separate account is used, management has ready access to information regarding the amount of returns or allowances that have been made.

Purchase Returns and Allowances is another temporary owner's equity account that is closed at the end of the accounting period. The purchase returns and allowances are subtracted from purchases on the income statement to arrive at Net Purchases.

Figure 8.8 Debit memorandum.

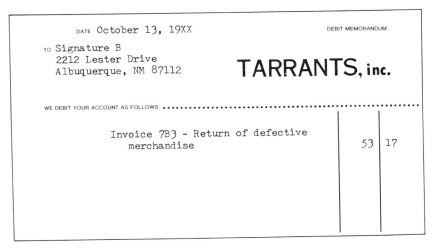

DATE October 13, 19XX

DEBIT MEMORANDUM

TO Signature B
2212 Lester Drive
Albuquerque, NM 87112

TARRANTS, inc.

WE DEBIT YOUR ACCOUNT AS FOLLOWS: ....

| Invoice 7B3 - Return of defective merchandise | 53 | 17 |

Transportation Costs

Most merchandising firms incur some costs related to the delivery of merchandise to customers. In retail firms, these costs are minimal since most sales are cash-and-carry or charge-and-carry. In wholesale firms, however, these costs are much higher since most goods are shipped to customers.

The terms under which goods are to be transported to a customer are stated on the invoice. If the seller is to assume the cost of transporting the goods, the terms are stated **FOB destination** (meaning free on board destination). If the buyer assumes the cost, the terms are stated **FOB shipping point**.

When the merchandise is shipped FOB destination, the amounts paid for shipping the goods represent an expense to the seller. The customer has no responsibility for the transportation costs. Usually a separate expense account called Transportation Out or Freight Out is used to record the costs. Sometimes the costs may be charged as Delivery Expense. The expense account is debited for the freight charges and Cash is credited. Accounts Receivable is debited and Sales is credited only for the price of the goods. Assume a $1,000 sale is made FOB destination. Freight costs are $50. On the seller's books the sale is recorded as follows:

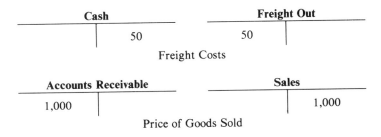

Cash		Freight Out	
	50	50	

Freight Costs

Accounts Receivable		Sales	
1,000			1,000

Price of Goods Sold

On the buyer's books, this is considered a purchase and is recorded as follows:

Accounts Payable		Purchases	
	1,000	1,000	

If the terms of sale are FOB shipping point, the shipping costs represent an expense to the buyer. The seller incurs no expense. Some firms record transportation costs as a direct debit to the Purchases account since in effect they add to the total purchase price of the goods. Usually, though, they are recorded in a separate expense account called Transportation In or Freight In. The buyer can handle transportation costs in either of two ways.

First, the merchandise can be sent collect to the buyer. In that case, the buyer pays the shipping costs upon receipt of the goods and enters the purchase in the following manner:

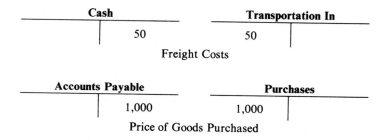

Cash		Transportation In	
	50	50	

Freight Costs

Accounts Payable		Purchases	
	1,000	1,000	

Price of Goods Purchased

The seller's books show only the price of the goods.

Accounts Receivable		Sales	
1,000			1,000

On the other hand, the seller may prepay the freight costs and charge them to the buyer. The transportation charges are added to the invoice for the goods. The entry on the seller's books is as follows:

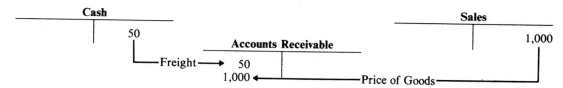

The entry on the buyer's books is as follows:

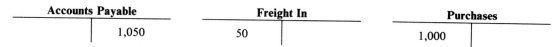

Accounts Payable		Freight In		Purchases	
	1,050	50		1,000	

The seller is reimbursed when the invoice is paid.

When cash or trade discounts are allowed on an invoice, the amount of the transportation charges is not included in the amount that is subject to the discount. Discounts are taken only on the actual price of the goods.

Transportation charges on any supplies or assets purchased for use in the business should be debited directly to the proper asset account.

Subsidiary Ledgers and Control Accounts

The general ledger contains all the accounts used by a firm. When a firm has numerous customers and creditors, the process of including individual accounts for all of them in the general ledger can create problems. The ledger becomes large and unwieldy. There is a greater chance for making posting errors as well as greater difficulty in locating them. The preparation of the financial statements also takes longer.

As a solution to this problem, it is customary to subdivide the general ledger. Large groups of similar individual accounts are placed in a separate ledger called a **subsidiary ledger**. The original ledger then contains only the asset, liability, and owner's equity accounts. It is still referred to as the general ledger. When a general ledger is subdivided, the accounts removed to a subsidiary ledger are represented in the general ledger by a summary account. The summary account is known as a **controlling** or **control account** and summarizes the information contained in the subsidiary ledger. The sum of the balances of the accounts in a subsidiary ledger must always agree with the balance of its control account.

Accounts in the subsidiary ledger are usually kept in alphabetical order on a three-column form similar to the one shown in figure 8.9. This form provides a current balance for a customer or a creditor at any time.

A merchandising firm generally keeps at least two subsidiary ledgers. (More can be used if necessary.) One is used to keep individual records for charge customers and is called a **subsidiary accounts receivable ledger**. Accounts in this ledger have debit balances except for rare instances when some unusual transaction has occurred, such as an overpayment of an

Figure 8.9 Three-column subsidiary ledger form.

Name_____

Address_____   Page_____

Date	Explanation	P/R	Debit	Credit	Balance	DR/CR

Figure 8.10 Schedule of accounts receivable.

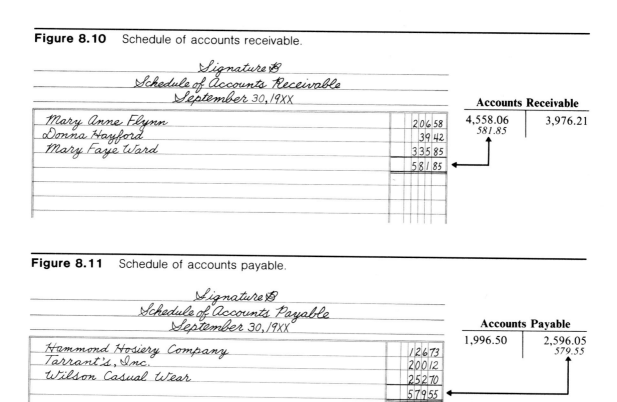

Signature B Schedule of Accounts Receivable September 30, 19XX			Accounts Receivable	
			4,558.06	3,976.21
Mary Anne Flynn	206 58		581.85	
Donna Hayford	39 42			
Mary Faye Ward	335 85			
	581 85			

Figure 8.11 Schedule of accounts payable.

Signature B Schedule of Accounts Payable September 30, 19XX			Accounts Payable	
			1,996.50	2,596.05
Hammond Hosiery Company	126 73			579.55
Tarrant's, Inc.	200 12			
Wilson Casual Wear	252 70			
	579 55			

account balance. The related control account in the general ledger is Accounts Receivable. This account shows only the total amounts owed a business by its charge customers. The subsidiary ledger provides the information about how much each customer owes and is the source of the information detailed on the itemized monthly statements sent to each customer.

A merchandising firm uses a second subsidiary ledger, called a **subsidiary accounts payable ledger**, to keep individual records for its creditors. The accounts in this ledger have credit balances except in instances where an account balance has been overpaid. The related control account is Accounts Payable. Accounts Payable shows only the total amounts owed to all creditors. The subsidiary ledger gives the details about the amounts owed to each creditor.

When the sums of the individual account balances from the subsidiary ledgers do not agree with their related control accounts, it is likely that a posting error has been made. The errors must be found and corrected.

Lists of individual accounts and their balances are prepared from each subsidiary ledger. The list of accounts prepared from the subsidiary accounts receivable ledger shows the amounts owed by each charge customer and is called a **schedule of accounts receivable** (fig. 8.10). The list prepared from the subsidiary accounts payable ledger shows the amounts owed to each creditor and is called a **schedule of accounts payable** (fig. 8.11).

Journalizing and Posting Procedures

In chapter 7, four commonly used special journals were described. A merchandising firm is likely to use a combination of all four of these special journals in addition to a general journal. In this chapter, however, we are more concerned with the way in which the sales and purchases journals might be used for greater efficiency. The books used by Signature B, a retail firm specializing in women's clothing, are used in all the examples.

Signature B uses a cash receipts journal for recording the receipt of cash from all sources (e.g., cash sales, payments on accounts). A cash payments journal is used to record the payment of cash for any purpose (e.g., cash purchases, payments on accounts). Portions of these journals are reproduced in figure 8.14.

Chapter 7 included examples of two alternate types of sales journals for use in recording sales of merchandise on account. Since Signature B must collect a retail sales tax, the three-column journal is more practical for that business. A portion of the journal used by Signature B is shown in figure 8.12. It includes transactions for the month of November.

The first sale in November was to Miss Julie Holt for $56.95. A sales tax of $2.28 was collected. The total amount of the invoice, $59.23, is written in the Accounts Receivable Dr. column. The amount of tax collected is written in the Sales Tax Payable Cr. column. Only the actual cost of the goods is recorded in the Sales Cr. column. Invoice 291 is the source document that provides the details for this entry. All sales of merchandise on account are recorded in this manner.

Signature B uses a one-column purchases journal, which is shown in figure 8.13. Only credit purchases of merchandise for resale are recorded

Figure 8.12 Three-column sales journal.

SALES JOURNAL   Page 36

Date	Inv. No.	Customer's Name	P/R	Accounts Receivable DR	Sales CR	Sales Tax Payable CR
19xx Nov 3	291	Julie Holt	✓	59 23	56 95	2 28
3	302	Donna Hayford	✓	204 62	196 75	7 87
5	312	Mary Faye Ward	✓	102 35	98 41	3 94

Figure 8.13   One-column purchases journal.

PURCHASES JOURNAL   Page 29

Date		Inv. No.	Creditor's Name	P/R	Amount
19xx Nov	2	310	Hammond Hosiery Company	✓	396 70
	4	311	Tarrant's, Inc.	✓	514 50
	4	312	Wilson Casual Wear	✓	672 50

in this journal. A portion of Signature B's purchases transactions for the month of November are included in this example. Invoice 310 provides the complete details for the first entry. Details of subsequent journal entries are provided by the invoices listed next to each purchase.

The posting procedure for these special journals was explained in chapter 7. The use of subsidiary ledgers alters this procedure slightly. Column totals from each special journal are posted to the general ledger accounts at the end of the month. Amounts recorded in any General column must be posted individually at regular intervals during the month. Individual posting to the accounts in the subsidiary ledgers must also be done (see p. 168). Individual posting to the subsidiary ledgers is usually done on a daily basis. As each amount is posted, a check mark is placed in the journal PR column. The posting may be done directly from the source document (sales ticket, invoice, credit memorandum), or it may be done from the journal itself. Posting from the source document is preferred. By doing so, the work can be divided among more persons, thereby providing a better means of internal control. Chances for recording or posting errors are also lessened. If posting is done from the source document, the posting reference in the subsidiary ledger account identifies that document. For example, CM for credit memorandum. If posting is done from a journal, the posting reference identifies the journal.

The Balance column of a subsidiary ledger account shows the current balance of the account. As each entry is recorded in the account, the new (or current) balance is entered in the Balance column. In an accounts receivable subsidiary ledger, the balance usually represents a debit balance. In an accounts payable subsidiary ledger, the balance usually represents a credit balance. Remember that the individual accounts in the subsidiary ledgers include postings for charges, payments, returns or allowances, and discounts.

The posting procedure from special journals, summary and individual, is illustrated in figure 8.14a through 8.14g. Only selected transactions have been recorded in the journals.

Figure 8.14a Posting from a cash receipts journal.

CASH RECEIPTS JOURNAL   Page 23

Date	Account Name	P/R	Cash DR	Accounts Receivable CR	Sales CR	Sales Tax Payable CR	General CR
19XX Nov 3	Donna Hayford	✓	76 91	76 91			
5	Mary Anne Flynn	✓	119 56	119 56			
19	Julie Holt	✓	59 23	59 23			
19	Cash Sales	✓	2460 35		2365 72	94 63	
25	Cash Sales	✓	3615 57		3476 51	139 06	
			6331 62	255 70	5842 23	233 69	
			(111)	(121)	(411)	(212)	

Figure 8.14b Posting from a cash payments journal.

CASH PAYMENTS JOURNAL   Page 21

Date	Ck. No.	Account Name	P/R	General DR	Accounts Payable DR	Purchases DR	Cash CR
19XX Nov 2	261	Tarrant's, Inc.	✓		316 17		316 17
2	262	Rent Expense	512	500 —			500 —
17	276	Office Furniture	141	246 —			246 —
28	284	Tarrant's, Inc.	✓		514 50		514 50
28	285	Wilson Casual Wear	✓		672 50		672 50
				746 —	1503 17		2249 17
				(✓)	(211)		(111)

Figure 8.14c Posting from a sales journal.

SALES JOURNAL   Page 36

Date	Inv. No.	Customer's Name	P/R	Accounts Receivable DR	Sales CR	Sales Tax Payable CR
19XX Nov 3	291	Julie Holt	✓	59 23	56 95	2 28
3	302	Donna Hayford	✓	204 62	196 75	7 87
5	312	Mary Faye Ward	✓	102 35	98 41	3 94
27	400	Mary Anne Flynn	✓	243 58	233 78	9 80
29	423	Julie Holt	✓	35 78	34 40	1 38
				1006 87	967 88	386 99
				(121)	(411)	(212)

Figure 8.14d Posting from a purchases journal.

PURCHASES JOURNAL   Page 29

Date		Inv. No.	Creditor's Name	P/R	Amount
19XX Nov	2	310	Hammond Hosiery Company	✓	396 70
	4	311	Tarrant's, Inc.	✓	514 50
	4	312	Wilson Casual Wear	✓	672 50
	24	320	Tarrant's, Inc.	✓	225 62
	26	324	Wilson Casual Wear	✓	167 19
			Purchases Dr / Accounts Payable Cr	511/211	3647 86

Figure 8.14e Posting to a general ledger.

GENERAL LEDGER

ACCOUNT   Cash   Account No. 111

Date		Item	P/R	Debit	Credit	Balance Debit	Balance Credit
19XX Nov	1	Balance	✓			9674 57	
	30		CR23	6331 62		16006 19	
	30		CP21		2249 17	13757 02	

ACCOUNT   Accounts Receivable   Account No. 121

Date		Item	P/R	Debit	Credit	Balance Debit	Balance Credit
19XX Nov	1	Balance	✓			2008 52	
	30		S36	10061 87		12070 39	
	30		CR23		255 70	11814 69	

ACCOUNT   Office Furniture   Account No. 141

Date		Item	P/R	Debit	Credit	Balance Debit	Balance Credit
19XX Nov	1	Balance	✓			2671 43	
	17		CP21	246 —		2917 43	

Figure 8.14e—*Continued*

ACCOUNT _Accounts Payable_   Account No. _211_

Date	Item	P/R	Debit	Credit	Balance Debit	Balance Credit
19xx Nov 1	Balance	√				1 40 2 70
30		P29		3 64 7 86		5 05 0 56
30		CP21	1 50 3 17			3 54 7 39

ACCOUNT _Sales Tax Payable_   Account No. _212_

Date	Item	P/R	Debit	Credit	Balance Debit	Balance Credit
19xx Nov 30		S36		3 86 99		3 86 99
30		CR23		2 33 69		6 20 68

ACCOUNT _Sales_   Account No. _411_

Date	Item	P/R	Debit	Credit	Balance Debit	Balance Credit
19xx Nov 30		S36		9 67 4 88		9 67 4 88
30		CR23		5 84 2 23		15 51 7 11

ACCOUNT _Purchases_   Account No. _511_

Date	Item	P/R	Debit	Credit	Balance Debit	Balance Credit
19xx Nov 30		P29	3 64 7 86		3 64 7 86	

ACCOUNT _Rent Expense_   Account No. _512_

Date	Item	P/R	Debit	Credit	Balance Debit	Balance Credit
19xx Nov 2		CP21	5 00 —		5 00 —	

Figure 8.14f Posting to an accounts receivable ledger.

ACCOUNTS RECEIVABLE LEDGER

Name _Mary Anne Flynn_
Address _1670 Lubbock St., Bakersfield, CA_

Date		Explanation	P/R	Debit	Credit	Balance	DR/CR
19xx Nov	1	Balance	✓			119 56	DR
	5		Ck		119 56	—o—	
	27		Inv 400	243 58		243 58	DR

Name _Donna Hayford_
Address _514 Appleton Way, Ruston, LA_

Date		Explanation	P/R	Debit	Credit	Balance	DR/CR
19xx Nov	1	Balance	✓			76 91	DR
	3		Ck		76 91	—o—	
	3		Inv 302	204 62		204 62	DR

Name _Julie Holt_
Address _1517 Roma, Albuquerque, NM_

Date		Explanation	P/R	Debit	Credit	Balance	DR/CR
19xx Nov	3		Inv 291	59 23		59 23	DR
	19		Ck		59 23	—o—	
	29		Inv 423	35 78		35 78	DR

Name _Mary Faye Ward_
Address _412 Pine Lane, Detroit, MI_

Date		Explanation	P/R	Debit	Credit	Balance	DR/CR
19xx Nov	1	Balance	✓			63 70	DR
	5		Inv 312	102 35		166 05	DR

Figure 8.14g Posting to an accounts payable ledger.

ACCOUNTS PAYABLE LEDGER

Name Hammond Hosiery Company

Address 510 Beltline, Plano, TX

Date		Explanation	P/R	Debit	Credit	Balance	DR/CR
19XX nov	2		Inv 310		396 70	396 70	CR

Name Tarrant's, Inc.

Address 5672 Williams St., New York, NY

Date		Explanation	P/R	Debit	Credit	Balance	DR/CR
19XX nov	1	Balance	✓			316 17	CR
	2		Ck 261	316 17		—o—	
	4		Inv 311		514 50	514 50	CR
	24		Inv 320		225 62	740 12	CR
	28		Ck 284	514 50		225 62	CR

Name Wilson Casual Wear

Address 956 Farris, Charlotte, NC

Date		Explanation	P/R	Debit	Credit	Balance	DR/CR
19XX nov	4		Inv 312		672 50	672 50	CR
	26		Inv 324		167 19	839 69	CR
	28		Ck 285	672 50		167 19	CR

Cost of Goods Sold

The calculation of net income or loss for a service enterprise is a simple procedure. Expenses are merely subtracted from revenue. The operating costs of the enterprise constitute the expenses and represent the total costs that must be taken into consideration. In determining the net income or loss for a merchandising firm, however, another kind of expense must be considered—the cost of goods sold. The **cost of goods sold** is the total cost of the merchandise sold during a period. It is an expense that must be subtracted from the net sales revenue for the period. **Net sales** is the total amount of sales less all sales returns, allowances, discounts, and transportation costs. The difference between the net sales of the period and the cost of goods sold is called the **gross margin** or **gross profit**.

The cost of goods sold is calculated by adding the beginning merchandise inventory to the net purchases of the period and then subtracting the ending merchandise inventory. **Net purchases** is the total amount of purchases less all purchase returns, allowances, discounts, and transportation costs. The transportation costs referred to are those incurred when goods are shipped FOB destination and the buyer must pay the freight (Freight In). The calculations for cost of goods sold are made directly on the income statement in the manner shown.

Revenue				
Gross Sales				$71,200
Less: Sales Returns				
and Allowances		560		
Sales Discounts		250	810	
Net Sales				$70,390
Cost of Goods Sold				
Mdse. Inv. Jan. 1, 19XX				
(Beginning)			25,100	
Purchases	$32,600			
Add: Freight In	55			
Cost of Delivered				
Goods	$32,655			
Less: Pur. Ret. and				
Allowances	426			
Purchase				
Discounts	325	751		
Net Purchases			31,904	
Mdse. available for sale			57,004	
Less: Mdse. Inv. Dec. 31, 19XX				
(Ending)			22,570	
Cost of Goods Sold				34,434
Gross Margin				$35,956

Gross Profit

After the gross margin has been determined, the operating expenses are subtracted from the gross margin to arrive at the net income or loss for the period.

The merchandising procedures explained in this chapter relate to manually operated systems of accounting. Manually operated systems are easier to understand and lend themselves more readily to learning situations. It should be noted, however, that all of the foregoing procedures may be accomplished by the use of mechanical, electronic, or electrical equipment. These mechanical or electronic means of processing data are explained in chapter 14.

Summary

Merchandising businesses are those whose primary source of revenue is from the sale of merchandise (p. 148). These firms use an accrual system of accounting rather than the cash system used by service enterprises (p. 148).

In merchandising firms, special accounts and procedures are used for handling transactions that involve the purchase and sale of merchandise. The amount of goods on hand at the beginning of the period plus the goods purchased during the period represents the Merchandise Inventory (p. 149). The receipt of revenue from sales of merchandise is recorded in a temporary owner's equity (revenue) account called Sales (p. 149). Goods purchased for resale represent an expense to a merchandising firm and are recorded in a temporary owner's equity (expense) account called Purchases (p. 154).

In merchandising firms, it is a common practice to offer discounts to buyers. Cash discounts are reductions in the amounts of invoices and are commonly offered as an incentive for early payment of amounts owed. These discounts are recorded as Sales or Purchase Discounts (pp. 155–57). Trade discounts, which are deductions from the wholesale catalog or list price of goods, may also be offered (p. 157).

Retail sales taxes are often levied on the gross sales price of merchandise. These taxes represent a liability to the collector (seller) and are recorded in a liability account called Sales Tax Payable (pp. 157–59).

Merchandise may on occasion be returned or a price adjustment (allowance) requested for various reasons. Credit or debit memorandums are issued to adjust or correct individual accounts for the price of the goods returned or for allowances made in the original price of the goods (pp. 159–61).

Most merchandising firms incur some expenses related to the delivery of merchandise to customers. These costs are the responsibility of the seller if the goods are shipped FOB destination. They are the responsibility of the buyer if shipped FOB shipping point (pp. 161–63).

Merchandising firms normally maintain subsidiary ledgers for individual charge customers and for creditors. Each subsidiary ledger is represented in the general ledger by a control account that summarizes the information contained in each subsidiary ledger. The sum of the balances of the individual accounts in each subsidiary ledger must always agree with the balance of their related control accounts. Individual accounts for charge customers are kept in a subsidiary accounts receivable ledger. Individual creditor accounts are kept in a subsidiary accounts payable ledger (pp. 163–65).

Special journals are used to facilitate the journalizing and posting of transactions involving the sale and purchase of merchandise (pp. 165–71).

When determining the net income or loss for a merchandising firm, the cost of goods sold must be taken into consideration. The cost of goods sold is an expense that must be subtracted from the net sales to arrive at the gross margin (profit). Operating expenses are then subtracted from the gross margin to determine the net income or loss for the period (pp. 172–73).

Key Terms

accrual system of accounting A system of accounting in which revenue is recorded in the period in which it is earned and expenses are recorded in the period in which they are incurred.

cash discount A reduction allowed in the amount of an invoice to encourage prompt payment of the invoice; to the seller, it is a Sales Discount, to the buyer, a Purchase Discount.

control account A general ledger account that summarizes the information contained in a related subsidiary ledger.

cost of goods sold The total cost of the merchandise that is sold during an accounting period.

credit (debit) memorandum A document given to a customer when merchandise is returned or an allowance in the price is made.

FOB destination Transportation arrangements whereby the seller pays the cost of the delivery of goods.

FOB shipping point Transportation arrangements whereby the buyer pays the cost of the delivery of goods.

gross margin (profit) The difference between the net sales of a period and the cost of goods sold.

merchandise inventory The total amount of goods on hand at the end of an accounting period.

merchandising business A firm whose primary source of revenue is from the sale of merchandise.

net purchases The total purchases—including transportation costs—less any returns, allowances, and discounts.

net sales The total sales less any returns, allowances, and discounts.

purchase invoice A document received by the buyer that contains details about a purchase.

purchase returns and allowances A contra expense account used by the buyer for recording the price for merchandise returned and price adjustments (allowances) on defective merchandise.

purchases Merchandise bought for resale.

realized revenue Cash or a claim to cash that is received in return for something of value given up.

retail sales tax A tax levied on the gross price of retail sales.

sales invoice (ticket) A document prepared by the seller containing details of a sale.

sales returns and allowances A contra revenue account used by the seller for recording the price of merchandise returned and price adjustments (allowances) on defective merchandise.

schedule of accounts payable A list of individual creditors and the amounts owed to each.

schedule of accounts receivable A list of individual charge customers and the amounts owed by each.

subsidiary accounts payable ledger A book containing individual ledger accounts for creditors.

subsidiary accounts receivable ledger A book containing individual ledger accounts for charge customers.

trade discount A reduction in the catalog or list price of merchandise offered by wholesalers.

Upon completion of this chapter, you should be able to:

1. Account for bad debts using the direct write-off and allowance methods.
2. Calculate the amount of bad debts losses based on sales and accounts receivable.
3. Understand the difference between an interest-bearing and a noninterest-bearing note.
4. Compute interest on a promissory note.
5. Journalize transactions relating to notes receivable.
6. Journalize transactions relating to notes payable.
7. Journalize transactions relating to accrued interest.

9 Accounting for Uncollectible Accounts and Promissory Notes

8. Define the following accounting terms:

accrued expense	maker
accrued revenue	maturity date
aging of accounts receivable	maturity value
allowance method	notes payable register
bad debt	notes receivable register
bank discount	payee
contingent liability	principal
direct write-off method	proceeds
discounting a note	promissory note
dishonored note	uncollectible account
interest	

In chapter 8, you learned that it is common practice for a merchandising firm to sell goods on a credit basis, or on account. Such sales represent an increase in the firm's assets (Accounts Receivable) and also an increase in revenue (Sales). Transactions involving credit sales are recorded at the time a sale is made even though the actual receipt of cash does not take place until a later time. This chapter discusses some of the problems that arise from the sale of goods on account.

Uncollectible Accounts

The extension of credit is a widespread business practice. It is used as a temporary substitute for cash in a large number of business transactions. The use of credit can increase the amount of sales, but its use is not without a certain element of risk. It is inevitable that companies doing business on a credit basis will find that some customers will not pay their accounts. The volume of charge sales as well as the credit policy of a firm influences the number of **uncollectible accounts.** In general, the number of uncollectible accounts is greater at the retail level where the granting of credit to customers is a common practice. However, most firms granting credit can expect some uncollectible accounts.

The fact that an account is uncollectible is not usually known immediately. Collection procedures may extend over a period of months before it becomes evident that an account is uncollectible. Thus, a sale recorded in one period may not prove to be uncollectible until a later accounting period. Only rarely will an uncollectible account be identified in the period in which the sale is made.

An account receivable that is determined to be uncollectible is called a **bad debt.** A bad debt represents an expense to the business and is debited to an expense account usually titled Bad Debts Expense or Uncollectible Accounts Expense. Other titles such as Loss from Doubtful Accounts or Loss from Uncollectible Accounts are also used.

Writing Off
Uncollectible
Accounts

As soon as an account is determined to be uncollectible, it can no longer be considered as an asset. It must be recognized as a loss (expense), and proper accounting for the loss must be made. There are two methods of accounting for, or writing off, bad debts—the direct write-off method and the allowance method.

Direct Write-off
Method

When the **direct write-off method** is used, an account is not written off as a loss until it has been determined that the account is uncollectible. The loss is then recorded in the period when the account is found to be uncollectible. For example, suppose that a firm sold merchandise worth $150 to Vicki Ward in November of last year. Attempts to collect the account have been unsuccessful. In August of the current year it is decided to write off the account as a bad debt. The journal entry to record the loss is:

Bad Debts Expense	150	
Accounts Receivable /		
Vicki Ward		150

This entry transfers the amount due on the account from Accounts Receivable to Bad Debts Expense. The loss is charged to the current year's expenses and reduces the Accounts Receivable. This entry also removes the amount due from Vicki Ward's subsidiary ledger account.

The direct write-off method is simple to use, but it is often criticized because it does not allow for proper matching of revenue and expenses. The sale is reported as revenue in the period in which the sale is made. However, the revenue from the sale and the expense from the loss are not usually reported in the same period because the loss is not written off until the account is found to be uncollectible. Most firms consider that a bad debt is actually incurred at the time the credit sale is made; therefore, it should be recorded in the same period even though the collection efforts may extend for longer periods of time. The direct write-off method violates this matching principle. It also causes incorrect amounts to be shown on the income statement and balance sheet. The net income for the accounting period in which the sale is made is overstated since the bad debt expense has not been reported. The net income is understated for the period in which the bad debts expense is finally reported because an expense related to a prior period is being reported. Furthermore, the amount of accounts receivables reported on the balance sheet is overstated until the account is written off.

Sometimes an account that has been written off is collected later. If that happens, the account is reinstated. In other words, the amount of the sale is transferred from Bad Debts Expense back to Accounts Receivable. Two entries need to be made—one to reinstate the account and one to record the payment. The journal entry to reinstate the account is:

Accounts Receivable / Vicki Ward	150	
Bad Debts Expense		150

The second journal entry to record the payment is then made in a routine manner, either in a combined journal or a cash receipts journal.

Cash	150	
Accounts Receivable /		
Vicki Ward		150

The direct write-off method is most commonly used by small businesses and professional enterprises that deal with only a limited amount of credit transactions. However, if the volume of credit sales is large, it is customary to use the allowance method of accounting for bad debts.

Allowance Method

Under the **allowance method,** an estimate is made of the amount of bad debts expected to result from the credit sales of an accounting period. The allowance (estimate) made for the expected losses (uncollectible accounts) is written off, or charged to the period in which the credit sales are made. This method permits a proper matching of revenue and expenses for the period as well as correct reporting of amounts on the income statement and balance sheet.

The allowance method specifies that the estimated bad debts be recorded at the end of each accounting period as an increase to expenses (Bad Debts Expense) and a decrease to assets (Accounts Receivable). Because it is not known at the time the bad debts are recorded which accounts will be uncollectible, the decrease cannot be recorded directly to Accounts Receivable. Unless the bad debts of specific customers can be identified in the subsidiary ledger, the Accounts Receivable control account cannot be credited directly. To do so would mean that the balance of the control account would not agree with the total of customers' account balances in the subsidiary ledger. For this reason, estimated bad debts are credited to a contra account called Allowance for Bad Debts. This account usually has a credit balance that decreases, or offsets, the debit balance of its related asset account, Accounts Receivable. The difference between the balances is the expected realizable value of the accounts receivables.

The estimated bad debts expense is recorded at the end of the accounting period by an adjusting entry debiting Bad Debts Expense and crediting Allowance for Bad Debts. Assume that the estimated bad debts expense for an accounting period is $200. The journal entry to record the expense is:

Bad Debts Expense	200	
Allowance for Bad Debts		200

Bad Debts Expense is reported on the income statement as an operating expense. Allowance for Bad Debts is reported on the balance sheet as a deduction from Accounts Receivable.

Accounts Receivable	2,100	
less Allowance for Bad Debts	200	1,900

The Bad Debts Expense account is closed at the end of the accounting period along with the other expense accounts. However, the Allowance for Bad Debts account is an open account whose balance is carried into the next period.

When a specific account is determined to be uncollectible, it is written off through the Allowance account rather than through the Bad Debts

Expense account. No expense needs to be recorded since it has already been estimated and recorded in the period in which the credit sale occurred. According to the allowance method, Vicki Ward's uncollectible account is written off against the Allowance for Bad Debts with the following entry:

Allowance for Bad Debts	150	
Accounts Receivable /		
Vicki Ward		150

As other accounts prove to be uncollectible, they are written off against the Allowance account in the same manner.

The amount of bad debts to be charged to an accounting period may be estimated in various ways. One method is to base the estimate on the credit sales of the period. The bad debts are expressed as a percentage of the total credit sales. If this method is used, the percentage is usually based on the past experience of a business or the experiences of similar businesses. If a company has total credit sales of $100,000 for the year and estimates that 1% of credit sales will be uncollectible, the bad debts expense for the year is estimated at $1,000 ($100,000 $\times$ 1%).

When the Bad Debts Expense is based on credit sales, the amount allowed for the losses each year will vary. The full amount of the estimated loss is recorded regardless of any balance in the Allowance for Bad Debts account. If the account has a credit balance of $150 and the estimated loss for the current year is $650, the amount of the adjustment is $650. The new balance is $800 ($150 + $650). The journal entry recording the estimated Bad Debts Expense is as follows:

Bad Debts Expense	650	
Allowance for Bad Debts		650

After posting, the ledger accounts look like this:

Allowance for Bad Debts		Bad Debts Expense	
	Bal 150	650	
	650		
	800		

This method is popular because it allows for an increase in the bad debts losses if the volume of credit sales goes up. Also, the percentage can be changed if it appears that the amount allowed for bad debts is either too high or too low.

Cash sales are not normally included in the estimate unless they are fairly small. If this is the case, the estimate is based on total net sales. Generally, sales returns and allowances are not considered unless they represent a relatively large proportion of the credit sales.

Table 9.1 Aging schedule of accounts receivable

Age Group (in days)	Total	Estimated Percentage	Estimated Loss
1– 30	$16,400	2%	$328
31– 60	900	4%	36
61– 90	700	10%	70
91–120	500	25%	125
			$559

Aging of Accounts Receivable

Some firms prefer to base their bad debt losses on accounts receivable. This process involves the **aging of accounts receivable.** Customers' accounts are analyzed to determine which amounts are unpaid and how long they have remained unpaid. The accounts are then assigned to groups according to the "age" or length of time they have been held. For example, the designated age groups might be 1–30 days past due, 31–60 days past due, 61–90 days past due, and 91–120 days past due. A specified percentage is then assigned to each age group. The percentage is based on the likelihood that accounts in a particular age group will become uncollectible (i.e., the older the unpaid account, the greater chance it will be uncollectible). The estimated bad debts loss is found by taking a percentage of the total of each age group and adding the results to arrive at one amount, which represents the expected loss.

The percentage applied to each age group varies. Since older accounts are most likely to prove uncollectible, a higher percentage is usually applied to them. An example of an aging schedule is presented in table 9.1. For this example, the estimated losses for the period are $559.

According to the aging method, before the adjustment for bad debts can be recorded, the current balance of Allowance for Bad Debts must first be considered. Assume that the Allowance account has a credit balance of $100 before the adjustment. If estimated losses are $559, only $459 has to be added to the present balance. The journal entry to record the expected losses is:

Bad Debts Expense	459	
Allowance for Bad Debts		459

After the entry is posted, the balance of the allowance account is $559, the amount of the expected losses.

Allowance for Bad Debts		Bad Debts Expense	
	Bal 100	459	
	459		
	559		

If the Allowance for Bad Debts account has a debit balance rather than the normal credit balance, another step is necessary to adjust the account at the end of the period. The adjusting entry must not only record the estimated bad debts loss for the period, but it must also record the amount needed to change the debit balance to a credit balance. Suppose in the previous example the Allowance account has a debit balance of $50 and the estimated bad debts for the period are $559. An adjusting entry of $609 ($559 + $50) must be made to cover the estimated losses and create a credit balance of $559. The following journal entry is made to record the adjusting entry:

Bad Debts Expense	609	
Allowance for Bad Debts		609

Allowance for Bad Debts		Bad Debts Expense	
Bal 50	609	609	
	559		

If an accurate estimate has been made of expected bad debts, the balance of the allowance account will be zero or near zero at the end of the accounting period. An accurate estimate also ensures a satisfactory match of expense and revenue. If the estimate is inaccurate, the balance may be too large or too small. A large credit balance (greater than the amount needed to provide for losses) indicates that the estimate of losses is too high. A large debit balance (smaller than the amount needed to provide for losses) indicates that the estimate of losses is too low.

If an account written off against the Allowance for Bad Debts is later collected, the write-off entry is reversed to reinstate the account. The payment is then recorded in a routine manner.

Accounts Receivable/Vicki Ward	150	
Allowance for Bad Debts		150
Cash	150	
Accounts Receivable/		
Vicki Ward		150

Worksheet Adjustments for Uncollectible Accounts

The adjustment procedure explained in chapter 5 is followed in recording the previous adjustments. The adjustments should first appear in the Adjustments columns of the worksheet so that correct amounts can be transferred to the financial statements. After completion of the worksheet and the financial statements, the entries are then made in the journal.

Promissory Notes

Up to this point we have been concerned with the importance of credit in retail sales. Usually retail credit sales are based on the buyer's signature on a sales ticket acknowledging agreement to pay later. However, credit is also granted by means of a more formal document called a promissory note (or note). A **promissory note** is a written unconditional promise to pay a specific person or bearer a specified sum of money either at a fixed future time or upon demand. It must be signed by the person or firm authorized to make the promise. The person to whose order the note is drawn is called the **payee.** To the payee, a promissory note is considered a note receivable (asset). The person who promises to pay the money is called the **maker.** To the maker, the note is a note payable (liability). The amount of money borrowed is called the **principal,** or the **face amount.** The date on which the note becomes due is called the **maturity date.** An example of a promissory note is shown in figure 9.1.

The exchange of a note for goods or services is common for credit periods over sixty days or for transactions involving large amounts of money. In addition, a note is often used to settle an open account or to borrow or lend money. Creditors may prefer to extend credit by use of a note rather than an open account because a note offers more security. Since it is an unconditional promise to pay, it represents a stronger legal claim if court action becomes necessary. It also is a negotiable instrument, which means that it can be transferred to another party in exchange for cash or merchandise.

A note may be either interest bearing or noninterest bearing. An interest-bearing note is one that requires the maker to pay a fee, known as **interest,** for the use of money over a period of time. The rate of interest to be charged is stated on the note. This interest represents an expense (In-

Figure 9.1 A promissory note.

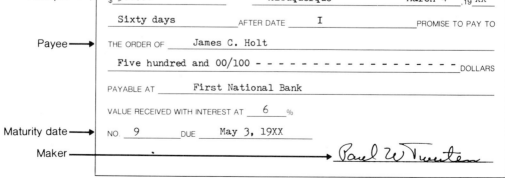

terest Expense) to the maker, while it represents revenue (Interest Income) to the payee. Figure 9.1 is an interest-bearing note and shows that Paul W. Tweeten must pay James C. Holt $500 plus 6 percent interest on May 3.

A noninterest-bearing note is one that makes no provision for interest on the note. However, if such a note is not paid when due, interest may be charged at the legal rate from the due date until it is paid. Also, in some cases where no rate of interest is stated, a note may still involve interest. For example, suppose you give a sixty-day noninterest-bearing note for $500 to a bank in return for a loan of $500 cash. The bank then gives you only $495 in cash. But when you repay the loan, you must pay the full $500. The $5 difference between the amount of cash received and the amount which must be repaid is, in effect, interest. However, this amount is called a **bank discount** rather than interest. The procedure of exchanging a note for less than its face amount is called **discounting a note.** The amount of the discount is considered interest expense at the time the note matures.

Computing Interest

The rate of interest shown on the face of the note usually represents an annual rate. The amount of interest is calculated for the time period of the note and must be paid on the maturity date unless the note is discounted.

The time period of a note may be expressed as a year or a fraction of a year; that is, as a certain number of days or months. When the time is expressed in months, each month represents 1/12 of a year. Interest on a note maturing in three months is computed for 3/12, or 1/4, of a year. When the time period is expressed in days, the interest is computed on the fraction of a year those days represent. A common business practice is to use a 360-day year; however, some institutions, such as banks and government agencies, use a 365-day year in computing interest. Interest for sixty days is computed for 60/360, or 1/6, of a year or 60/365, depending on the method used.

When the time period of a note is expressed in days, the exact number of days must be counted to determine the due date. For example, a ninety-day note dated August 12 is due on November 10. The due date is determined as follows:

Days in August	31
Date of note	− 12
Days remaining in August	19
Days in September	+ 30
Days in October	+ 31
Total	80
Due date, November	10
	90

The date the note is issued is excluded, but the maturity date is counted.

If the time is expressed in months, the due date is determined by counting the number of months from the date of issue of the note. The due date of a four-month note dated April 10 is August 10.

Interest is computed by the following formula:

$$\text{Principal} \times \text{Rate} \times \text{Time} = \text{Interest}$$

Thus, the interest on a sixty-day, 6 percent, $1,000 note is computed as follows:

$$\$1,000 \times \frac{6}{100} \times \frac{60}{360} = \$10.00$$

A shortcut to computing interest called the sixty-day, 6 percent method is often used. Sixty days represents 1/6 of a year (60/360), and 1/6 of 6 percent is 1 percent. The amount of interest is then computed quickly by determining 1 percent of the principal, or moving the decimal point two places to the left. For example, interest on $695 at 6 percent for sixty days is $6.95. Using the standard interest formula, interest is computed for this example as follows:

$$\$695 \times \frac{6}{100} \times \frac{60}{360} = \$6.95$$

Another variation of this shortcut, called the six-day, 6 percent method, is also commonly used. Interest is calculated by moving the decimal point three places to the left. Either of these methods can be used for any combination of days and percentages.

Notes Receivable

Promissory notes are most commonly accepted by firms for two reasons: (1) in exchange for goods or services and (2) as settlement of an open account receivable. These notes are assets to the receiving firm or person and are debited to an account called Notes Receivable.

When a note is accepted in exchange for goods or services, the Notes Receivable account is debited for the face amount of the note and the Sales account is credited. While the note may be interest bearing or noninterest bearing, no interest is recorded until payment of the note is received. When an interest-bearing note is issued, the principal of the note plus the interest, which is known as the **maturity value,** is paid on the maturity date. The amount of interest is recorded as revenue on the books of the payee.

Suppose that a sixty-day, 8 percent note for $700 is received from Maurice Ward in exchange for merchandise. The entry to record the acceptance of the note debits Notes Receivable for the principal only.

Notes Receivable	700	
Sales		700

When Maurice Ward pays the note at the end of the sixty days, he pays a total of $709.33 (principal plus interest). The journal entry to record the payment is:

Cash	709.33	
Notes Receivable		700.00
Interest Income		9.33

After these transactions are posted, the ledger accounts appear as follows:

Cash		Notes Receivable	
709.33		700	700

Sales		Interest Income	
	700		9.33

Interest Income is a temporary owner's equity account that is reported on the income statement as Other Income.

Sometimes a customer who has purchased merchandise on account will fail to pay the account on time. In situations where an extension of time is needed, the seller may require that the customer convert the account receivable into a note receivable. For example, assume that the Williams and Walls account has a past-due balance of $600. The seller offers to settle the account in exchange for a sixty-day, 6 percent note for $600. The journal entry to record this transaction is as follows:

Notes Receivable	600	
Accounts Receivable/		
Williams and Walls		600

The entry changes the asset from an account receivable to a note receivable and brings the balance of the Williams and Walls account to zero. Upon receipt of the payment of the note, the journal entry becomes:

Cash	606	
Notes Receivable		600
Interest Income		6

The ledger accounts appear as follows:

Cash		Accounts Receivable	
606		600	600

Notes Receivable		Interest Income	
600	600		6

The holder of a note receivable may use the note to obtain cash or to pay a debt (account payable). When a note is used to obtain cash, it is usually transferred (sold) to a bank in return for the cash. This procedure is also called discounting a note since the amount of cash received is the maturity value of the note less a discount (interest charged by the bank).

If the note being discounted is noninterest bearing, the maturity value is the same as the principal. Therefore, the bank discount is computed on the face amount for the time remaining from the date of discount to maturity. For example, if a sixty-day, noninterest-bearing note for $500 dated August 6 is transferred to the bank on September 5, the note is discounted from September 5 to the maturity date. If the bank charges a 6 percent discount rate, the discount for thirty days is $2.50 ($500 $\times$ 6/100 $\times$ 30/360 = $2.50). The amount of cash received by the payee is $497.50, which equals the maturity value ($500) less the bank discount ($2.50). The amount received by the payee is called the **proceeds.** The discount of the noninterest-bearing note is recorded by the following journal entry:

Cash	497.50	
Interest Expense	2.50	
Notes Receivable		500

If the note being discounted is interest bearing, the same procedure is followed. However, the stated interest must be added to the principal to determine the maturity value. The bank discount is then applied to the maturity value. For example, assume that the note in the previous example bears an interest rate of 5 percent. The discount is computed in the following manner:

Maturity value of note dated August 6		$504.17
Principal	$500.00	
plus interest at 5% for 60 days	4.17	
Discount period September 5 to November 5—30 days		
Discount amount: $504.17 at 6% for 30 days		2.52
Proceeds		$501.65

The journal entry to record this transaction is:

Cash	501.65	
Interest Income		1.65
Notes Receivable		500.00

The cash received in this transaction is more than the value of the note exchanged for it; therefore, the excess represents revenue and is reported as Interest Income. If the amount of cash received is less than the value of the note, the difference would represent an expense and would be recorded as a debit to Interest Expense.

A note receivable may be applied against an account payable. Notes used for this purpose are applied against the account payable at their discount value. Computation of the discount value is the same as previously explained. However, in a transaction of this type, Accounts Payable rather than Cash is debited for the proceeds.

When a note receivable is discounted, the original payee endorses the note over to a new payee. The maker must then pay the new holder of the note the maturity value on the due date. Under ordinary circumstances, discounting eliminates the endorser from the transaction. However, if the maker defaults on the note, the endorser is responsible for payment of the note. For this reason, the discounting of a note receivable creates a **contingent liability** for the endorser until the due date of the note. If at maturity the maker pays the note, the contingent liability is discharged. The endorser has no further responsibility. If, however, the maker does not pay the note at maturity, the contingent liability becomes an actual one, and the endorser must pay the maturity value of the note.

It is customary to indicate the amount of any contingent liabilities on the balance sheet. This is usually done with a notation to the effect that the firm is "contingently liable for notes receivable, which have been discounted in the amount of. . . ."

If the maker of a note fails to pay the note on the due date, the note is said to be **dishonored.** In that event, the amount of the dishonored note plus any interest due is transferred back to the Accounts Receivable account. If the Williams and Walls note (recorded on p. 185) is dishonored, the journal entry is as follows:

Accounts Receivable / Williams and Walls	606	
Notes Receivable		600
Interest Income		6

This entry reverts the note, together with the interest, back to the customer's account. At this point, some other means of collecting the amount is necessary. Occasionally, the holder of a note will turn the note over to a bank for collection. Most banks charge a fee for this service, which is recorded on the books of the holder as an expense.

Usually, carbon copies of all notes receivable are kept by the payee; however, some firms prefer to keep a separate record of each note receivable,

Figure 9.2 Notes receivable register.

Date of Receipt	No.	By Whom Payable	Date Made M	D	Y	Time	When Due J	F	M	A	M	J	J	A	S	O	N	D
19XX Apr 1	1	J. L. Graham	Apr	1	19XX	60 d.					31							
17	2	Floyd Hanson	Apr	17	19XX	90 d.							16					

especially if the number is large. The record is called a **notes receivable register** (see fig. 9.2). If a notes receivable register is used, its related control account in the general ledger is Notes Receivable. The balance of the Notes Receivable account should agree with the total balance of unpaid notes in the register.

Notes Payable

Promissory notes are given for a variety of reasons: (1) to purchase merchandise or other assets, (2) to obtain a cash loan, and (3) to extend the payment time on an account payable. These notes represent liabilities to the maker and are credited to an account called Notes Payable. They may be interest bearing or noninterest bearing.

When a note is given to purchase an asset, the transaction is recorded by debiting the asset account (or Purchases if merchandise is involved) and crediting Notes Payable. Later, when payment is made, if the note is noninterest bearing, Notes Payable is debited and Cash is credited for the face amount of the note. If the note is interest bearing, the principal plus the amount of interest must be repaid. Notes Payable is debited for the principal, and Interest Expense is debited for the amount of the interest. The credit to Cash is for the total amount paid (principal plus interest).

Transactions involving notes given in settlement of an account payable are recorded by debiting Accounts Payable and crediting Notes Payable. Assume that a firm has an overdue account of $1,000, which it owes to a

Amount	Interest		Discounted		Date Paid	Remarks
	Rate	Amount	Bank	Date		
620 —	6%	6 20			May 31	
800 —	9%	18 —			Jul 16	

creditor, Luke, Inc. The firm offers a ninety-day, 4 percent, $1,000 note in settlement of the overdue account. The transaction is recorded as:

Accounts Payable/Luke, Inc.	1,000	
Notes Payable		1,000

Accounts Payable		Notes Payable
1,000	1,000	1,000

When the note is paid, payment is recorded as follows:

Notes Payable	1,000	
Interest Expense	10	
Cash		1,010

Cash	Notes Payable		Interest Expense
1,010	1,000	1,000	10

There are a variety of ways in which notes given to secure bank loans can be handled. Probably the most common method is to borrow money with an interest-bearing note. In this situation, the full amount of the note is received in cash. Upon maturity, the borrower repays the face amount of the note plus interest. For example, when $500 cash is received in exchange for a sixty-day, 6 percent note, the borrower records the transaction in the following manner:

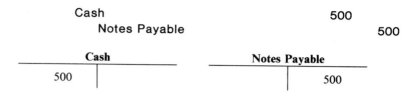

When the note is paid, the following journal entry is made:

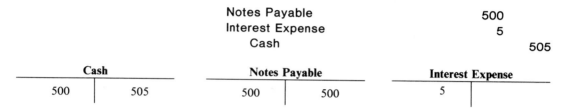

If the note given is noninterest bearing, interest in the form of a discount is collected in advance. The borrower receives the proceeds in cash. For a sixty-day, $500 noninterest-bearing note for which the bank charges a 6 percent discount, the following journal entry is made:

Figure 9.3   Notes payable register.

NOTES PAYABLE REGISTER

Date of Issue	No.	To Whom Payable	Date Made			Time	When Due											
			M	D	Y		J	F	M	A	M	J	J	A	S	O	N	D
19XX Jan 3	1	First National Bank	Jan	3	19XX	30d.		2										
Feb 15	2	The Acme Brick Company	Feb	15	19XX	60d.				16								

		Cash		495	
		Interest Expense		5	
		Notes Payable			500

Cash		Notes Payable		Interest Expense	
495			500	5	

When the note matures, the face amount of the note must be paid and the journal entry appears as follows:

| | Notes Payable | | 500 | |
| | Cash | | | 500 |

Cash		Notes Payable	
	500	500	500

The interest charged is recorded when the loan is made, so no further entry is necessary.

If the number of notes payable is relatively small, it is not necessary to keep a separate register, although many firms prefer to do so. The register is called a **notes payable register.** Its related control account in the general ledger is Notes Payable. The total amount of notes unpaid in the register must agree with the balance of the control account. One form of a Notes Payable register is shown in figure 9.3.

Amount	Interest		Date Paid	Remarks
	Rate	Amount		
200 —	6%	1 —	Feb 2	
450 —	8%	6 —		Settlement of Dec. 10 inv.

Accrued Interest

It has been shown that some expenses that are incurred on a daily basis during an accounting period are not recorded as they occur. Because these expenses gradually increase during the period, they are said to accrue and are known as **accrued expenses** (sometimes called **accrued liabilities**). These expenses must be recorded in the period in which they are incurred even though they are not paid until a later period. Interest that has accrued on notes payable falls in this category of accrued expenses.

You have also learned that revenue should be accounted for in the period in which it is earned even though the cash is not received until a later period. Like accrued expenses, some types of revenue accrue each day of an accounting period, although the revenue is not recorded immediately. This revenue is known as **accrued revenue** (also **accrued assets**). Interest that has accrued on notes receivables is an example of accrued revenue.

The interest expense and revenue that is accruing each day of an accounting period must be recorded in the period in which it is earned or incurred. Therefore, at the end of the period, adjustments must be made for any unrecorded interest expense and revenue.

Any interest receivable that has accrued over the period must be recorded as an asset and as revenue. Any interest payable that has accrued must be recorded as a liability and as an expense. The amounts to be recorded are obtained either from the face of the notes outstanding or from the note registers. The accrued interest receivable on all outstanding notes receivable is calculated in the same manner as the accrued interest expense on all outstanding notes payable. Two adjusting entries are made to record this information on the books.

Suppose that a firm has two outstanding interest-bearing notes receivable at the end of the accounting period. The accrued interest receivable on these notes is $11.75. The adjusting entry is:

Accrued Interest Receivable	11.75	
Interest Income		11.75

Accrued Interest Receivable is reported as a current asset on the balance sheet. Interest Income is reported as Other Income on the income statement.

Suppose also that a firm has three outstanding interest-bearing notes payable with accrued interest of $16.40. The adjusting entry is:

Interest Expense	16.40	
Accrued Interest Payable		16.40

Interest Expense is reported on the income statement, and Accrued Interest Payable is reported as a current liability on the balance sheet.

As you have already learned, these adjusting entries are recorded first in the Adjustments columns of the worksheet.

Summary

A firm that sells merchandise on a credit basis usually finds that some accounts are uncollectible. The uncollectible accounts are bad debts, which represent an expense to the firm (p. 176). There are two commonly used methods of accounting for bad debts: the direct write-off method and the allowance method (pp. 176–81). Usually, the allowance method is the more practical of the two since it permits a better matching of the revenue and expense for an accounting period. The estimated bad debts expense of a period is charged against the sales of that period. The estimate of expected losses is based on the sales of the period or on the unpaid accounts receivable (pp. 178–81).

Promissory notes are another means of granting or receiving credit. They are often preferred to accounts receivable because they have a stronger legal status and are negotiable (p. 182).

Promissory notes may be interest bearing or noninterest bearing (p. 182). Interest is computed by applying the formula: principal $\times$ rate $\times$ time (pp. 182–84). Interest paid by the maker of a note represents an expense. Interest received by the payee of a note represents revenue.

Notes may be transferred to a bank or another party before the due date. This process is called discounting (pp. 186–87), and it imposes a contingent liability on the person transferring the note (p. 187).

Interest on notes accrues each day of an accounting period although the interest is not being recorded daily. Because accrued interest must be accounted for at the end of the period, adjusting entries are made to record the amount of accrued interest (p. 192).

Key Terms

accrued expense An expense incurred during an accounting period that has not been paid or recorded; sometimes called accrued liability.

accrued revenue Revenue earned during an accounting period that has not been recorded; sometimes called accrued asset.

aging of accounts receivable The grouping of accounts receivable according to the length of time they have been held.

allowance method A method of accounting for bad debts that estimates the amount of bad debts expected to result from the credit sales of an accounting period. The expected losses are recorded in the period in which the credit sales are made.

bad debts Accounts receivable that are uncollectible.

bank discount The difference between the principal of a note and the amount of cash received for the note.

contingent liability A potential liability assumed by the endorser of a discounted note if the maker defaults.

direct write-off method A method of accounting for bad debts that writes off an account as a bad debt at the time the account becomes uncollectible.

discounting a note receivable The exchange of a note receivable for cash or payment of a debt.

dishonored note A note that is not paid by the maker on the due date.

interest A fee charged for the use of money over a period of time.

maker The firm or person who signs a promissory note.

maturity date The date on which a note becomes due.

maturity value The amount the maker must pay on the due date of a note; the principal plus interest.

notes payable register A subsidiary record containing detailed information about each note payable.

notes receivable register A subsidiary record containing detailed information about each note receivable.

payee The firm or person to whose order a promissory note or check is drawn.

principal The face amount of a promissory note.

proceeds The amount of cash received when a note receivable is discounted.

promissory note A written unconditional promise to pay a specific person or bearer a specified sum of money either at a fixed future time or on demand.

uncollectible account An account receivable that cannot be collected.

Objectives

Upon completion of this chapter, you should be able to:

1. Calculate depreciation on long-lived assets using the following methods:

   straight-line   sum-of-the-years'-digits
   declining balance   units-of-production

2. Journalize and post transactions involving the disposal of long-lived assets.

3. Determine the cost of ending merchandise inventory using the following methods:

   first-in, first-out (FIFO)   lower-of-cost-or-market
   last-in, first-out (LIFO)   gross profit
   weighted average   retail

10 Accounting for Depreciation and Inventory

4. Define the following accounting terms:

amortization

book value

declining balance method

depletion

FIFO method

functional depreciation

gross profit method

intangible asset

LIFO method

long-lived asset

lower-of-cost-or-market method

net cost

personal property

physical depreciation

real property

retail method

straight-line method

sum-of-the-years'-digits method

tangible asset

units-of-production method

wasting asset

weighted average method

You are already familiar with the terms *depreciation* and *merchandise inventory.* The concept of depreciation was first introduced in chapter 4 where one simple method for determining depreciation was explained. In this chapter, that method is expanded upon, and several other methods of determining depreciation are described.

Merchandise inventory, which was discussed in chapter 8, is presented in greater detail in this chapter.

Accounting for Depreciation

Long-Lived Assets and Depreciation

As explained in chapter 4, *long-lived*, or fixed, assets are those that are used in the operation of the business for a number of years. Long-lived assets are classified as either real property or personal property. **Real property** includes land and anything that is attached to it. **Personal property** includes all assets owned other than real property. Common examples of personal property are furniture, equipment, motor vehicles, patents, and copyrights.

Long-lived assets can also be classified by their physical properties. Assets having physical substance, such as land, furniture, and equipment, are called **tangible assets.** Those having no physical substance, such as patents, leases, copyrights, and goodwill, are known as **intangible assets.**

Most long-lived assets lose their usefulness over a period of years even though they may never be totally used up. However, there are some long-lived assets that are actually used up or exhausted. Those assets are classified as **wasting assets.** Examples of such assets are oil and gas wells, mines, and timber.

The same principle of depreciation applies in all of these classifications: a portion of the cost of each asset is written off as an expense at the end of each period. However, different terms are generally used to describe the writing-off process. For tangible assets (with the exception of land, which is not depreciated), the writing-off process is called **depreciation.** For intangible assets, the process is called **amortization.** For wasting assets, the process is called **depletion.** We are primarily concerned with accounting for the tangible assets in this chapter.

Depreciation is the loss of usefulness of an asset. The loss of usefulness may result from two things:

1. **Physical depreciation** is a decline in usefulness caused by use and exposure to the elements. Physical depreciation is continuous, but various factors can offset its rate. The useful life of an asset can be prolonged by regular maintenance. Likewise, assets used indoors will normally deteriorate more slowly than those used outdoors.

2. **Functional depreciation** is a loss of usefulness attributable to inadequacy or obsolescence. An asset becomes inadequate when it can no longer meet the demands of the job it was intended to perform. Improved technology often results in an asset becoming obsolete even though it may actually have some years of usefulness left.

The depreciation process has two basic purposes: (1) to allocate the cost of a long-lived asset as an expense over its useful life and (2) to show the decreasing value of the asset each period. Three factors that must be considered in the depreciation process are the cost of the asset, the expected useful life of the asset, and its market value at the end of its useful life.

The amount recorded for a long-lived asset is the total cost of installation and preparation of the asset prior to its use. This amount includes the purchase price of the asset plus transportation charges, sales taxes, installation costs, and any other costs that may be incurred in placing the asset into service. The amount is debited to the proper asset account, and the offsetting credit is to Cash or a liability account, such as Accounts Payable or Notes Payable. If a company gives a note to purchase a computer worth $5,000 on which a $200 installation charge must be paid, the asset account is debited for $5,200. The liability account is credited for the same amount.

Computer		Notes Payable	
5,200			5,200

The useful life of an asset and its market value at retirement cannot be accurately determined at the time the asset is purchased. The accountant can only estimate these things. There are no hard-and-fast rules on which to base estimates; usually they are based on past experience or the experience of others. However, some industry trade associations and government agencies do publish statistical information that can serve as a guideline.

The estimate of the market value of a depreciable asset at the time of retirement is called its **salvage value.** Salvage value is also referred to as *residual, scrap,* or *trade-in* value. The original cost less the salvage value equals the depreciable cost of the asset. The depreciable cost is the amount that is depreciated over the useful life of the asset.

A month is ordinarily the smallest unit of time considered in depreciating an asset. An asset acquired or disposed of before the fifteenth of the month is considered to have been owned as of the first day of the month and is therefore depreciated for the full month. An asset acquired or disposed of after the fifteenth of the month is considered to have been owned as of the last of the month. Therefore, no depreciation is calculated until the following month.

| Methods for Determining Depreciation | There are several different methods of calculating the depreciation on long-lived assets. The four most commonly used methods, straight-line, units-of-production, declining balance, and sum-of-the-years'-digits, are discussed here. |

| Straight-Line Method | The **straight-line method** of determining depreciation is the simplest to use. It is based on the assumption that an asset will experience a steady loss of value over its useful life. Therefore, an equal amount of an asset's depreciable cost is apportioned as an expense during each full period of its useful life. The amount of depreciation is calculated by dividing the total amount to be depreciated by the estimated years of useful life. To illustrate this method, assume that the purchase price of a piece of office equipment is $3,100. It has an estimated useful life of five years and an estimated salvage value of $100. The annual depreciation is computed as follows: |

$$\frac{\$3,100 \text{ (cost)} - \$100 \text{ (salvage value)}}{5 \text{ years (estimated life)}} = \frac{\$3,000}{5} = \$600 \text{ annual depreciation}$$

In this example (assuming the asset is held the full five years), $600 depreciation will be charged as an expense for each of the five years of estimated life.

Some assets are assumed to possess no salvage value. If the salvage value is assumed to be zero, the annual depreciation is computed as follows:

$$\frac{\$3,100 \text{ (cost)} - \$0 \text{ (salvage value)}}{5 \text{ years (estimated life)}} = \frac{\$3,100}{5} = \$620 \text{ annual depreciation}$$

The straight-line method is often preferred because it reflects the fact that many assets depreciate on a relatively even basis.

| Units-of-Production Method | The **units-of-production method** determines depreciation based on the output of an asset. The depreciation expense for each period is determined by the number of units produced. If the asset is not used, no depreciation is recorded. |

The first step in the units-of-production method is to calculate the amount of depreciation for a single unit of production, or output. The total number of units produced during an accounting period is then multiplied by the single unit amount to arrive at the annual depreciation. Assume that a truck purchased for $6,000, with a salvage value of $1,000, is expected to have a service life of 100,000 miles. The depreciation per unit is computed as follows:

$$\frac{\$6,000 \text{ (cost)} - \$1,000 \text{ (salvage value)}}{100,000 \text{ miles (expected life)}} = \frac{\$5,000}{100,000} = \$0.05 \text{ (depreciation per mile)}$$

If the truck is driven 15,000 miles the first year, the depreciation expense for the year is $750 (15,000 × $0.05). If during the second year the truck is driven only 10,000 miles, the depreciation expense for that year would be $500 (10,000 × $0.05).

The units-of-production method of determining depreciation is usually preferred over the straight-line method in situations where the usage of an asset varies considerably. In such instances, this method provides a more accurate representation of expenses and revenue.

Declining Balance Method

The **declining balance method** of determining depreciation provides for a declining depreciation charge over the estimated life of an asset. It is based on the assumption that an asset is more useful during its early years and will lose more value in its early years than it will in later years. It assumes, too, that repair and maintenance expenses will be lower in the early years; therefore, a larger amount of depreciation should be taken in the early years to offset the increasing repair and maintenance expenses in the later years.

The most common procedure for figuring depreciation according to this method is to double the straight-line depreciation rate and apply that rate to the declining book value of the asset. The **book value,** often called the *undepreciated cost,* of an asset is its original cost less any accumulated depreciation. For an asset with an expected life of five years, the rate is 40 percent, which is double the straight-line rate of 20 percent (100% ÷ 5 years). The declining balance method as it applies to an asset costing $2,000 is illustrated in the following example:

Year 1	$2,000	Cost of asset	$2,000	
	x .40	Depreciation rate	−800	
	$800.00	Accumulated depreciation for year	$1,200	Book value at end of year 1
Year 2	$1,200		$1,200	
	x .40		−480	
	$480.00	Accumulated depreciation for year	$ 720	Book value at end of year 2

Table 10.1 shows the declining balance method as it applies for the full five years of expected life.

Table 10.1   Declining-balance method

Year	Annual Depreciation	Accumulated Depreciation	Book Value
0	—	—	$2,000.00
1	$800.00	$ 800.00	1,200.00
2	480.00	1,280.00	720.00
3	288.00	1,568.00	432.00
4	172.80	1,740.80	259.20
5	103.68	1,844.48	155.52

The salvage value is ignored in determining the depreciation rate. With this method the asset cost can never be fully depreciated. However if a salvage value has been estimated, the asset should not be depreciated below the salvage value. For example, if a salvage value of $200 has been estimated for the described asset, the depreciation for the fifth year would be $59.20 ($259.20 — $200.00) instead of $103.68.

Use of the declining balance method is in keeping with IRS laws, which allow for accelerated depreciation of long-lived assets. Under IRS regulations, a depreciation rate of up to twice the yearly straight-line rate is permissible on assets that are purchased new and that have a service life of three years or more.

Sum-of-the-Years'-Digits Method

The **sum-of-the-years'-digits method** of determining depreciation is similar to the declining balance method. It too provides for greater depreciation in the early years of estimated life of an asset. However, this method takes into account the salvage value of an asset. The annual depreciation is based on an asset's depreciable cost. With this method, an asset can be depreciated fully or to the exact amount of estimated salvage value.

To compute the annual depreciation, the asset's net cost (or gross cost if no salvage value is estimated) is multiplied by a fraction. The fraction applied is successively smaller each year, which results in a steady decrease in the amount of depreciation each year of estimated life of the asset. The denominator of the fraction, which remains constant, is the sum of the digits representing the years of the asset's life. The numerator, which changes every year, is the number of years of useful life. The largest number is used as the numerator for the first year's depreciation. For example, if an asset has an estimated useful life of five years, the denominator is 15, the sum of the years 5 + 4 + 3 + 2 + 1. The numerator for the first year is 5. The depreciation expense for the first year is 5/15 of the net cost of the asset. For the second year, it is 4/15 of the net cost, and so on. The calculation of depreciation using the sum-of-the-years'-digits is illustrated in table 10.2. The depreciation is computed for an asset costing $5,000 with a salvage value of $500 and an estimated life of five years.

Table 10.2 Sum-of-the-years'-digits method

Year	Rate	Net Cost	Annual Depreciation	Accumulated Depreciation	Book Value End of Year
0	—	—	—	—	$5,000
1	5/15	$4,500	$1,500	$1,500	3,500
2	4/15	4,500	1,200	2,700	2,300
3	3/15	4,500	900	3,600	1,400
4	2/15	4,500	600	4,200	800
5	1/15	4,500	300	4,500	500

It should be noted that in the discussion of each of the depreciation methods it was assumed that the first use of an asset coincided with the beginning of an accounting period. In actual practice, an asset is more likely to be placed into use at a time other than the first day of an accounting period. It is necessary, therefore, to prorate the depreciation for the first year according to the length of time the asset was owned. For example, assume that an asset costing $1,500 purchased on July 1 is expected to serve ten years with no salvage value. Annual depreciation, calculated on a straight-line basis, amounts to $150 ($1,500 ÷ 10). At the end of the first accounting period, the depreciation is prorated for six months rather than a full year. Depreciation expense for the asset for six months amounts to $75 ($12.50 a month × 6 months). Thereafter, the depreciation is calculated for a full year, unless the asset is disposed of prior to the end of an accounting period. If this were the case, the depreciation would again be prorated for that portion of the year that the asset was owned.

Comparison of Depreciation Methods

Table 10.3 shows the accumulated depreciation using three of the methods described. The units-of-production method is not included since it is based upon the usage of an asset rather than a fixed period of time. The calculations are based on an asset costing $1,500 with an expected salvage value of $100 at the end of five years.

Table 10.3 Comparison of three depreciation methods

Year	Straight-Line Depreciation	Straight-Line Book Value	Declining Balance Depreciation	Declining Balance Book Value	Sum-of-the-Years'-Digits Depreciation	Sum-of-the-Years'-Digits Book Value
0	—	$1,500	—	$1,500.00	—	$1,500.00
1	$280	1,220	$600.00	900.00	$466.67	1,033.33
2	280	940	360.00	540.00	373.33	660.00
3	280	660	216.00	324.00	280.00	380.00
4	280	380	129.60	194.40	186.67	193.33
5	280	100	77.76	116.64	93.33	100.00

The straight-line method provides for equal amounts of depreciation each year while both the declining balance and sum-of-the-years'-digits methods provide for a higher amount of depreciation in the earlier years with a steady decline in the remaining years. The straight-line method is the simplest to use, but accountants often choose one of the other two methods for the tax advantage to be gained. Either the declining balance or the sum-of-the-years'-digits methods will reduce the income tax liability in the earlier years of an asset's life. Advantages can be gained in later years when the higher costs for repairs and maintenance are offset by lower depreciation amounts.

Worksheet Adjustments for Depreciation

Depreciation is usually recorded by an adjusting entry made at the end of each accounting period. As you already know, the adjustments appear first on the worksheet. The procedure for adjustments was explained in chapter 5.

The amount of depreciation is debited to an expense account, Depreciation Expense. A contra asset account, Accumulated Depreciation, is used to record the credit. The use of the contra account makes it possible to retain the original cost of the asset as well as to show the exact amount of accumulated depreciation. It also makes it possible to quickly determine the asset's book value. The credit balance of the contra account subtracted from the debit balance of its related asset account represents the book value of the asset.

Office Equipment		Accumulated Depreciation—Office Equipment	
1,000		—	400	= $600 (book value)

Usually a separate Accumulated Depreciation account is kept for each long-lived asset. Although it is not standard practice, separate Depreciation Expense accounts may also be kept.

A deviation from the usual procedure of recording depreciation at the end of the year occurs when a long-lived asset is disposed of. In such a situation, the depreciation (to the nearest full month) is recorded at the time of disposal. Otherwise, it would not be possible to determine whether a loss or gain has been made on the disposal transaction.

Disposal of Long-Lived Assets

Depreciable long-lived assets eventually become unusable. When that happens, they may be discarded, sold, or traded in on the purchase of another asset. Regardless of the method of disposal, the book value of the asset must be removed from the accounts. To do this, the asset account must be credited for the cost of the asset, and the related accumulated depreciation account must be debited for the amount of depreciation at the time of disposal. Several different asset disposal situations are illustrated in the following pages.

Long-lived assets may be discarded (or retired) when it is determined that they are no longer useful to the business. Such an event may involve a loss, depending on whether or not the asset has been fully depreciated. If an asset has been fully depreciated, no loss results. For example, assume that office equipment costing $1,500 with no salvage value and an estimated life of five years is fully depreciated at the time it is discarded. The journal entry to record the disposal is:

Accumulated Depreciation—Office Equipment	1,500	
Office Equipment		1,500

After posting, both the asset and its accumulated depreciation are removed from the accounts. The general ledger accounts appear as follows:

Office Equipment		Accumulated Depreciation—Office Equipment	
1,500	1,500	1,500	300
			300
			300
			300
			300

Suppose that the equipment in the example is discarded at the end of the fourth year when it has a book value of $300. The journal entry becomes:

Accumulated Depreciation—Office Equipment	1,200	
Loss on disposal of asset	300	
Office Equipment		1,500

A loss is realized since the asset is disposed of before it is fully depreciated. The loss is considered to be an expense. It is reported on the income statement as Other Expense.

In the event a depreciable asset is discarded before the end of the accounting period, it is necessary to record accumulated depreciation for that portion of the year the asset was owned. Only after the depreciation is brought up to date are the asset and accumulated depreciation removed from the books. If a fully depreciated asset is not disposed of immediately, it remains on the books until such time as it is discarded, but no further depreciation is taken on it.

When a depreciable long-lived asset is sold, the accumulated depreciation must first be brought up to date so that the book value of the asset can be determined. If the asset is sold for more than the book value, a gain is recorded. If the asset is sold for less than the book value, a loss results. If the asset is sold at the book value, there is no gain or loss. The journal entries for each of these types of transactions are shown in the following list. Assume that a typewriter has been purchased for $900 and has an estimated life of ten years. The typewriter is then sold at the end of six years. The general ledger accounts appear as follows:

Office Equipment		Accumulated Depreciation—Office Equipment	
900	—	90	= $360 (book value)
		90	
		90	
		90	
		90	
		90	

1. The typewriter is sold for $360 cash. No gain or loss is recorded since the book value is the same as the selling price.

Cash	360	
Accumulated Depreciation—Office Equipment	540	
Office Equipment		900

2. The typewriter is sold for $400 cash. A gain of $40 results since the selling price is higher than the book value.

Cash	400	
Accumulated Depreciation—Office Equipment	540	
Gain on sale of asset		40
Office Equipment		900

3. The typewriter is sold for $300 cash. A loss of $60 is recorded since the selling price is below the book value.

Cash	300	
Loss on sale of asset	60	
Accumulated Depreciation—Office Equipment	540	
Office Equipment		900

A gain on the sale of an asset is considered as revenue. It appears in the income statement as Other Income. A loss on the sale of an asset is considered an expense. It is reported on the income statement under the heading of Other Expense.

Trade-In of an Asset   Sometimes an asset is traded in on another asset rather than sold. The allowance for a trade-in is deducted from the sales price of the new asset. The difference represents the balance owed (referred to as *boot*) by the buyer. A loss or gain can result on such a transaction depending on whether the trade-in allowance is less or more than the book value. However, income tax laws state that no gain or loss can be recognized (recorded) on the exchange of similar assets. So the cost of the new asset is recorded as the book value of the old asset plus any cash actually paid for the new asset. For exchanges that do not involve similar kinds of assets, gains or losses can be recognized.

Assume that the typewriter in the earlier illustration is traded in after three years on a new typewriter that costs $1,500. Depreciation of $90 each year has been recorded. The accumulated depreciation is $270 so the book value is $630 ($900 − $270) at the time of trade-in. A trade-in allowance of $700 is given. The cash to be paid is $800 ($1,500 − $700). In a transaction of this type, no gain or loss can be recognized so the cost of the new asset is recorded as $1,430 ($630 + $800). A gain of $70 ($700 − $630) actually results but cannot be recorded because similar assets are involved in the trade-in. The journal entry to record the exchange is:

Office Equipment (new)	1,430	
Accumulated Depreciation—Office Equipment	270	
Office Equipment (old)		900
Cash		800

Using the same figures, assume that the old typewriter is traded in on a new office intercom system valued at $1,500. Since the typewriter is not exchanged for a similar asset, the gain can be recognized, and the transaction is recorded as:

Office Equipment (new)	1,500	
Accumulated Depreciation—Office Equipment	270	
Office Equipment (old)		900
Gain on sale of asset		70
Cash		800

Generally, accumulated depreciation is recorded at the end of an accounting period (as has been the case in the preceding examples). However, there are occasions when a depreciable asset is disposed of (sold, traded, or discarded) at a time other than the end of the accounting period. In that event, depreciation of the asset must be determined for that portion of the period that has elapsed since the last depreciation was recorded. The

Table 10.4 Calculation of group depreciation rate

Asset	Cost	Salvage Value	Estimated Life	Annual Depreciation
Tables	$1,000	$100	10 years	$ 90
Desks	2,500	500	20 years	100
Chairs	1,500	200	10 years	130
Total	$5,000	$800		$320

accumulated depreciation (to the nearest month) for the interval between the date of the last entry and the disposition date must first be recorded before any other calculations are made relating to the depreciation of the asset.

In the previous examples, the depreciation has been computed on individual assets. However, depreciation can be computed for groups of assets as well. A single rate can be applied to a group of assets having common characteristics, such as office furniture. The group, or composite, rate is based on averages. Table 10.4 shows how a group rate is determined.

$$\frac{\$320 \text{ (annual depreciation)}}{\$5,000 \text{ (cost)}} = .064 = 6.4\% \text{ composite rate}$$

The composite rate of 6.4% is applied to the total group cost to arrive at the annual depreciation for the group. It is assumed that the composition of the group will change little over the years. The rate will also remain the same unless significant changes occur.

If the depreciation is calculated on a group rate, it is not related to any specific item. Nor is any gain or loss recognized on any particular item. At the time of disposal, the asset account is credited for the cost of the asset. The accumulated depreciation account is debited for the difference between the cost and the salvage or trade-in value. It is expected that any deficiencies in the depreciation will balance out over the years.

A business with a large number of depreciable long-lived assets usually prefers to keep relatively few accounts in the general ledger and to support those control accounts with subsidiary records for each asset. The subsidiary records should contain information regarding the acquisition and disposal dates of the asset, the depreciation charged each period, the accumulated depreciation, and any other information that is considered pertinent.

A detailed explanation of the procedures for figuring depreciation on wasting and intangible assets is not presented here since the basic principles are similar to those already discussed for tangible assets.

Accounting for Inventory

Importance of Inventory

As you learned in chapter 8, merchandise inventory is the amount of merchandise on hand at the beginning of the accounting period. It represents an asset to a firm. A firm begins an accounting period with a certain amount of inventory on hand. At intervals during the period, other inventory is added. At the end of the accounting period it is necessary to determine the value of the goods on hand as well as the cost of goods sold. The cost of goods sold is deducted from the period's sales in the calculation of a gross margin for the period. The cost of the remaining goods on hand is carried forward into the next period as inventory. In other words, costs are matched against revenue. It is important, therefore, that an accurate record of merchandise inventory be kept. Failure to do so can result in a misstatement of the net income for a period. If the inventory on hand is understated, the cost of goods sold will be overstated. The result is an understatement of net income. The reverse is true if the inventory is overstated.

The two systems of accounting for merchandise inventory—periodic and perpetual—were briefly mentioned in chapter 8. The periodic system involves the actual counting of goods on hand at the end of a period, while under the perpetual system, a current count of inventory is kept at all times.

Because no entries are made to the merchandise inventory account during the accounting period under the periodic system, it is necessary to make a complete physical count of inventory at the end of the period. Under the perpetual system, a separate record is kept for each type of merchandise. The record is usually kept on an inventory card, which shows the current inventory for each item. The card usually shows dates and quantities purchased as well as dates and quantities sold. However, at least once a year, it is necessary to check the accuracy of these records by taking a physical inventory.

While the accountant is usually not responsible for taking inventory, he or she should, nevertheless, be familiar with the process.

Determining Inventory on Hand

The inventory on hand is determined by counting the quantity of each type of merchandise the business owns. The counting may be done by regular full-time employees, or it may be necessary to hire additional part-time help. Usually the persons taking the inventory work in pairs. One person counts the inventory, and the other records the count on inventory sheets. Only that merchandise owned by the business should be included in the count. After the counting has been completed, a third person records the unit cost for the items. Other persons may be used to multiply the units by the appropriate unit cost.

Determining Cost of Inventory

The assignment of a cost to inventory can be complicated. For instance, an inventory can consist of a number of identical items that were purchased at different times and at different prices. It is up to the accountant to determine the appropriate cost to be applied to the units on hand. To make the job of valuing inventory easier, several methods of valuation have been developed. The four most commonly used methods are discussed in the following pages.

First-In, First-Out Method

The **first-in, first-out method (FIFO)** assumes that the first items purchased are the first ones sold and that ending inventories are made up of the most recent purchases. To illustrate this and other methods of inventory valuation, the following data is used:

January 1, beginning inventory	10 units	@	$10.00	=	$100
Purchases during the year					
First purchase	20 units	@	$11.00	=	220
Second purchase	10 units	@	$12.50	=	125
Third purchase	5 units	@	$13.00	=	65
Total cost of 45 units available for sale					$510
On hand, end of year, 15 units					

According to the FIFO method, the fifteen units on hand represent the most recently purchased units. The process for determining the cost of units on hand involves working backward through the purchases until a sufficient quantity is obtained to cover the inventory on hand. The value of the ending inventory is calculated as follows:

5 units	@	$13.00	=	$ 65
10 units	@	12.50	=	125
15 units				$190

The value of the inventory on hand is $190. The cost of goods sold is $320 ($510 − $190).

FIFO is perhaps the most widely used of the inventory valuing methods primarily because it conforms to the actual business practice of moving older goods out of stock first. In addition, the most recent costs are assigned to the current inventory.

Last-In, First-Out Method

The **last-in, first-out method (LIFO)** is based on the assumption that the most recently purchased items are the first items sold. The remaining inventory consists of the oldest items purchased. The LIFO method stipulates that the cost of inventory on hand is determined by working forward from the beginning inventory through the purchases until sufficient units are obtained to cover the ending inventory. Using the given data, the cost of the inventory is calculated as follows:

10 units	@	$10.00	=	$100
5 units	@	11.00	=	55
15 units				$155

The value of the ending inventory is $155. The cost assigned to goods sold is $355 ($510 − $155).

The LIFO method has a major disadvantage in that it does not represent the actual physical movement of goods in a business. Seldom are the newest purchases moved out first. However, the use of the LIFO method is preferred by some firms because it results in the most recent costs being charged against the current revenue. Thus, earnings are not likely to be greatly distorted by fluctuating prices. Certain tax advantages can also be gained. A lower net earnings figure results because of the higher cost assigned to the goods sold.

Weighted Average Method

The **weighted average method** of valuing inventory takes into consideration the quantity and the price of the inventory items. According to this method, the same amount of cost is assigned to identical units. To determine the weighted average cost per unit, the cost of the total number of units available for sale is divided by the total units available for sale. (The beginning inventory as well as any purchases during the period are included in determining the unit cost.) The number of units in the ending inventory is multiplied by the weighted average figure. Referring to the same data used in the previous illustrations, the cost of the fifteen units is calculated as follows:

$$\frac{\$510 \text{ (total cost of units available for sale)}}{45 \text{ (total units available for sale)}} = \$11.33 \text{ weighted average unit cost}$$

$$\$11.33 \times 15 \text{ (units on hand)} = \$169.95$$

The value of the ending inventory is $169.95. The cost of goods sold is $340.05 ($510 − $169.95).

The weighted average method of assigning cost to inventory is best suited to firms that purchase a large volume of homogeneous goods and store them in a common area. For example, this method might be appropriate for a grain-processing firm or a chemical distributor.

Lower-of-Cost-or-Market Method

Another frequently used method of valuing inventory is the **lower-of-cost-or-market method,** which assigns the cost or market value, whichever is lower, to the inventory units. When this method is used, *cost* refers to the cost calculated by the FIFO or weighted average method. Tax laws do not permit the use of the lower of LIFO cost or market. *Market* refers to the cost of replacing the inventory units.

To illustrate this method, the examples for figuring FIFO and weighted average will be used. In this example, assume that the market price to replace the items is $11.00.

When compared with the FIFO cost, it is seen that the market price of $11.00 is lower than FIFO cost (5 units @ $13.00; 10 units @ $12.50). Therefore, the cost assigned to the ending inventory is $165 (15 × $11.00). The cost of goods sold is $345 ($510 − $165).

When compared with the weighted average cost ($11.33), the market price of $11.00 is also lower. The value of the ending inventory is again calculated as $165.

The lower-of-cost-or-market method may be applied to each item in the inventory, to classes of inventory, or to the total inventory.

This method is based on a principle of *conservatism* that provides for recording of losses on goods before they are sold. If market prices are lower than cost, it is assumed that a reduced profit will result when the goods are sold. The anticipated loss should be recognized and recorded in the period in which the decline in prices occurs. However, gains or unrealized profits caused by increases in market prices are not recorded before the goods are sold. For example, if the ending inventory has a cost of $10,000 and a market value of $12,000, the increase is not recognized or recorded. However, if the market value is $8,000, the inventory is valued at $8,000 and the loss recognized.

Comparison of Methods

In a market where prices remain unchanged, all of the methods described would yield the same cost figures. However, in a market where prices fluctuate, each method may yield a different result. Table 10.5 shows the differences among the methods. The examples were based on a period in which prices were rising.

Table 10.5 Comparison of inventory cost valuation methods

	FIFO	LIFO	Weighted Average	Cost or Market
Total cost of merchandise available for sale	$510	$510	$510.00	$510
Ending inventory	190	155	169.95	165
Cost of goods sold	$320	$355	$340.05	$345

Each of these methods has certain advantages. FIFO most realistically reflects the actual movement of goods—oldest out first. Also, the inventory amount reported on the balance sheet is closest to current replacement cost since the latest prices are reflected in the inventory valuation. LIFO minimizes the effect of price changes and produces the least fluctuation in net income. Current costs are more closely matched with current revenue. LIFO also offers certain tax advantages. During periods of rising prices, it assigns the greatest amount to cost of goods sold, which results in a lower net income and concurrently a lower taxable income. The weighted average method tends to smooth out price fluctuations, and the lower-of-cost-or-market method recognizes loss from an inventory price decline in the period in which the decline occurs. Reported income is reduced in the period of the price decline. On the other hand, more normal profit margins are realized in the period of sale.

There are, of course, certain disadvantages associated with each of these methods. FIFO tends to magnify the effect of price changes, resulting in a greater over-or understatement of income. LIFO does not realistically picture the movement of goods for most firms—newest out first. The merchandise inventory reported on the balance sheet does not always approximate current replacement costs since the amount represents older and lower unit costs. The biggest disadvantage to the weighted average method is the time required to assemble the data needed for the calculations. This method can entail a rather lengthy, expensive search through files of invoices, especially if a large volume and variety of merchandise is involved. It would also be possible to manipulate income by using this method. If a purchase of a large amount of goods at a high price was made after the last sale of the period, the average unit cost would change. In turn, the amount assigned to cost of goods sold would also change.

Any of these methods of valuing inventory are acceptable. No one of them can be considered the only correct one. It is possible to apply one method to a particular class of inventory and a different method to another class of inventory.

The choice of one method does not rule out changing to another if conditions warrant a change. However, if a change is made, the reason for the change and its effects must be reported in the company's financial statements.

It is also important that the method(s) chosen be followed consistently from year to year. Without some measure of consistency, it is difficult to make valid or meaningful comparisons of financial statements from year to year.

Certain factors other than the invoice price must be taken into account when computing inventory costs. Purchase discounts and shipping charges enter into the computations. However, it is not necessary to adjust each item of inventory for these costs. Usually the amount of the ending inventory is reduced by a percentage determined by the relationship of the discounts and shipping charges to purchases for the year.

Estimating Inventory

In addition to calculating the exact cost of inventory at the end of a year, it is sometimes necessary to estimate inventories. For instance, sometimes interim financial statements may need to be prepared. In such cases, an estimate of inventory and cost of goods sold is sufficient. Two common methods of estimating inventory are the gross profit method and the retail method.

Gross Profit Method

The **gross profit method** is based on the gross profit realized on sales during the period. The net sales for the period are reduced by the normal gross profit percentage to arrive at the estimated cost of goods sold from the total goods available for sale. To illustrate, assume that the beginning inventory is $50,000, the net purchases for the month amount to $75,000, and the net sales amount to $150,000. The estimated gross profit is 30% of net sales. The ending inventory for the month can be estimated in the following manner:

Beginning merchandise inventory		$ 50,000
Net purchases		75,000
Merchandise available for sale		$125,000
Net sales	$150,000	
less estimated Gross Profit on sales ($150,000 × 30%)	45,000	
Estimated Cost of Goods Sold		$105,000
Estimated Ending Inventory		$ 20,000

This method is useful not only for preparing interim financial statements but also to test the accuracy of inventories taken through a physical count. The method is also useful in estimating the cost of inventories that have been destroyed by fire or other disaster.

The method is based on the assumption that the rate of gross profit has been relatively stable and is expected to remain so in the future. Unless that percentage of gross profit is stable, the calculations will be inaccurate. It should be remembered too that calculations made using this method are only reasonable estimates, not exact figures.

Retail Method

The **retail method** of estimating inventories is based on the relationship of the cost of merchandise available for sale to the retail price of that same merchandise. This method is widely used by retail businesses, such as department stores. The retail value of the ending inventory is calculated by subtracting the amount of retail sales from the retail value of the total goods available for sale. The estimated cost of the ending inventory is determined by multiplying the estimated retail inventory by the ratio of cost to selling price. An illustration of the retail method follows:

	Cost	Retail
Beginning merchandise inventory	$25,000	$ 40,000
Net purchases	53,000	90,000
Merchandise available for sale	$78,000	$130,000
less Net sales		110,000
Ending merchandise inventory at retail		$ 20,000

Ratio of Cost to Retail price $\frac{\$78,000}{\$130,000} = 60\%$

Ending merchandise inventory at cost (60% of $20,000) = $12,000

This method also facilitates the preparation of interim financial statements. In addition, once the cost-retail ratio has been established, it can be used to convert an inventory priced at retail to its approximate cost. An estimate of inventory shortages can also be made using this method.

The merchandise inventory account is brought up to date by end-of-the-period adjustment which will be discussed in chapter 11.

Summary

Long-lived assets are broadly classified as tangible, intangible, or wasting assets (p. 198). These assets depreciate in value over a period of years. The portion of the cost of an asset that depreciates each year represents an expense to a firm. An adjusting entry to record the depreciation expense is made at the end of each accounting period. A contra asset account, Accumulated Depreciation, is credited for the accumulated depreciation (p. 204).

Four commonly used methods of calculating depreciation are the straight-line, units-of-production, declining balance, and sum-of-the-years'-digits methods (pp. 200–03).

Long-lived assets eventually become unusable and are discarded, sold, or traded in. The disposal of a long-lived asset may result in a gain or loss depending upon whether or not the asset is fully depreciated. Both the asset and its accumulated depreciation are removed from the books at the time of disposal (pp. 204–07). Depreciation can be computed for groups of assets as well as for individual assets (p. 208).

At the end of an accounting period it is necessary to assign costs to the ending merchandise inventory and to the goods that have been sold during the period (p. 209). There are several methods for determining the cost of inventory based on actual costs: FIFO, LIFO, weighted average, and lower-of-cost-or-market. All of these methods are considered acceptable, and often more than one method is used in determining the cost of inventory (pp. 210–13).

Two other methods that are based on estimated costs are also used: the gross profit method and the retail method. These methods are useful when interim financial statements must be prepared or when estimates must be made of the cost of inventories that have been destroyed (pp. 214–15).

Once the ending inventory has been determined, it is entered on the books by an end-of-the-period adjustment.

Key Terms

amortization The process of writing off an intangible asset as an expense.

book value The cost of an asset less accumulated depreciation; often called *undepreciated cost*.

declining balance method A method for calculating depreciation that assigns a greater amount of depreciation to the early years of an asset's life with a steady decrease in the amount charged to depreciation in the remaining years.

depletion The process of writing off a wasting asset as an expense.

FIFO method A method of assigning costs to inventory based on the assumption that the first goods purchased are the first goods sold.

functional depreciation The loss of usefulness of an asset because of inadequacy or obsolescence.

gross profit method A method for estimating cost of inventory; a percentage of gross profit is applied to the sales of the period.

intangible asset An asset that has no physical substance.

LIFO method A method of assigning costs to inventory based on the assumption that the last goods purchased are the first goods sold.

long-lived asset An asset that is expected to be used in the operation of a business for a number of years.

lower-of-cost-or-market method A method of assigning cost to inventory in which lower cost or market price is applied to units on hand.

net cost The gross cost of an asset less its estimated salvage value.

personal property All assets other than real property.

physical depreciation A decline in usefulness of an asset caused by use or exposure to the elements.

real property Land and anything that is attached to the land.

retail method A method for estimating cost of inventory based on a ratio of cost to retail price.

straight-line method A method for calculating depreciation that assigns equal amounts of depreciation to equal periods of time.

sum-of-the-years'-digits method A method for calculating depreciation that assigns greater amounts of depreciation to the early years of an asset's life.

tangible asset An asset that has physical substance.

units-of-production method A method for calculating depreciation that is based on the output or production of an asset multiplied by a constant cost per unit.

wasting asset A long-lived asset that is eventually consumed or exhausted.

weighted average method A method of assigning an average cost to inventory units based on both the quantity and cost of units.

Objectives

Upon completion of this chapter, you should be able to:

1. Prepare a worksheet for a merchandising firm.
2. Prepare classified financial statements for a merchandising firm.
3. Journalize and post adjusting and closing entries for a merchandising firm.
4. Journalize and post reversing entries for accrued revenue and expense.

11 Adjusting and Closing Process for a Merchandising Firm

5. Define the following accounting terms:

classified financial statements

current assets

current liabilities

fixed assets

general expenses

long-term investments

long-term liabilities

prepaid expenses

reversing entry

selling expenses

Chapter 5 presented the procedures for adjusting and closing the books of a professional enterprise. Although the same basic procedures are followed in adjusting and closing the books of a merchandising firm, this chapter also considers the variations necessary for applying these procedures to a merchandising firm.

The Worksheet

As previously defined, a worksheet is an informal statement prepared at the end of the accounting period. It permits the accountant to gather in one place all the data necessary for bringing the accounts up to date, preparing the financial statements, and getting the books ready for the transactions of a new accounting period.

In chapter 5, you learned how to prepare a ten-column worksheet. The same form (fig. 11.1) and procedures are used in preparing the worksheet for a merchandising firm.

To review briefly: At the end of the accounting period, these activities are performed prior to the preparation of the worksheet. The general ledger accounts are footed and balanced. The subsidiary ledgers are proved against their respective control accounts in the general ledger. A trial balance is taken to verify the equality of the debit and credit balances in the general ledger. The trial balance is prepared in the first two columns of the worksheet rather than as a separate statement. Any errors found are corrected before proceeding further with the worksheet. The trial balance for Signature B appears on the worksheet shown in figure 11.1.

The accounts listed below the trial balance totals do not appear in the trial balance because there are no balances in those accounts to record. However, because all the accounts are affected in some way by the adjustments to be made, they must be listed on the worksheet.

Adjustments

Some ledger accounts must be adjusted to bring their balances up to date before preparing the financial statements. These adjustments appear first in the Adjustments columns of the worksheet. The data needed for adjusting the accounts of Signature B are as follows:

1. Ending merchandise inventory, $28,900.
2. Prepaid insurance expired, $225.
3. Supplies used, $296.
4. Depreciation of store equipment, 10 percent a year, $421.40.
5. Accrued bank credit card expense, $236.25.
6. Uncollectible accounts, ½ percent of credit sales, $579.10.
7. Interest accrued on notes payable, $33.33.

These adjustments, illustrated in the worksheet, are explained on the following pages.

| Merchandise Inventory | The balance of Merchandise Inventory at the end of one accounting period is the same as the balance at the beginning of the next period. During the year, however, the inventory level fluctuates. Inventory is increased by purchases of additional merchandise and decreased by sales of merchandise. The balance of Merchandise Inventory is seldom the same at the beginning and the end of an accounting period. In the worksheet in figure 11.1, the $26,740 balance in the Trial Balance Dr. column represents the merchandise inventory at the beginning of the accounting period without adjustments for purchases and sales of merchandise. Therefore, the Merchandise Inventory account must be adjusted at the end of the period to show the value of the inventory at that time. Two adjustments are necessary—one to clear the beginning balance from the Merchandise Inventory account, the other to record the new balance of inventory on hand at the end of the period. These adjustments are identified on the worksheet by the letters (a) and (b). |

The first adjustment (a) transfers the beginning Merchandise Inventory balance, $26,740, to the Expense and Revenue Summary account where it will later be included in the determination of the net income for the period. Expense and Revenue Summary is debited for $26,740. Merchandise Inventory is credited for the same amount.

The second adjustment (b) records the amount of the ending inventory, $28,900, in the Merchandise Inventory account. (The procedures for determining the value of the ending inventory were explained in chapter 10.) The ending inventory of $28,900 is debited to Merchandise Inventory and credited to Expense and Revenue Summary.

Since the first adjustment crediting Merchandise Inventory leaves the account with a zero balance, the second adjustment debiting Merchandise Inventory records the proper balance for the account at the end of the period. The credit to Expense and Revenue Summary makes it possible for the ending inventory to also be included in the determination of the net income for the period.

Prepaid Insurance

The $675 balance in the Prepaid Insurance account represents a prepaid premium for a three-year policy against theft, fire, smoke, and water damage to the store's contents. On December 31, one year of the premium, $225, has expired. The asset account, Prepaid Insurance, is reduced by the amount that has expired, and that same amount is transferred to the proper expense account. Item (c) on the worksheet, which records this change, debits Insurance Expense and credits Prepaid Insurance for $225.

If a firm has several insurance policies, a supplementary record, called an insurance policy record, may be kept. This record contains complete information about each policy and provides the accountant with information concerning the amount of expired insurance that must be charged as an expense.

Figure 11.1 Worksheet for Signature B.

Signature B
Worksheet
For the Year Ended December 31, 19XX

Account Name	Acct. No.	Trial Balance Debit	Trial Balance Credit	Adjustments Debit	Adjustments Credit	Adjusted Trial Balance Debit	Adjusted Trial Balance Credit
Cibola National Bank	111	17400 —				17400 —	
Petty Cash	113	100 —				100 —	
Accounts Receivable	121	115820 —				115820 —	
Allowance for Bad Debts	012		10256		(g) 57910		68166
Merchandise Inventory	131	26740 —		(b) 28900	(a) 26740 —	28900 —	
Prepaid Insurance	141	675 —			(c) 225 —	450 —	
Supplies	151	562 —			(d) 296 —	266 —	
Store Equipment	161	4214 —				4214 —	
Acc. Depr.-Store Equipment	016		42140		(e) 42140		84280
Accounts Payable	211		91220 —				91220 —
Notes Payable	212		5000 —				5000 —
Sales Tax Payable	213		2600 —				2600 —
Mary Beth Flynn, Capital	311		571904				571904
Mary Beth Flynn, Drawing	312	10090 —				10090 —	
Sales	411		210700 —				210700 —
Sales Returns & Allowances	041	3010 —				3010 —	
Purchases	511	151450 —				151450 —	
Pur. Returns & Allowances	051		1980 —				1980 —
Purchases Discount	052		7320 —				7320 —
Rent Expense	512	9600 —				9600 —	
Salary Expense	513	22647 —				22647 —	
Payroll Tax Expense	514	1908 —				1908 —	
Utilities Expense	515	1346 —				1346 —	
Telephone Expense	516	461 —				461 —	
Advertising Expense	517	7160 —				7160 —	
Bank Credit Card Expense	518	2564 —		(f) 23625		280025	
Miscellaneous Expense	519	526 —				526 —	
Interest Expense	520	265 —		(h) 3333		29833	
		376538 —	376538 —				
Accrued Interest Payable	221				(h) 3333		3333
Accrued Bank Credit Card Payable	222				(f) 23625		23625
Expense and Revenue Summary	313			(a) 26740 —	(b) 28900 —	26740 —	28900 —
Depreciation Expense	521			(e) 42140		42140	
Supplies Expense	522			(d) 296 —		296 —	
Bad Debts Expense	523			(g) 57910		57910	
Insurance Expense	524			(c) 225 —		225 —	
				574308	574308	40670808	40670808
Net Income							

Income Statement		Balance Sheet	
Debit	Credit	Debit	Credit
		17400 —	
		100 —	
		115820 —	
			68166
		28900 —	
		450 —	
		266 —	
		4214 —	
			84280
		91220 —	
		5000 —	
		2600 —	
			5719404
		10090 —	
	210700 —		
3010 —			
151450 —			
	1980 —		
	7320 —		
9600 —			
22647 —			
1908 —			
1346 —			
461 —			
7160 —			
280025			
526 —			
29833			
			3333
			23625
26740 —	28900 —		
42140			
296 —			
57910			
225 —			
2294608	248900 —	177240 —	15780808
194392			1943192
248900 —	248900 —	177240 —	177240 —

Prepaid Insurance is listed as an asset. However, it actually represents a business expense that has been paid in advance but that is not wholly consumed during the accounting period. This type of asset is often called a **prepaid expense.**

Supplies

The Supplies account is another example of a prepaid expense. It represents an asset to the company until the supplies are consumed. Rather than adjust the asset account every time a portion of the supplies is used, one adjustment is made at the end of the accounting period. The adjustment for the supplies used is similar to the adjustment for expired insurance.

At the beginning of the accounting period, Signature B had supplies on hand worth $562. At the end of the period the records show that $296 worth of supplies were used during the period. This amount is debited to Supplies Expense and credited to Supplies. This adjustment is identified as item (d) on the worksheet.

Depreciation

Signature B has only one long-lived asset subject to depreciation, Store Equipment. The equipment has an expected useful life of ten years with no salvage value. Signature B uses the straight-line method of figuring depreciation (which was explained in chapter 10). Using this method, the yearly depreciation rate is 10 percent (100% ÷ 10), and the annual depreciation expense is $421.40 (10% of $4,214). The adjustment for depreciation is recorded by debiting Depreciation Expense and crediting Accumulated Depreciation—Store Equipment, item (e) on the worksheet, for $421.40.

Accrued Bank Credit Card Expense

Bank credit card expense represents an accrued expense; that is, an expense that builds or accrues over a period of time but that has not been recorded. It also represents an accrued liability until such time as it is actually paid. Even though this expense is not paid until later, it must be recorded during the period in which the related bank credit card sales were made.

Signature B has accrued a bank credit card expense of $236.25 as of December 31, which will not be paid until January. The accrued expense (liability) is recorded by debiting Bank Credit Card Expense and crediting Accrued Bank Credit Card Payable. This adjustment is identified as item (f) on the worksheet.

Uncollectible Accounts

Past experience has shown that ½ percent of Signature B's credit sales usually prove to be uncollectible. Thus, $579.10 (.005 × $115,820) is charged as bad debts expense. The adjustment, item (g), is made by debiting Bad Debts Expense and crediting Alowance for Bad Debts.

Item (h) on the worksheet records the interest that has accrued on an outstanding $5,000, 6 percent, ninety-day note payable. The note is dated November 21, so interest has accrued for forty days but has not been recorded. The accrued interest of $33.33 is recorded by debiting Interest Expense and crediting Accrued Interest Payable.

After these entries are recorded in the Adjustments columns of the worksheet, the two columns are totaled to prove the equality of debits and credits. Next, the amounts in the Trial Balance columns, which reflect the changes brought about by the adjustments, are extended to the Adjusted Trial Balance columns. Also note that both the debit and credit amounts for Expense and Revenue Summary are also extended to the Income Statement columns. It is not necessary to determine the difference between the two amounts since both amounts are reported on the income statement.

When the equality of the debits and credits in the Adjusted Trial Balance columns has been proved, the balances of the asset, liability, and owner's equity accounts are transferred to the Balance Sheet columns of the worksheet. The balances of the Expense and Revenue Summary account and the revenue and expense accounts are transferred to the Income Statement columns. The worksheet is then completed, and the net income or net loss determined in the manner explained in chapter 5.

According to the worksheet in figure 11.1, Signature B has a net income of $19,431.92 for the year ended December 31, 19XX.

Financial Statements

The account balances have been sorted on the worksheet according to the statements in which they appear. Financial statements can be prepared quickly and easily once the worksheet has been completed. The procedures for preparing the financial statements for a professional enterprise were explained in chapter 3. Those statements were relatively simple since few accounts were used. In a merchandising firm, however, the statements are somewhat more detailed and usually involve a greater number of accounts. For this reason, the items on the statements are often grouped into classifications, in which case the statements are called **classified financial statements.** Classifying the accounts on the statements simplifies the analysis and interpretation of the data.

Income Statement

The income statement is usually prepared first. The two most widely used methods for preparing the income statement are the single-step and the multiple-step methods. The income statement in chapter 3 was prepared in the single-step form, so-called because total expenses are subtracted from total revenue. Merchandising firms usually find the multiple-step form (fig.

11.2) more suitable for reporting the results of their operations. The multiple-step income statement is so-called because it contains several sections, each one listed in a sequence that culminates in the determination of the net income.

Figure 11.2 Multiple-step income statement.

```
                                    Signature B
                                 INCOME STATEMENT
                         For the Year Ended December 31, 19XX

Operating Revenue:
  Sales                                                              $210,700.00
      less Sales Returns and Allowances                                 3,010.00
  Net Sales                                                          $207,690.00

Cost of Goods Sold:
  Merchandise Inventory, January 1, 19XX              $ 26,740.00
      Purchases                        $151,450.00
      less: Purchases, Returns
         and Allowances      $1,980.00
         Purchase Discount    7,320.00        9,300.00
  Net Purchases                                        142,150.00
  Merchandise Available for Sale                      $168,890.00
      less Merchandise Inventory, December 31, 19XX     28,900.00
         Cost of Goods Sold                                           139,990.00
Gross Profit on Sales                                                $ 67,700.00

Operating Expenses:
  Rent Expense                                        $  9,600.00
  Depreciation Expense                                     421.40
  Salary Expense                                       22,647.00
  Payroll Tax Expense                                   1,908.00
  Utilities Expense                                     1,346.00
  Supplies Expense                                        296.00
  Telephone Expense                                       461.00
  Advertising Expense                                   7,160.00
  Bank Credit Card Expense                              2,800.25
  Bad Debts Expense                                       579.10
  Insurance Expense                                       225.00
  Miscellaneous Expense                                   526.00
     Total Operating Expenses                                          47,969.75
Income from Operations                                               $ 19,730.25

Other Expenses:
  Interest Expense                                                        298.33

Net Income                                                           $ 19,431.92
```

The income statement for Signature B for the year ended December 31, 19XX, is shown in figure 11.2. The multiple-step income statement for a merchandising firm is described in the following list:

1. The total of all sales of merchandise is reported in the Operating Revenue section (sometimes labeled *Revenue from Sales*). Sales Returns and Allowances and Sales Discounts (if discounts are allowed) are subtracted from the total sales to determine net sales.

2. The cost of the goods sold during the period is shown in the Cost of Goods Sold section. The procedure for determining cost of goods sold was explained in chapter 8.

3. The gross profit on sales is determined by subtracting the cost of goods sold from net sales.

4. All the expenses incurred within the normal operations of the business are reported in the Operating Expenses section. These expenses are often classified further either as selling or as general, or administrative, expenses. **Selling expenses** are those directly connected with the sale of merchandise. **General,** or **administrative, expenses** are those incurred in the operation of the business that are not a part of the actual process of selling. The operating expenses have not been classified on the income statement in figure 11.2; however, it is usually desirable to do so with a larger business.

5. The income from operations, or operating income, is determined by subtracting total operating expenses from the gross profit on sales. If the total operating expenses are larger than the gross profit on sales, a *loss from operations* results.

6. Some firms have income or expenses from sources other than those connected with its normal operations (e.g., income from the sale of an asset or interest paid on an outstanding debt). Special sections on the income statement labeled Other Income and Other Expenses are used to record these items. They are offset against each other. If the total of Other Income exceeds the total of Other Expenses, the difference is added to the Income from Operations. If the opposite is true, the difference is subtracted from the Income from Operations.

7. The final figure on the income statement represents the net income or net loss from all sources. Operating expenses are subtracted from the gross profit on sales to determine this amount.

Balance Sheet   The two most widely used forms for the balance sheet were illustrated in chapter 3. The account form lists assets on the left-hand side of the statement, and liabilities and owner's equity are listed on the right-hand side. The totals of both sides must equal. The report form (fig. 11.3) presents the three sections one under the other. The total of the assets section must equal the combined total of the other two sections (liabilities and owner's equity).

In the balance sheet illustrated in chapter 3 (fig. 3.4), all assets were listed in one group and all liabilities in another. However, when a balance sheet contains a number of accounts, as with a merchandising firm, it is more useful to classify assets and liabilities. A classified balance sheet

Figure 11.3 Classified balance sheet.

Signature B
BALANCE SHEET
December 31, 19XX

ASSETS

Current Assets:			
Cibola National Bank			$ 17,400.00
Petty Cash			100.00
Accounts Receivable		$115,820.00	
less Allowance for Bad Debts		681.66	115,138.34
Merchandise Inventory			28,900.00
Prepaid Insurance			450.00
Supplies			266.00
Fixed Assets:			
Store Equipment		4,214.00	
less Accumulated Depreciation		842.80	3,371.20
Total Assets			$165,625.54

LIABILITIES

Current Liabilities:			
Accounts Payable		$ 5,000.00	
Notes Payable		91,220.00	
Sales Tax Payable		2,600.00	
Accrued Interest Payable		33.33	
Accrued Bank Credit Card Payable		236.25	
Total Current Liabilities			$ 99,089.58

OWNER'S EQUITY

Mary Beth Flynn, Capital:			
Capital, January 1, 19XX		$ 57,194.04	
Net Income for Year	$19,431.92		
less Withdrawals	10,090.00		
Net Increase		9,341.92	
Capital, December 31, 19XX			66,535.96
Total Liabilities and Owner's Equity			$165,625.54

prepared in report form for Signature B on December 31, 19XX, is shown in figure 11.3. Assets and liabilities are usually classified into the following groups:

1. **Current assets** are cash and other assets that are expected to be converted to cash or used up within the normal operating period of the business or one year, whichever is longer. Cash, receivables, merchandise inventory, and prepaid expenses are the major types of current assets. These assets are listed on the balance sheet in the order of their *liquidity;* that is, how quickly the asset can be converted into cash or used. Cash, of course, is the most liquid so it is listed first. The receivables are usually listed next because they are turned into cash as soon as the customers pay their bills. Merchandise Inventory represents goods the business has on hand and expects to sell within the accounting period. Prepaid expenses, such as rent, insurance, and supplies, are also considered to be current assets since they are generally used up during the normal operating cycle.
2. **Fixed assets** are relatively long-lived assets that are used in the operation of the business. The firm does not expect to convert them to cash or use them up in the near future. Some typical fixed assets are land, buildings, and equipment. These assets are sometimes labeled as Long-lived Assets, Plant Assets, or Plant and Equipment.
3. Some firms also use a third classification, **long-term investments.** These assets consist of securities, such as stocks and bonds, that are converted to cash eventually but not within the current accounting period. If this classification is used, it is listed on the balance sheet between Current and Fixed Assets.
4. **Current liabilities** are those debts and obligations that must be paid within one operating cycle or one year, whichever is longer. Accounts Payable, Salaries Payable, and Taxes Payable also fall in this category. Current liabilities are listed on the balance sheet in the order in which they must be paid. They are normally paid from Current Assets.
5. **Long-term liabilities** are debts that are not due for a relatively long time, usually more than one year. A mortgage on land or buildings represents a long-term liability.

A year is typically used as the maximum limit for current accounts. A shorter period can be used, although that is rarely the case.

Generally, the owner's equity section is not classified when a business is owned by one person. However, corporations or partnerships may find it desirable to classify the owner's equity section also.

After the financial statements have been prepared, the adjustments shown
on the worksheet are journalized and posted. The balances of the ledger
accounts then agree with the amounts reported in the financial statements.
The adjusting entries for Signature B are shown in figure 11.4.

Next, the closing entries are journalized and posted. All of the temporary owner's equity accounts (revenue and expenses and their related
accounts) are closed to the Expense and Revenue Summary account, which
reduces their balances to zero. The Expense and Revenue Summary account
then contains all the balances pertaining to inventory, sales, purchases, and
expenses. The balance of this account represents the net income or loss for
the period and is closed to the owner's Capital account. This closing entry
reduces the Expense and Revenue Summary account balance to zero also.
The last closing entry closes the balance of the owner's Drawing account
to the Capital account. The amounts for the closing entries are taken from

Figure 11.4   Adjusting entries for Signature B.

GENERAL JOURNAL   Page 1

Date		Explanation	P/R	Debit	Credit
19xx		Adjusting Entries			
Dec	31	Expense and Revenue Summary		26740 —	
		Merchandise Inventory			26740 —
	31	Merchandise Inventory		28900 —	
		Expense and Revenue Summary			28900 —
	31	Insurance Expense		225 —	
		Prepaid Insurance			225 —
	31	Supplies Expense		296 —	
		Supplies			296 —
	31	Depreciation Expense		421 40	
		Accumulated Depr.—Store Eqpt.			421 40
	31	Bank Credit Card Expense		236 25	
		Accrued Bank Credit Card Payable			236 25
	31	Bad Debts Expense		579 10	
		Allowance for Bad Debts			579 10
	31	Interest Expense		33 33	
		Accrued Interest Payable			33 33

the Income Statement columns of the worksheet with the exception of the amount for the owner's Drawing account. This amount is taken from the debit column of the Balance Sheet section of the worksheet. The closing entrie for Signature B are shown in figure 11.5.

After the adjusting and closing entries for Signature B have been posted, the Expense and Revenue Summary and the Capital accounts appear as shown in figure 11.6. The entries have been labeled in figure 11.6 to show clearly what has happened. They are not labeled in actual practice. The complete ledger is not shown since you are already familiar with the journalizing and posting procedures from previous chapters.

Figure 11.5   Closing entries for Signature B.

GENERAL JOURNAL   Page 1

Date	Explanation	P/R	Debit	Credit
19XX	Closing Entries			
Dec 31	Sales		210700 —	
	Purchase Returns and Allowances		1980 —	
	Purchase Discounts		7320 —	
	Expense and Revenue Summary			220000 —
31	Expense and Revenue Summary		202728 08	
	Sales Returns and Allowances			3010 —
	Purchases			151450 —
	Rent Expense			9600 —
	Depreciation Expense			421 40
	Salary Expense			22647 —
	Payroll Tax Expense			1908 —
	Utilities Expense			1346 —
	Supplies Expense			296 —
	Telephone Expense			461 —
	Advertising Expense			7160 —
	Bank Credit Card Expense			2800 25
	Bad Debts Expense			579 10
	Insurance Expense			225 —
	Miscellaneous Expense			526 —
	Interest Expense			298 33
31	Expense and Revenue Summary		19431 92	
	Mary Beth Flynn, Capital			19431 92
31	Mary Beth Flynn, Capital		10090 —	
	Mary Beth Flynn, Drawing			10090 —

Figure 11.6 Expense and Revenue Summary and Capital accounts after posting.

ACCOUNT _Expense and Revenue Summary_   Account No. _313_

Date		Item	P/R	Debit	Credit	Balance	
						Debit	Credit
19XX Dec	31	Beginning Inventory	J1	26740 —		26740 —	
	31	Ending Inventory	J1		28900 —		2160 —
	31	Sales, Pur. Ret. & Allow., Pur. Disc.	J1		220000 —		222160 —
	31	Sales Ret. & Allow., Pur., Expense	J1	202728 08			19431 92
	31	Net Income	J1	19431 92			— 0 —

ACCOUNT _Mary Beth Flynn, Capital_   Account No. _411_

Date		Item	P/R	Debit	Credit	Balance	
						Debit	Credit
19XX Jan	1	Balance	✓		57194 04		57194 04
Dec	31	Net Income	J1		19431 92		76625 96
	31	Drawing	J1	10090 —			66535 96

Postclosing Trial Balance

Once the temporary owner's equity accounts have been closed, only the asset, liability, and owner's equity accounts have balances. A postclosing trial balance is then prepared to verify the equality of the debit and credit balances of the open accounts. This statement insures that the accounts are ready for recording transactions in the next accounting period. The postclosing trial balance for Signature B appears in figure 11.7. The balances on this statement agree with the amounts appearing on the balance sheet shown in figure 11.3.

Reversing Entries

Another step in the accounting cycle, which is not absolutely necessary but often useful, involves reversing certain of the adjusting entries after the closing of the books has been completed. Many accountants reverse the adjustments for accrued expenses and revenue. If a **reversing entry** is made, the next transactions that occur in connection with the account involved in the adjusting entry can be made in a routine manner. A reversing entry also permits all revenue and expense to be properly allocated to the period in which it was earned or incurred.

For example, Signature B has accrued a bank credit card expense of $236.25 for December, which will not actually be paid until January. After the adjusting and closing entries have been posted, the accounts are as shown in figure 11.8. The reversing entry for the bank credit card expense

Figure 11.7 Postclosing trial balance for Signature B.

Signature B
Postclosing Trial Balance
December 31, 19XX

Account Name	Debit	Credit
Cibola National Bank	17400 —	
Petty Cash	100 —	
Accounts Receivable	11 58 20 —	
Allowance for Bad Debts		681 66
Merchandise Inventory	28900 —	
Prepaid Insurance	450 —	
Supplies	266 —	
Store Equipment	4214 —	
Acc. Depr.-Store Equipment		842 80
Accounts Payable		91220 —
Notes Payable		5000 —
Sales Tax Payable		2600 —
Accrued Interest Payable		33 33
Accrued Bank Credit Card Payable		236 25
Mary Beth Flynn, Capital		66535 96
	167150 —	167150 —

Figure 11.8 Bank credit card accounts after posting.

ACCOUNT Accrued Bank Credit Card Payable   Account No. 222

Date		Item	P/R	Debit	Credit	Balance Debit	Balance Credit
19XX Dec	31		J1		236 25		236 25

ACCOUNT Bank Credit Card Expense   Account No. 518

Date		Item	P/R	Debit	Credit	Balance Debit	Balance Credit
19XX Dec	31	Balance	✓			2564 —	
	31		J1	236 25		2800 25	
	31		J1		2800 25	— 0 —	

adjustment is shown in figure 11.9. After the reversing entry is posted, the accounts appear as shown in figure 11.10.

The credit balance in the liability account has been removed, and the epense account now has a credit balance of $236.25. When the accrued bank credit card expense for December is paid in January, the amount will be debited to Bank Credit Card Expense and credited to Cash. The expense account will then be in balance. Later when credit card expense for January is recorded, there will be no problem with trying to figure how much of the January balance should be charged to the year just ended and how much to the new year.

Signature B also has accrued interest expense in the amount of $33.33 on a $5,000, 6 percent, ninety-day note. After the adjusting and closing entries have been posted, the accounts appear as shown in figure 11.11.

Figure 11.9 Reversing entry for the bank credit card expense adjustment.

GENERAL JOURNAL   Page 1

Date	Explanation	P/R	Debit	Credit
19xx				
Jan 1	*Reversing Entry*			
	Accrued Bank Credit Card Payable		236 25	
	Bank Credit Card Expense			236 25

Figure 11.10 Bank credit card accounts after posting of reversing entry.

ACCOUNT _Accrued Bank Credit Card Payable_   Account No. 222

Date		Item	P/R	Debit	Credit	Balance Debit	Balance Credit
19xx Dec	31		J1		236 25		236 25
19xx Jan	1		J1	236 25			—0—

ACCOUNT _Bank Credit Card Expense_   Account No. 518

Date		Item	P/R	Debit	Credit	Balance Debit	Balance Credit
19xx Dec	31	Balance	✓			2564 —	
	31		J1	236 25		2800 25	
	31		J1		2800 25	—0—	
19xx Jan	1		J1		236 25		236 25

Figure 11.11 Interest accounts after posting.

ACCOUNT _Accrued Interest Payable_   Account No. _221_

Date		Item	P/R	Debit	Credit	Balance Debit	Balance Credit
19xx Dec	31		J1		33 33		33 33

ACCOUNT _Interest Expense_   Account No. _520_

Date		Item	P/R	Debit	Credit	Balance Debit	Balance Credit
19xx Dec	31	Balance	✓			265 —	
	31		J1	33 33		298 33	
	31		J1		298 33	— 0 —	

Figure 11.12 Reversing entry for the accrued interest expense adjustment.

GENERAL JOURNAL   Page __1__

Date	Explanation	P/R	Debit	Credit
19xx	Reversing Entry			
Jan 1	Accrued Interest Payable		33 33	
	Interest Expense			33 33

To reverse the adjustment for accrued interest expense, the journal entry in figure 11.12 is made. After posting the reversing entry, the Accrued Interest Payable account has a zero balance and the Interest Expense account has a credit balance of $33.33. Later when the note is paid, the transaction can be journalized and posted in the standard manner. The Interest Expense account will then have a debit balance of $41.67, which is the amount of interest incurred in the year in which the note is paid (fig. 11.13).

Reversing entries are made as soon as the books have been closed at the end of the accounting period. Usually, however, the entries are dated the first day of the new period.

The reversing procedure simplifies the accounting for accruals. The portion of any payment of an expense or receipt of revenue that pertains to the new accounting period is automatically shown as the balance of the expense or revenue account involved.

Figure 11.13 Interest account after posting of note payment.

ACCOUNT _Interest Expense_ Account No. _520_

Date		Item	P/R	Debit	Credit	Balance	
						Debit	Credit
19XX Dec	31	Balance	✓			2 6 5 —	
	31		J1	33 33		2 9 8 33	
	31		J1		2 9 8 33	— 0 —	
19XX Jan	1		J1		3 3 —		3 3 —

Summary

The end-of-the-period activities for a merchandising firm are basically the same as those for a professional enterprise (p. 220). The basic difference lies in the number and type of adjusting entries and the format used for preparing the financial statements (pp. 220–25).

Financial statements for a merchandising firm are usually more detailed than those for a professional enterprise. The accounts are classified to facilitate analyzing and interpreting the data (pp. 225–29).

There is no difference in the manner in which adjusting and closing entries are journalized and posted for a merchandising firm (pp. 230–32). However, in addition to the adjusting and closing entries, there is another type of journal entry that is commonly included in the end-of-the-period activities. Journal entries, called reversing entries, are made to reverse the adjustments for accrued revenue and expenses (pp. 232–35). These reversing entries are not actually necessary, but they simplify the accounting for accrued expenses and revenue. Reversing entries make it possible for all revenue and expense to be allocated to and routinely recorded in the period in which it was earned or incurred.

Key Terms

classified financial statements Financial statements in which the accounts have been grouped into classifications.

current assets Cash and other assets that are expected to be converted to cash or used up within the normal operating period of the business or one year, whichever is longer.

current liabilities Debts and obligations that must be paid within one operating cycle or one year, whichever is longer.

fixed assets Assets with a relatively long life that are not expected to be converted to cash or used up in the near future; sometimes called long-lived assets or plant assets.

general expenses Expenses incurred in the operation of the business that are not a part of the actual process of selling merchandise; sometimes called administrative expenses.

long-term investments Securities that are converted to cash eventually but not within the current accounting period.

long-term liabilities Debts that are not due for a relatively long time, usually more than one year.

prepaid expenses Business expenses that have been paid in advance but that are not wholly consumed during the accounting period; they are listed as assets at the time of purchase.

reversing entry A journal entry made on the first day of a new accounting period to reverse the adjustments for accruals.

selling expenses Expenses incurred in the operation of the business that are directly related to the sale of merchandise.

Upon completion of this chapter, you should be able to:

1. Compute an employee's gross earnings.
2. Determine employee payroll deductions for:

   FICA taxes   other taxes
   federal income taxes   voluntary deductions

3. Compute federal income tax withholdings by the wage-bracket table and the percentage method.
4. Complete a payroll register.
5. Journalize the entry to record a payroll.
6. Prepare an employee's individual earnings record.

12 Accounting for Payroll Employee

7. Define the following accounting terms:

employee	payroll register
employee's individual earnings record	pegboard accounting
employer	percentage method
fair labor standards act	piece rate
federal income tax	salary
federal insurance contributions act	taxable earnings
FICA taxes	time-sharing
gross earnings	wage-bracket method
independent contractor	wages
net pay	withholding allowances
paycheck	

Up to this point, the discussion of payroll procedures has been deliberately limited. Wages and salaries have been mentioned only in regard to the expense they represent to a business. In the previous examples of journal entries involving payroll expenses, only gross amounts have been shown. No deductions from gross pay have been calculated. In this chapter and chapter 13 all of the records and procedures relevant to payroll accounting will be discussed in detail.

Necessity of Payroll Records

The payment of wages and salaries represents one of the major expenses of a typical business. The computing and recording of the payroll, as well as the handling of payroll-related transactions, requires a large portion of an accountant's time.

Detailed payroll records are a necessity for any business. Complete, accurate records must be kept of what is owed each employee at the end of each pay period. This information is needed so that proper accounting for payroll expenses can be made. In addition, a variety of federal, state, and local taxes are imposed on both employers and employees; therefore, detailed records are necessary to verify that the correct amount of taxes has been submitted to the appropriate taxing agencies.

It is also a common practice for most firms to provide for voluntary withholdings from employees' pay for such things as insurance, retirement, and savings bonds. It is essential, therefore, that complete records of these withholdings and the disposition of the withheld funds be kept.

Employer-
Employee
Relationship

An **employer** is a business or person for whom one performs a service. Not all persons who perform services for a business or another person are employees. Only those persons under the control or direction of the business or person for whom the services are performed are classified as **employees.** For example, a factory worker, a sales clerk, and a secretary are considered employees.

Some persons are hired to perform a job or service for a business or another person but are not subject to the control or direction of that business or person. These persons are classified as **independent contractors** rather than employees. Independent contractors are responsible for the results of their services and usually receive a fee for services performed. A public accountant and a management consultant are classified as independent contractors.

Payroll accounting is concerned only with the records associated with the employer-employee relationship; therefore, payments to independent contractors are not included in a firm's payroll records.

Types of Remuneration	Remuneration to employees is usually classified according to the type of work performed and the period of time covered. Remuneration for managerial or administrative work is usually called a **salary.** A salary is ordinarily expressed as a fixed monthly or yearly amount. Remuneration for either skilled or unskilled labor is usually referred to as **wages.** Wages may be expressed on an hourly, weekly, or piece-rate basis. If a **piece-rate** basis is used, employees are paid at a certain rate for each unit of production.

In addition to a basic salary or wage, an employee may receive supplemental income in the form of commissions, bonuses, profit sharing, or cost-of-living adjustments. Commissions and bonuses are usually paid for work performed in excess of an expected minimum.

Employees are generally paid by check or in cash. In some instances, however, payment is made in the form of merchandise, meals, lodging, or some other property. If payment is made in this manner, the face value of the property or service must be determined.

In actual practice, the terms *wages* and *salaries* are often used interchangeably; however, the Internal Revenue Service uses the term wages for all types of remuneration.

Employee Earnings

Fair Labor Standards Act	An employee's rate of pay is based upon an agreement between the employer and the employee. However, the minimum wage an employee may receive and the maximum number of hours an employee may work at the minimum wage rate are regulated by law. Employers engaged in interstate commerce come under the regulation of the **federal Fair Labor Standards Act,** also called the Wages and Hour Law. This act sets forty hours as the maximum time to be worked each week at the regular rate. It also stipulates that all hours worked in excess of forty hours must be compensated at a minimum rate of one and one-half times the regular rate (time and a half). (Some companies pay double the regular rate for hours worked on Sundays or holidays.)

This act also sets a minimum hourly rate of pay. The rate has been revised numerous times since the passage of the act in 1938. The current rate is $3.35 per hour.

The Fair Labor Standards Act also requires that employers keep detailed records for each employee showing compliance with the provisions of the act. Some executive, administrative, and professional employees are exempt from the minimum wage and overtime provisions of the act.

Gross Earnings	The amount an employee earns is known as **gross earnings,** or **gross pay.** Gross earnings are the total earnings before any deductions. Gross earnings are based on the total time worked during a payroll period. For employees paid on an hourly basis, a record of the number of hours worked by each employee must be kept. This can be accomplished in a number of ways—

record books, time sheets, time clocks. More recently, some employers are using punched cards to record hours worked for computer-operated payroll systems.

To illustrate the computation of an hourly employee's earnings, assume that Marvin Miller is paid at a regular rate of $14 an hour for a forty-hour week. He receives time and a half for hours in excess of forty hours per week. During the week of December 17, he worked forty-six hours. His gross pay is computed as follows:

Hours at regular rate	(40 × $14)	$560.00
Hours at overtime rate	(6 × $21)	126.00
Gross earnings		$686.00

Normally, gross earnings for a person who is exempt from the provisions of the Fair Labor Standards Act are simply the amount of the salary. However, if a salaried employee does receive overtime pay, the regular hourly rate must first be computed. For example, assume that Mary Ward receives a salary of $1,500 a month. She is entitled to overtime pay at a rate of time and a half her regular hourly rate for any time worked in excess of forty hours per week. Her overtime pay is computed as follows:

$1,500 × 12 months	=	$18,000 annual pay
$18,000 ÷ 52 weeks	=	$346.15 per week
$346.15 ÷ 40 hours	=	$8.65 regular hourly rate
$8.65 × 1.5	=	$12.98 overtime rate

To calculate Mary Ward's gross earnings, multiply the number of overtime hours by the overtime rate and add that amount to her regular salary.

Deductions from Earnings

Employees are not paid the total amount of their gross earnings because of the various deductions that must be subtracted from the gross amount. Some of these deductions are required by law, such as income taxes and social security taxes. Others are voluntary deductions authorized by the employee, such as insurance premiums, savings bonds, and charitable contributions.

Social Security Taxes (FICA)

The federal social security programs were established by the **Federal Insurance Contributions Act (FICA)** in 1935. The programs provide for old-age and disability benefits, insurance benefits to survivors, and health insurance for the aged (Medicare). These programs are funded by taxes paid by employees and employers.

FICA taxes are paid in equal amounts by both the employer and employee. The tax is based on the annual gross earnings of an employee up to a certain maximum amount. The rate and the maximum amount are

Figure 12.1   Social Security Employee Tax Table (1981 figures).*

The FICA withholding table, for employee's share of tax only, is extended to only $100 of wages. To compute the FICA withholding for wages over $100 either multiply the total wage by 6.65% or use the multiples of the tax on $100 wages. The multiples are listed at the end of the table.

Example 1.—Wage paid subject to FICA is $400.09₁ The amount of FICA tax to be withheld is:

on	$400.00	$26.60
on	.09	
total		$26.60

Example 2.—Wage paid subject to FICA is $1,289.62. The amount of FICA tax to be withheld is:

on	$1,000.00	$66.50
on	200.00	13.30
on	89.62	5.96
total		$85.76

Social Security Employee Tax Table

6.65 percent employee tax deductions

Wages		Tax to be withheld	Wages		Tax to be withheld	Wages		Tax to be withheld	Wages		Tax to be withheld
At least	But less than		At least	But less than		At least	But less than		At least	But less than	
$0.00	$0.09	$0.00	$8.73	$8.90	$.59	$17.54	$17.70	$1.17	$26.35	$26.51	$1.76
.09	.25	.01	8.90	9.06	.60	17.70	17.87	1.18	26.51	26.68	1.77
.25	.41	ᴖᴖ	9.06	9.22	ᴖ ᴖ	17.87	18.03		ᴖᴖ ᴖᴖ	26.84	ᴖ ᴖ
ᴖᴖ		ᴖ ᴖ			3.25			3.96	1 ᴖ ᴖ		.68
38.10	38.26	2.54	48.86	49.03	3.25	59.63	59.79	3.97	70.40	70.56	4.69
38.26	38.42	2.55	49.03	49.19	3.26	59.79	59.96	3.98	70.56	70.72	4.70
38.42	38.59	2.56	49.19	49.35	3.28	59.96	60.12	3.99	70.72	70.89	4.71
38.59	38.75	2.57	49.35	49.52	3.29	60.12	60.28	4.00	70.89	71.05	4.72
38.75	38.91	2.58	49.52	49.68	3.30	60.28	60.45	4.01	71.05	71.21	4.73
38.91	39.08	2.59	49.68	49.84	3.31	60.45	60.61	4.02	71.21	71.38	4.74
39.08	39.24	2.60	49.84	50.00	3.32	60.61	60.77	4.04	71.38	71.54	4.75
39.24	39.40	2.61	50.00	50.17	3.33	60.77	60.93	4.05	71.54	71.70	4.76
39.40	39.56	2.62	50.17	50.33	3.34	60.93	61.10	4.06	71.70	71.86	4.77
39.56	39.73	2.64	50.33	50.49	3.35	61.10	61.26	4.07	71.86	72.03	4.78
39.73	39.89	2.65	50.49	50.66	3.36	61.26	61.42	4.08	72.03	72.19	4.79
39.89	40.05	2.66	50.66	50.82	3.37	61.42	61.59	4.09	72.19	72.35	4.81
40.05	ᴖᴖ		ᴖᴖ.82	ᴖ		ᴖᴖ	ᴖ ᴖ				
ᴖᴖ	ᴖᴖ	5.43	ᴖᴖ.ᴖᴖ	ᴖ.ᴖᴖ	5.84	ᴖᴖᴖ		6.24	99.76	ᴖᴖ.ᴖᴖ	6.64
81.82	81.98	5.44	87.85	88.01	5.85	93.89	94.05	6.25	99.92	100.00	6.65
81.98	82.14	5.46	88.01	88.18	5.86	94.05	94.21	6.26			
82.14	82.31	5.47	88.18	88.34	5.87	94.21	94.38	6.27	The multiples of the withholding for FICA on $100 are		
82.31	82.47	5.48	88.34	88.50	5.88	94.38	94.54	6.28			
82.47	82.63	5.49	88.50	88.67	5.89	94.54	94.70	6.29	Wage	Tax to be withheld	
82.63	82.79	5.50	88.67	88.83	5.90	94.70	94.87	6.30	$100	$ 6.65	
82.79	82.96	5.51	88.83	88.99	5.91	94.87	95.03	6.31	200	13.30	
82.96	83.12	5.52	88.99	89.16	5.92	95.03	95.19	6.32	300	19.95	
83.12	83.28	5.53	89.16	89.32	5.93	95.19	95.36	6.33	400	26.60	
83.28	83.45	5.54	89.32	89.48	5.94	95.36	95.52	6.35	500	33.25	
83.45	83.61	5.55	89.48	89.65	5.96	95.52	95.68	6.36	600	39.90	
83.61	83.77	5.56	89.65	89.81	5.97	95.68	95.85	6.37	700	46.55	
83.77	83.94	5.58	89.81	89.97	5.98	95.85	96.01	6.38	800	53.20	
83.94	84.10	5.59	89.97	90.14	5.99	96.01	96.17	6.39	900	59.85	
84.10	84.26	5.60	90.14	90.30	6.00	96.17	96.33	6.40	1,000	66.50	

*Amounts in the Taxes to be Withheld columns are approximate due to the unavailability of complete FICA forms at the time of printing.

determined by Congress and can be changed by Congress at any time. Currently, the rate is 6.65 percent for employees and employers (a total of 13.30%) on the first $29,700 earned during a year. The employee's share of the tax is collected by the employer through payroll deductions each pay period.

The FICA tax to be withheld can be computed by multiplying the employee's **taxable earnings** by the current tax rate. For example, assume that an employee earns $240 during a pay period, all of which is taxable. Based on the current rate of 6.65 percent, the employee's FICA taxes are $15.96 ($240 × 6.65%).

Employers can also use a Social Security Employee Tax Table (excerpts of which are shown in fig. 12.1) to determine the FICA tax. If the tax table is used, the employee's FICA taxes on $240 are computed as follows:

FICA tax on $200		$13.30
FICA tax on 40		2.66
	Total	$15.96

Since the FICA tax is levied only on the first $29,700 earned during a year, it is necessary to determine what amount of an employee's wages are taxable in the pay period in which this base is reached. Only those wages that bring the gross earnings up to $29,700 are taxable. For example, assume that an employee's gross earnings to date are $29,500. The employee's total wages for the current pay period are $490. Only $200 is taxable ($29,700 − $29,500) because it represents the difference between the employee's current earnings and the taxable limit for FICA taxes for the year. The remaining $290 is not taxed since the base has been reached. The employee's FICA taxes for the current pay period are $13.30 ($200 × 6.65%). The employee's earnings are not subject to FICA taxes during the remainder of the year.

Every person covered by FICA is required to have a social security number. A person is assigned a social security number by the Social Security Administration after completing Form SS-5, Application for Social Security Number. The number is the employee's identification number for the social security program. It also is used by the Internal Revenue Service as a tax identification number. In addition, it is often used as an identification number for a variety of purposes and by a variety of institutions, such as banks, businesses, and colleges.

Federal Income Taxes

Employers are required by law to withhold a portion of each employee's earnings for **federal income taxes.** The amount to be withheld from each employee's paycheck is determined by the (1) gross earnings, (2) marital status, and (3) number of withholding allowances (exemptions) claimed.

Each employee is entitled to the following **withholding allowances**:

1. One for self.
2. One for spouse if spouse does not claim it for him- or herself.
3. One for each dependent. A dependent is a close relative who receives less than $1,000 a year and who receives more than half of his or her support from the taxpayer claiming him or her.
4. Additional allowances if the employee or the employee's spouse is sixty-five or older or blind.
5. Special withholding allowances based on expected excessive itemized deductions, alimony payments, or tax credits for child care expenses, earned income, or credit for the elderly.

Figure 12.2   Form W-4, Employee Withholding Allowance Certificate.

Form **W-4** (Rev. October 1979)	Department of the Treasury—Internal Revenue Service **Employee's Withholding Allowance Certificate**

Print your full name ▶

Your social security number ▶

Address (including ZIP code) ▶

Marital status: ☐ Single   ☐ Married   ☐ Married, but withhold at higher Single rate

Note: *If married, but legally separated, or spouse is a nonresident alien, check the single block.*

1 Total number of allowances you are claiming (from line F of the worksheet on page 2) . . . .

2 Additional amount, if any, you want deducted from each pay (if your employer agrees) . . . . $

3 I claim exemption from withholding because (see instructions and check boxes below that apply):

  a ☐ Last year I did not owe any Federal income tax and had a right to a full refund of **ALL** income tax withheld, **AND**

  b ☐ This year I do not expect to owe any Federal income tax and expect to have a right to a full refund of **ALL** income tax withheld. If both

    a and b apply, enter "EXEMPT" here . . . . ▶

  c If you entered "EXEMPT" on line 3b, are you a full-time student? . . . . ☐ Yes ☐ No

Under the penalties of perjury, I certify that I am entitled to the number of withholding allowances claimed on this certificate, or if claiming exemption from withholding, that I am entitled to claim the exempt status.

Employee's signature ▶   Date ▶   , 19

Employer's name and address (including ZIP code) (FOR EMPLOYER'S USE ONLY)   Employer identification number

- Detach along this line -

▲   *Give the top part of this form to your employer; keep the lower part for your records and information*   ▲

Purpose

The law requires that you complete Form W-4 so that your employer [illegible] Federal income tax

- 1 for yourself,
- 1 if you are 65 or older, and
- 1 [illegible] are blind.

E. Allowances for estimated itemized deductions and alimony.—If you expect to [illegible] your deductions or [illegible]

(The last two allowance categories are not considered in the computation of the income taxes to be withheld from an employee's paycheck. However, these allowances are taken into consideration when an employee computes and reports earnings and taxes at the end of the year.)

An employee may also choose to claim no withholding allowances. By choosing to claim no withholding allowances, an employee pays a larger amount of taxes during the year. However, when the tax return is filed, the employee has little or no additional taxes to pay or, in many cases, receives a refund of the amount overpaid during the year.

The number of withholding allowances that an employee claims is reported on a Form W-4, Employee's Withholding Allowance Certificate (fig. 12.2). The amount of federal income tax withheld is determined by the information provided on the Form W-4.

The amount of federal income tax to be withheld can be determined in either of two ways: (1) by the **wage-bracket method** or (2) by the **percentage method.** Most employers prefer to use a wage-bracket table.

The Internal Revenue Service furnishes employers with tables that indicate how much tax to withhold for married and single taxpayers for daily, weekly, biweekly, semimonthly, monthly, and miscellaneous pay periods. The wage-bracket table shown in figure 12.3 is from the wage-bracket table for married persons paid on a weekly basis.

The example of Marvin Miller's wages is used again to illustrate the use of the wage-bracket table. Marvin Miller is married and claims four withholding allowances. From the table, it is determined that federal income taxes of $138.60 are to be withheld from the $686 he earned. His wage bracket and the federal income tax to be withheld are circled on the tax table.

Figure 12.3 Wage-bracket table.

MARRIED Persons — WEEKLY Payroll Period

And the wages are—		And the number of withholding allowances claimed is—										
At least	But less than	0	1	2	3	4	5	6	7	8	9	10 or more
		The amount of income tax to be withheld shall be—										
$300	$310	$47.50	$43.00	$39.00	$34.90	$30.90	$26.90	$23.40	$19.90	$16.50	$13.00	$10.00
310	320	49.90	45.30	41.10	37.00	33.00	28.90	25.20	21.70	18.30	14.80	11.50
320	330	52.30	47.70	43.20	39.10	35.10	31.00	27.00	23.50	20.10	16.60	13.20
330	340	54.70	50.10	45.50	41.20	37.20	33.10	29.10	25.30	21.90	18.40	15.00
340	350	57.10	52.50	47.90	43.30	39.30	35.20	31.20	27.20	23.70	20.20	16.80
350	360	59.50	54.90	50.30	45.70	41.40	37.30	33.30	29.30	25.50	22.00	18.60
360	370		57.30	52.70			39.40	35.40		27.30	23.80	20.40
	660	156.00			134.60	127.00			107.90			
660	670	159.70	152.60	145.40	138.30	131.20	124.10	117.30	111.10	105.00	98.80	92.70
670	680	163.40	156.30	149.10	142.00	134.90	127.80	120.70	114.30	108.20	102.00	95.90
680	690	167.10	160.00	152.80	145.70	138.60	131.50	124.40	117.50	111.40	105.20	99.10
690	700	170.80	163.70	156.50	149.40	142.30	135.20	128.10	121.00	114.60	108.40	102.30
700	710	174.50	167.40	160.20	153.10	146.00	138.90	131.80	124.70	117.80	111.60	105.50
710			171.10	163.90			142.60	135.50		121.20	114.80	
	810	211.50			190.10	183.00			161.70			
810	820	215.20	208.10	200.90	193.80	186.70	179.60	172.50	165.40	158.20	151.10	144.00
820	830	218.90	211.80	204.60	197.50	190.40	183.30	176.20	169.10	161.90	154.80	147.70
830	840	222.60	215.50	208.30	201.20	194.10	187.00	179.90	172.80	165.60	158.50	151.40
840	850	226.30	219.20	212.00	204.90	197.80	190.70	183.60	176.50	169.30	162.20	155.10
		37 percent of the excess over $850 plus—										
$850 and over		228.10	221.00	213.90	206.80	199.70	192.50	185.40	178.30	171.20	164.10	157.00

Figure 12.4 Percentage Method Income Tax Withholding Table.

Percentage Method Income Tax Withholding Table

Payroll period	One withholding allowance
Weekly	$19.23
Biweekly	38.46
Semimonthly	41.66
Monthly	83.33
Quarterly	250.00
Semiannually	500.00
Annually	1,000.00
Daily or miscellaneous (each day of the payroll period)	2.74

Figure 12.5 Tables for Percentage Method of Withholding.

TABLE 1. WEEKLY Payroll Period

(a) SINGLE person—including head of household:

If the amount of wages is:		The amount of income tax to be withheld shall be:	of excess over—
Not over $27		0	
Over—	But not over—		
$27	—$63	15%	—$27
$63	—$131	$5.40 plus 18%	—$63
$131	—$196	$17.64 plus 21%	—$131
$196	—$273	$31.29 plus 26%	—$196
$273	—$331	$51.31 plus 30%	—$273
$331	—$433	$68.71 plus 34%	—$331
$433		$103.39 plus 39%	—$433

(b) MARRIED person—

If the amount of wages is:		The amount of income tax to be withheld shall be:	of excess over—
Not over $46		0	
Over—	But not over—		
$46	—$127	15%	—$46
$127	—$210	$12.15 plus 18%	—$127
$210	—$288	$27.09 plus 21%	—$210
$288	—$369	$43.47 plus 24%	—$288
$369	—$454	$62.91 plus 28%	—$369
$454	—$556	$86.71 plus 32%	—$454
$556		$119.35 plus 37%	—$556

TABLE 2. BIWEEKLY Payroll Period

(a) SINGLE person—including head of household: | **(b) MARRIED person—**

If the tax is computed using the percentage method, a certain amount is allowed for each withholding allowance, as shown in the Percentage Method Income Tax Withholding Table (fig. 12.4). The amount is multiplied by the number of allowances the employee claims on Form W-4. The product is subtracted from the employee's gross earnings, which determines the amount of earnings subject to federal income taxes. The amount to be withheld is then determined by using the appropriate Table for Percentage Method of Withholding provided by the IRS (fig. 12.5).

According to the percentage method, Marvin Miller's income tax is $138.99 and is computed as follows:

Total earnings		$686.00
One allowance	$19.23	
Allowances claimed	× 4	76.92
Amount subject to withholding		$609.08
Tax to be withheld from Table 1,		
married person		
Tax on first $556		$119.35
Tax on remainder	$53.08 × .37	19.64
Total to be withheld		$138.99

Other Taxes

In addition to federal withholding taxes, there are often state and city income taxes that must also be collected. These taxes are handled in much the same manner as federal income taxes. Deductions are determined in the same manner, and appropriate tax tables are furnished by state and city governments.

Other Deductions

Payroll deduction for payment of taxes is required; this tax withholding process is mandated by law. However, there are some voluntary deductions that an employee may authorize. Voluntary deductions most commonly involve payment of life insurance premiums, medical and hospital insurance premiums, savings plans, retirement plans, and charitable contributions. These deductions are computed individually for each employee. If an employee is a member of a union, there may also be deductions for union dues. Deductions for union dues are agreed upon by the employer and the union with written consent from the employee.

Net Pay

All deductions must be subtracted from the employee's gross earnings; the remainder represents the employee's **net pay**, or **take-home pay.** In the following example, Marvin Miller's net pay is computed. As stated earlier, the applicable FICA tax rate is 6.65 percent on the first $29,700. Miller's gross earnings so far this year are $29,490. He has authorized deductions of $50.00 for life insurance, $15.60 for group hospital insurance, and $20.00 for U.S. savings bonds.

Gross earnings		$686.00
Deductions		
FICA tax	$13.97	
Federal income tax	138.60	
Life insurance	50.00	
Group hospital insurance	15.60	
U.S. savings bonds	20.00	238.17
Net pay		$447.83

Mr. Miller had cumulative earnings of $29,490 prior to this week's earnings of $686. After adding the week's gross earnings to the cumulative earnings for the year, the total earnings for the year are $30,176. Therefore, only the portion of this week's earnings that brings the total to $29,700 ($29,700 − $29,490 = $210) is subject to FICA taxes.

When computing federal income tax, there is no need to consider cumulative earnings since there is no maximum on the amount of wages subject to income taxes. The total wages each pay period are subject to income taxes. Thus, $138.60 represents the income tax on the entire $686.

Payroll Records

The necessity for payroll records has already been pointed out. Payroll records are used to satisfy the informational needs of a business as well as to fulfill the requirements of various federal and state agencies. The three payroll records most commonly used are the payroll register, the paycheck, and the employee's individual earnings record.

Figure 12.6 Payroll register.

PAYROLL REGISTER

Name	Employee No.	No. of With. Allowances	Marital Status	Earnings				Taxable Earnings					
				Regular	Over-time	Total	Cumulative Total	Unemploy. Compen.	F.I.C.A.	F.I.C.A. Tax	Federal Inc. Tax	Life Ins.
Cunico, Gerald C.	2	4	M	550 —	90 —	640 —	30,310 —		30 —	2 —	123 80	20 —
Jackson, Connie L.	5	1	S	410 —		410 —	5,300 —	410 —	410 —	27 27	90 70	
Miller, Marvin C.	3	4	M	560 —	126 —	686 —	30,176 —		210 —	13 97	138 60	50 —
Smith, Dorothy	4	2	M	300 —		300 —	15,600 —		300 —	19 95	39 —	
Stoughton, Charles R.	1	3	M	540 —		540 —	30,250 —				97 30	25 —
				2,360 —	216 —	2,576 —	111,636 —	410 —	950 —	63 19	489 40	95 —

At the end of each pay period, the payroll data are compiled and summarized in a **payroll register.** The payroll register is a multicolumn form containing complete information about the hours worked, pay rate, gross earnings, deductions, and net pay for each employee. The form of the register varies depending upon the number of employees and the extent to which automation is used. One form of payroll register typically used by a firm with a small number of employees is shown in figure 12.6.

Most of the column headings are self-explanatory. The Cumulative Total column under the Earnings section is used to accumulate data regarding the employee's total gross earnings from the beginning of the year to the current date. This column makes it easy for the accountant to note when an employee has reached the maximum base for FICA and other taxes. The two columns under the heading of Taxable Earnings are used in computing the employer's payroll taxes (to be discussed in chapter 13).

After the data for each employee have been entered in the payroll register, the column totals should be cross-verified. Cross-verification of the payroll register in figure 12.6 is shown as follows:

Regular earnings		$2,360.00
Overtime earnings		216.00
Gross earnings		$2,576.00
Deductions:		
FICA taxes	$ 63.19	
Federal income taxes	489.40	
Life insurance	95.00	
Group hospital insurance	70.20	
Other (U.S. savings bonds)	30.00	747.79
Net amount of payroll		$1,828.21

For period ending *Dec. 17, 19XX*

Deductions						
Group Hospital Ins.	Other		Total	Date	Net Pay	Ck. No.
26 40			172 20	12/17	467 80	405
13 20			131 17	12/17	278 83	406
15 60	U.S. Savings 20	—	238 17	12/17	447 83	407
	U.S. Savings 10	—	68 95	12/17	231 05	408
15 —			137 30	12/17	402 70	409
70 20		30 —	747 79		1,828 21	

Figure 12.7 Paycheck and stub.

Paycheck

The amount the employee receives for the pay period is shown in the payroll register column headed Net Pay. The number of the check issued in payment of the wages is also recorded. Each employee's **paycheck** is accompanied by a statement that shows much of the same information contained in the payroll register—total earnings, deductions, etc. While this information may be shown on a separate statement, it is usually shown on a detachable stub attached to the paycheck. The stub is detached and retained by the employee. A typical payroll check and its stub are shown in figure 12.7.

Employee's Individual Earnings Record

Employers are required to keep an individual earnings record for each employee. An **employee's individual earnings record** contains cumulative data on the hours worked, gross earnings, deductions, and net pay. This data is needed by the employer to compile the various tax reports required by law. In addition, the data accumulated in the individual earnings record are used:

1. To compute the employer's state and federal payroll tax returns.
2. To show when each employee's wages have reached the tax-exempt base for FICA and federal and state unemployment taxes.
3. To provide data for the withholding statement (Form W-2) given to the employee at the end of the year.

A portion of Marvin Miller's individual earnings record is shown in figure 12.8. The information contained in the earnings record is transferred from the payroll register.

Space is provided in the earnings record for quarterly subtotals and yearly totals. These totals facilitate the preparation of various quarterly and yearly tax reports.

Figure 12.8 Employee earnings record.

EMPLOYEE EARNINGS RECORD

Week	Period Ending	Earnings Regular	Earnings Overtime	Earnings Total	Deductions F.I.C.A.	Federal Inc. Tax	Group Life Ins.	Group Hospital Ins.	Other	Total	Net Pay Amount	Taxable Earnings Accumulated
	Totals 2nd Quarter	7,280 —	108 —	7,388 —	491 30	1,282 82	650 —	202 80	260 —	2,886 92	4,501 08	
1	7/7	560 —		560 —	37 24	97 60	50 —	15 60	20 —	220 44	339 56	16,768 —
2	7/14	560 —		560 —	37 24	97 60	50 —	15 60	20 —	220 44	339 56	17,328 —
3	7/21	560 —		560 —	37 24	97 60	50 —	15 60	20 —	220 44	339 56	17,888 —
4	7/28	560 —	42 —	602 —	40 03	110 40	50 —	15 60	20 —	236 03	365 97	18,490 —
5	8/5	560 —		560 —	37 24	97 60	50 —	15 60	20 —	220 44	339 56	19,050
6	8/12	560 —		560 —	37 24	97 60	50 —	15 60	20 —	220 44	339 56	19,610
7	8/19	560 —	66 —	626 —	41 63	116 80	50 —	15 60	20 —	244 03	381 97	20,236 —
8	8/26	560 —		560 —	37 24	97 60	50 —	15 60	20 —	220 44	339 56	20,796 —
9	9/3	560 —		560 —	37 24	97 60	50 —	15 60	20 —	220 44	339 56	21,356 —
10	9/10	560 —	21 —	581 —	38 64	104 —	50 —	15 60	20 —	228 24	352 76	21,937 —
11	9/17	560 —		560 —	37 24	97 60	50 —	15 60	20 —	220 44	339 56	22,497 —
12	9/24	560 —		560 —	37 24	97 60	50 —	15 60	20 —	220 44	339 56	23,057 —
13	10/01	560 —		560 —	37 24	97 60	50 —	15 60	20 —	220 44	339 56	23,617 —
	Totals 3rd Quarter	7,280 —	129 —	7,409 —	492 70	1,307 20	650 —	202 80	260 —	2,912 70	4,496 30	
1	10/8	560 —		560 —	37 24	97 60	50 —	15 60	20 —	220 44	339 56	24,177 —
2	10/15	560 —		560 —	37 24	97 60	50 —	15 60	20 —	220 44	339 56	24,737 —
3	10/22	560 —	42 —	602 —	40 03	110 40	50 —	15 60	20 —	236 03	365 97	25,339 —
4	10/29	560 —	105 —	665 —	44 22	131 20	50 —	15 60	20 —	261 02	403 98	26,004 —
5	11/05	560 —	105 —	665 —	44 22	131 20	50 —	15 60	20 —	261 02	403 98	26,669 —
6	11/12	560 —		560 —	37 24	97 60	50 —	15 60	20 —	220 44	339 56	27,229 —
7	11/19	560 —		560 —	37 24	97 60	50 —	15 60	20 —	220 44	339 56	27,789 —
8	11/26	560 —		560 —	37 24	97 60	50 —	15 60	20 —	220 44	339 56	28,349 —
9	12/03	560 —	21 —	581 —	38 64	104 —	50 —	15 60	20 —	228 24	352 76	28,930 —
10	12/10	560 —		560 —	37 24	97 60	50 —	15 60	20 —	220 44	339 56	29,490 —
11	12/17	560 —	126 —	686 —	13 97	138 60	50 —	15 60	20 —	238 17	447 83	30,176 —
12	12/24	560 —		560 —		97 60	50 —	15 60	20 —	183 20	376 80	30,736 —
13												
	Totals 4th Quarter											
	Yearly Totals											

Name Marvin E. Miller

Address 6212 Larchmont Rd., Okla. City, OK 74831

Social Security No. _____ Clock No. 3

Rate $14.00
Withholding Exemptions 4
Group Life Ins. $50.00
Group Hospital Ins. $15.60
Marital Status M

The information contained in a payroll register must be journalized and posted to the general ledger. The payroll register itself serves as a supplementary record and is the basis for the journal entry that transfers the payroll information to the proper ledger accounts.

The employee's gross earnings represent an expense to the employer. They are debited to an expense account called Wage Expense, or Salary Expense. In some cases, several payroll expense accounts are used, each one recording wages of specific types of employees; i.e., Office Wage Expense, Sales Wage Expense.

The amounts withheld from the employees' gross wages represent liabilities to the employer until such time as they are paid to the appropriate parties. For example, FICA taxes collected from the employees are liabilities until they are remitted to the proper taxing agency; amounts deducted for insurance premiums are liabilities until they are paid to the companies providing the insurance coverage. Separate liability accounts are credited for each type of deduction, such as FICA Tax Payable and Life Insurance Premiums Payable. When the amounts deducted are remitted to the appropriate parties, the proper liability account is debited and Cash is credited.

The journal entry to record the payroll shown in figure 12.6 is as follows:

Wage Expense	2,576.00	
FICA Tax Payable		63.19
Federal Income Tax Payable		489.40
Life Insurance Premiums Payable		95.00
Group Hospital Insurance Premium Payable		70.20
U.S. Savings Bonds Payable		30.00
Cash		1,828.21

Notice that Wage Expense is debited for the total gross earnings of all employees. The credit to Cash is for the total (or net) amount actually paid to all employees (net pay). After posting, the ledger accounts look like this:

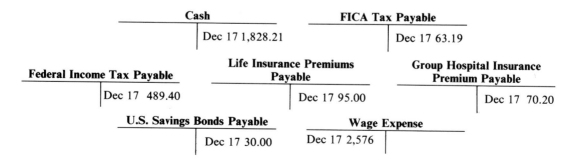

Payment to employees may be made (1) by checks drawn on a firm's regular account, (2) in cash, or (3) by payroll checks drawn on a special checking account established for the payment of the payroll.

If a firm has a small number of employees, the payroll checks will likely be drawn on the firm's regular checking account. A separate journal entry can be made for each employee's pay; however, this is not necessary. The entire amount paid to all employees can be recorded in one entry. The detailed information contained in the payroll register can be used as a reference when necessary.

When employees are paid in cash, one check is drawn for the amount of the payroll and cashed. The money is put into individual pay envelopes. Upon receiving the pay envelope, the employee signs a receipt as evidence that payment has been received.

A firm with a large number of employees usually prefers to establish a special checking account for the issuance of payroll checks (fig. 12.7). When the payroll register is completed, a single check is drawn on the firm's regular checking account for the total amount to be paid and deposited in the special payroll account. Individual checks for each employee are drawn on the special account, and the numbers are written in the payroll register. The use of a special payroll account simplifies not only the preparation and distribution of the checks but also the preparation of the bank reconciliations. This method also provides some measure of internal control, because the same person usually does not reconcile both the special payroll account and the regular checking account. The use of a special payroll account also offers additional security since it avoids the necessity of having a large amount of cash on hand on paydays and of sorting the cash into individual pay envelopes.

Use of Pegboard or Automated Systems

Payroll records can be prepared manually or electronically. Systems have been devised for both methods to allow the simultaneous preparation of all three payroll records—the payroll register, the paycheck, and the earnings record. This is called the *write-it-once principle*. It greatly reduces the time it takes to prepare payrolls and increases accuracy.

The **pegboard accounting system**, which makes it possible to record data on several forms at one writing, is often used for manually prepared payrolls. The pegboard contains a series of evenly spaced metal pegs along the edge or in the middle of the board. Special forms with punched holes fit over the pegs. The forms are usually made of NCR (no carbon required) paper, which allows the information to be reproduced on all forms at one time without using carbon paper.

The payroll register, paycheck, and earnings record are aligned on the pegboard so that information is entered on all three records simultaneously. Figure 12.9 shows the pegboard system as it is used in preparing a payroll.

Figure 12.9 Pegboard system of payroll accounting.

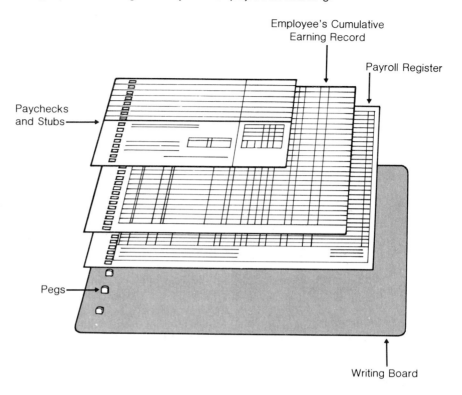

Employee's Cumulative
Earning Record

Payroll Register

Paychecks
and Stubs

Pegs

Writing Board

Companies with a large number of employees often find that an automated system is more efficient in preparing payroll records. The data output for automated systems can be structured to provide more information than manual systems.

There are alternatives for companies too small to justify having their own electronic systems. Service bureaus and some commercial banks offer payroll services on a contract basis for small and middle-sized businesses. Another alternative is the use of **time-sharing.** Several businesses can own or rent a computer jointly. Each business is connected with the computer via a telephone line, and information is fed to the computer by means of a typewriter-printer console located at each company's office.

Summary

Detailed payroll records are necessary for proper accounting for payments to employees, recording of payroll expenses, and payment and reporting of various federal and state taxes (p. 242).

The wages an employee receives are regulated by the Federal Fair Labor Standards Act (p. 243). Employees' regular and overtime earnings are computed in accordance with the provisions of this act (pp. 243–44).

Employers are required by law to withhold certain amounts from employees' earnings for FICA and federal income taxes (pp. 244–49). In addition, there are certain voluntary deductions that can be authorized by addition, there are certain voluntary deductions that can be authorized by an employee (p. 249).

There are three records common to most payroll systems: (1) the payroll register, (2) the paycheck, and (3) the employee's individual earnings record. These records contain detailed information regarding the earnings and withholdings for each employee for each pay period. This information is used for recording the payroll as well as for computing and reporting taxes (pp. 250–53).

Payroll records may be prepared manually or electronically. The pegboard system is a convenient method of preparing a payroll manually (pp. 255–56). Automated systems are usually more practical for companies with a large number of employees. Service bureaus and time-sharing plans can provide automated services for smaller companies (p. 256).

Key Terms

employee One who performs a service for payment and is under the control or direction of the business or person for whom the service is performed.

employee's individual earnings record A supplementary payroll record that shows the yearly cumulative earnings and deductions for each employee.

employer A business or person for whom one performs a service.

Fair Labor Standards Act A federal law covering all employers engaged in interstate commerce, which establishes minimum wage and overtime pay requirements.

federal income tax Tax levied by the federal government, which is based on an individual's earnings.

Federal Insurance Contributions Act A federal law taxing employees and employers for support of a national social security program providing retirement, medical, and death benefits.

FICA taxes Taxes collected equally from employees and employers to support the social security programs.

gross earnings An employee's total earnings before any deductions.

independent contractor One who sells services to a business for a fee but is not an employee of the business.

net pay The amount of pay an employee receives after deductions; often called take-home pay.

paycheck Check issued by a business as remuneration for an employee's work.

payroll register A supplementary payroll record that summarizes information about gross earnings and deductions of all employees for a specific pay period.

pegboard accounting A manual system of accounting that permits the recording of payroll information on all three payroll records at one time.

percentage method A method of computing employee income tax withholdings.

piece-rate A means of compensating employees based on the number of units an employee produces.

salary Remuneration for employees engaged in managerial or administrative work; usually expressed as a fixed monthly or yearly amount.

taxable earnings The amount of an employee's earnings that are subject to federal and state income taxes. A certain base amount of these earnings is also subject to FICA and unemployment taxes.

time-sharing A way of providing automated payroll accounting to small companies, whereby several businesses jointly own or rent time on a computer.

wage-bracket method A method of determining employee income tax withholdings by use of tables furnished by the Internal Revenue Service.

wages Remuneration for skilled or unskilled labor, usually expressed on an hourly, weekly, or piece-rate basis.

withholding allowances Exemptions allowed on the federal income tax.

Objectives

Upon completion of this chapter, you should be able to:

1. Compute an employer's payroll expenses for:

   FICA taxes   State unemployment taxes

   federal unemployment taxes (FUTA)

2. Journalize the entry to record the employer's payroll tax expense.

3. Journalize the entries to record the payment of the employer's payroll taxes and payroll liabilities.

4. Compute and record accrued salary expenses and liabilities.

13 Accounting for Payroll Employer

---

5. Define the following accounting terms:

accrued wages
employer identification number
federal unemployment tax act
FUTA taxes

merit-rating
state unemployment taxes
unemployment insurance

In this chapter we will continue the discussion of procedures and records relevant to payroll accounting. Chapter 12 was devoted largely to the procedures used to determine employee wages and the payroll records that must be kept for each employee. This chapter will deal mainly with the payroll taxes levied against employers and the procedures for reporting and paying those taxes.

Employer's Payroll Taxes

Thus far our discussion of taxes has centered on payroll taxes that are withheld by the employer from the employees' earnings. The taxes withheld from employees are considered as liabilities to the employer rather than expenses. No expense is incurred by the employer because the taxes are levied directly on the employee. The employer serves only as a collection agent for the government and is liable for the amount of taxes withheld only until payment to the government has been made. However, employers themselves are also subject to certain federal and state taxes. Such taxes are also based upon employees' earnings but, unlike the taxes withheld from employees, are considered an operating expense of the employer. An expense is incurred because the taxes are levied on the employer and therefore must be paid by the employer directly to the government.

FICA Tax

It has already been mentioned that the tax levied under the Federal Insurance Contributions Act applies both to employees and employers. The tax rate and the maximum earnings on which the tax must be paid by the employer are the same as those that apply to employees; therefore, the employer's FICA taxes are the same as those withheld from employees. The amounts may sometimes differ slightly due to rounding amounts computed for individual employees.

The employer's FICA taxes may be computed in either of two ways: (1) by multiplying the total of the Taxable Earnings FICA column in the payroll register by the current tax rate or (2) by using the Social Security Employee Tax Table (fig. 12.1). Using the first method, the employer's FICA taxes on the payroll in figure 12.6 are computed as follows:

$950 × 6.65% = $63.18 Employer's FICA taxes

If the Social Security Employee Tax Table is used, the employer's FICA taxes on $950 are computed as follows:

FICA tax on $900	$59.85
FICA tax on 50	3.33
Total	$63.18

The $63.18 is a liability to the employer (as well as an expense) until it is paid. Only one liability account, FICA Tax Payable, is used to record both the employer and employee FICA taxes. After the entries to record the employer and employee FICA taxes are posted, the ledger account looks like this:

FICA Tax Payable

	Dec 16 63.19 (employees)
	16 63.18 (employer)

The $.01 difference in the employee and employer FICA taxes is due to the rounding factor mentioned earlier.

Federal Unemployment Compensation Tax (FUTA)

The **Federal Unemployment Tax Act** provides for an unemployment insurance program that is jointly administered by the federal and state governments. Any person who becomes unemployed through no fault of his or her own is entitled to unemployment compensation for a limited period of time.

Under this jointly administered program, the federal government does not directly compensate unemployed workers. It provides a portion of the funds needed by the states to administer their programs. Each state has its own unemployment insurance program under which it pays benefits to unemployed workers.

The unemployment insurance program is funded by a payroll tax levied on the *employer only*. The Federal Unemployment Tax Act stipulates that a tax must be levied on employers of four or more persons or those who employ one or more persons for some portion of a day in each of twenty weeks in the calendar year or those who paid $1,500 or more in wages during any quarter of the current or preceding calendar year. The current rate is 3.4% on the first $6,000 of earnings paid to a covered employee during the calendar year. However, the act also stipulates that an employer can take a credit against the FUTA tax for contributions paid into a state unemployment fund. The maximum credit allowance for contributions to a state fund is 2.7% of the first $6,000 of each employee's gross wages. Therefore, the FUTA rate is actually 0.7% (3.4% − 2.7%) of the taxable wages.

The total earnings subject to the FUTA tax are shown in the Taxable Earnings Unemployment Compensation column of the payroll register. The FUTA tax for the payroll in figure 12.6 is computed as follows:

$$\$410 \times 0.7\% = \$2.87 \text{ Employer's FUTA tax}$$

This $2.87 represents a liability to the employer until it is paid. It is recorded in a liability account, FUTA Tax Payable, and as an expense in a Payroll Tax Expense account.

Every state has an unemployment compensation program through which benefits are paid to eligible unemployed workers. Each state administers its own program, but a portion of the state's administrative expenses comes from federal funds generated by the Federal Unemployment Tax Act. The state's portion of the program is financed through **state unemployment taxes** imposed on the employer. Although the rates may vary among states, most impose the maximum rate of 2.7% of the first $6,000 of wages paid each employee. This 2.7% represents the credit an employer is allowed against the 3.4% FUTA tax levied by the federal government.

In most states, there is also a **merit-rating system** whereby employers with a history of low unemployment pay less than the maximum rate. Employers who qualify for a lower rate are still entitled to the maximum 2.7% credit against the federal unemployment tax. On the other hand, employers with a history of high or irregular unemployment can be assessed penalties in excess of the maximum rate. This system is designed to promote the stabilization of employment and to reduce unemployment.

The Taxable Earnings Unemployment Compensation column of the payroll register in figure 12.6 indicates that $410 of the week's earnings are taxable for unemployment compensation The employer's taxes for state unemployment compensation are computed as follows:

$$\$410 \times 2.7\% = \$11.07 \text{ State unemployment taxes}$$

The state unemployment tax of $11.07 is also a liability to the employer until it is paid. It is recorded in a liability account, State Unemployment Tax Payable, and as an expense in a Payroll Tax Expense account.

Recording Taxes

The employer's payroll taxes are considered expenses of the business and are debited to a separate expense account called Payroll Tax Expense. These taxes are also considered as liabilities and are credited to separate liability accounts—FICA Tax Payable, FUTA Tax Payable, State Unemployment Tax Payable.

The employer must record the taxes in the period in which the corresponding payroll occurs, even though the taxes are not usually paid until a later time. The journal entry to record the payroll tax expense and liabilities for the weekly payroll is as follows:

Payroll Tax Expense	77.12	
FICA Tax Payable		63.18
FUTA Tax Payable		2.87
State Unemployment Tax Payable		11.07

After the entry is posted, the ledger accounts look like this:

Payroll Tax Expense		FICA Tax Payable	
Dec 17 77.12		Dec 17 63.19 (employees)	
		Dec 17 63.18 (employer's)	

FUTA Tax Payable		State Unemployment Tax Payable	
	Dec 17 2.87		Dec 17 11.07

Reporting and Paying Taxes

Federal and state governments have established time schedules that employers must follow in reporting and paying payroll taxes. These schedules are based on the calendar year, regardless of the fiscal year a firm may employ for its accounting records.

Payment of federal income taxes and FICA taxes (employee and employer) is made by depositing the taxes in a Federal Reserve Bank or in an approved commercial bank depository. The schedule for remitting the deposits depends upon the amount of the taxes.

If the total FICA and federal income taxes withheld for one month is more than $200 but less than $2,000, the total must be deposited within fifteen days after the end of the month. If taxes total $2,000 or more during any month, four deposits must be made each month: on the seventh, fifteenth, twenty-second, and last day of the month. For taxes of less than $200, no deposit need be made until the last day of the month following the end of the quarter.

Each deposit is accompanied by a Federal Tax Deposit Form 501 (fig. 13.1). Each Form 501 is preinscribed with the form number and the

Figure 13.1   Federal Tax Deposit Form 501.

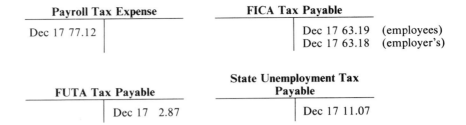

IRS return number to which the deposit relates. An **employer identification number** is also preprinted. Anyone who is required to report employee taxes or give tax statements to employees must have an employer identification number. An employer identification number is issued upon completion of a Form SS-4, Application for Employer Identification Number.

When the taxes are paid (deposited), a journal entry debiting each of the liability accounts and crediting Cash is made. The following journal

Figure 13.2 Employer's Quarterly Federal Tax Return.

Form **941**
(Rev. April 1980)
Department of the Treasury
Internal Revenue Service

Employer's Quarterly Federal Tax Return

Your name, address, employer identification number, and calendar quarter of return. (If not correct, please change) ▶

Name (as distinguished from trade name) — Date quarter ended
Trade name, if any — Employer identification number
Address and ZIP code

T
FF
FD
FP
I
T

If address is different from prior return, check here ▶ ☐

1 Number of employees (except household) employed in the pay period that includes March 12th (complete for first quarter only) . . . . .
2 Total wages and tips subject to withholding, plus other compensation . . . . . →
3 Total income tax withheld from wages, tips, annuities, gambling, etc. . . . . .
4 Adjustment of withheld income tax for preceding quarters of calendar year . . . . .
5 Adjusted total of income tax withheld . . . . . →
6 Taxable FICA wages paid . . . . . $........ multiplied by 12.26% = TAX . .
7 Taxable tips reported . . . . . $........ multiplied by 6.13% = TAX . .
8 Total FICA taxes (add lines 6 and 7) . . . . . →
9 Adjustment of FICA taxes (see instructions) . . . . .
10 Adjusted total of FICA taxes . . . . . →
11 Total taxes (add lines 5 and 10) . . . . .
12 Advance earned income credit (EIC) payments, if any (see instructions) . . . . .
13 Net taxes (subtract line 12 from line 11) . . . . .

Record of Federal Tax Deposits (See instructions on page 4)

Deposit period ending:		I. Tax liability for period	II. Date of deposit	III. Amount deposited
Overpayment from previous quarter. . . .				
First month of quarter	1st through 7th day			
	8th through 15th day			
	16th through 22d day			
	23d through last day			
A First month total . . . . A				
Second month of quarter	1st through 7th day			
	8th through 15th day			
	16th through 22d day			
	23d through last day			
B Second month total . . . . B				
Third month of quarter	1st through 7th day			
	8th through 15th day			
	16th through 22d day			
	23d through last day			
C Third month total C				
D Total for quarter (add items A, B, and C) .				
E Final deposit made for quarter. (Enter zero if the final deposit made for the quarter is included in item D)				

14 Total deposits for quarter (including final deposit made for quarter) and overpayment from previous quarter. (See instructions for deposit requirements on page 4.) . . . . .
Note: *If undeposited taxes at the end of the quarter are $200 or more, deposit the full amount with an authorized financial institution or a Federal Reserve bank according to the instructions on the back of the Federal Tax Deposit Form 501. Enter this deposit in the Record of Federal Tax Deposits and include it on line 14.*
15 Undeposited taxes due (subtract line 14 from line 13—this should be less than $200). Pay to Internal Revenue Service and enter here . . . . . →
16 If line 14 is more than line 13, enter overpayment here ▶ $ and check if to be: ☐ Applied to next return, or ☐ Refunded.
17 Number of Forms W-4 enclosed. Do not send originals. (See General and Specific Instructions.) . . . . .
18 If you are not liable for returns in the future, write "FINAL" (see instructions) ▶ Date final wages paid ▶

Under penalties of perjury, I declare that I have examined this return, including accompanying schedules and statements, and to the best of my knowledge and belief it is true, correct, and complete.

Date ▶ Signature ▶ Title ▶

Please file this form with your Internal Revenue Service Center (see instructions on "Where to File").

Form **941** (Rev. 4-80)

entry is made to record the payment of the FICA taxes and federal income taxes for the payroll in figure 12.6:

FICA Tax Payable	126.37	
Federal Income Tax Payable	489.40	
Cash		615.77

After the entry is posted, the ledger accounts look like this:

Cash		Federal Income Tax Payable		FICA Tax Payable	
	615.77	489.40	489.40	126.37	63.19
					63.18

At the end of every quarter (March, June, September, December), the employer is required to file a Form 941, Employer's Quarterly Federal Tax Return (fig. 13.2). The form includes information about each employee's taxable wages, the total federal income tax withheld, and the total FICA taxes (employer's and employees) for the quarter. Any deposits made during the quarter are deducted from the totals. Form 941 must be filed by the last day of the month following the end of the quarter. A journal entry is made to record the amount of any taxes remitted with Form 941. The proper liability accounts are debited and Cash is credited for the amount remitted.

FUTA taxes are computed on a quarterly basis. If the amount of the tax is $100 or less, no quarterly deposit is necessary. The total quarterly tax is merely added to the amount for deposit for the next quarter. If the tax exceeds $100, the total must be deposited on or before the last day of the month immediately following the end of the quarter. A preinscribed Federal Tax Deposit Form 508 must accompany the deposit (fig. 13.3).

Figure 13.3 Federal Tax Deposit Form 508.

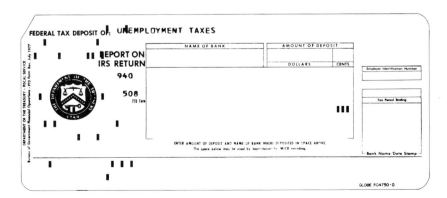

Figure 13.4 Employer's Annual Federal Unemployment Tax Return.

| Form **940** Department of the Treasury Internal Revenue Service | **Employer's Annual Federal Unemployment Tax Return** | **1979** |

If Incorrect, make any necessary change ▶

Name (as distinguished from trade name)

Trade name, if any

Address and ZIP code

Calendar Year
1979
Employer identification number

```
T
FF
FD
FP
I
T
```

A Have you paid all required contributions to your State unemployment fund by the due date of Form 940? . . . . . ☐ Yes ☐ No

If you check the "Yes" box, enter amount of contributions timely paid to your State unemployment fund . . . ▶

B Are you required to pay contributions to only one State? . . . . ☐ Yes ☐ No

If you check the "Yes" box: (1) Enter the name of the State that you are required to pay contributions to . . ▶
(2) Enter your State experience rate(s) for 1979 (see instructions for Part V, columns 4 and 5) . ▶ %, %. %

Part I   Computation of Taxable Wages (To Be Completed by All Taxpayers)

1 Total payments (including exempt payments) during the calendar year for services of employees . . . .

| Exempt Payments | | Amount paid | |

2 Exempt payments. (Explain each exemption shown, attaching additional sheets if necessary) ▶

3 Payments for services in excess of $6,000. Enter only the excess over the first $6,000 paid to individual employees exclusive of exempt amounts entered on line 2. Do not use State wage limitation . . . .

4 Total exempt payments (add lines 2 and 3) . . . .

5 Total taxable wages (subtract line 4 from line 1). (If any portion is exempt from State contributions, see instructions) . ▶

Part II   Tax Due or Refund (Complete if You Checked the "Yes" boxes in Both Items A and B Above)

1 FUTA tax. Multiply the wages on line 5, Part I, by .007 and enter here . . . .

2 (a) Delaware wages included on line 5, Part I . ▶ $.................... multiplied by .003 . . .

  (b) Pennsylvania wages included on line 5, Part I . ▶ $.................... multiplied by .003 . . .

3 Total FUTA tax (add lines 1, 2a, and 2b) . . . .

4 Less: Total FUTA tax deposited from line 5, Part IV . . . .

5 Balance due (subtract line 4 from line 3—this should not be over $100). Pay to Internal Revenue Service . . ▶

6 Overpayment (subtract line 3 from line 4) . . . . ▶

Part III   Tax Due or Refund (Complete if You Checked the "No" Box in Either Item A or Item B Above)

1 Gross FUTA tax. Multiply the wages on line 5, Part I, by .034 . . . .

2 Maximum credit. Multiply the wages on line 5, Part I, by .027 . . . .

3 Enter the smaller of the amount on line 11, Part V, or line 2, above . . . .

4 (a) Delaware wages included on line 5, Part I . ▶ $.................... multiplied by .003

  (b) Pennsylvania wages included on line 5, Part I . ▶ $.................... multiplied by .003

5 Credit allowable (subtract lines 4a and 4b from line 3) . . . .

6 Net FUTA tax (subtract line 5 from line 1) . . . .

7 Less: Total FUTA tax deposited from line 5, Part IV . . . .

8 Balance due (subtract line 7 from line 6—this should not be over $100). Pay to Internal Revenue Service . . ▶

9 Overpayment (subtract line 6 from line 7) . . . . ▶

Part IV   Record of Federal Tax Deposits for Unemployment Tax (Form 508)

	a. Quarter	b. Liability by period	c. Date of deposit	d. Amount of deposit	
1	First				
2	Second				
3	Third				
4	Fourth				

5 Total FUTA tax deposited (add column d, lines 1 through 4) (do not include contributions paid to State) . ▶

If you will not have to file returns in the future, write "Final" here (see general instruction "Who Must File") . . ▶

Under penalties of perjury, I declare that I have examined this return, including accompanying schedules and statements, and to the best of my knowledge and belief, it is true, correct, and complete, and that no part of any payment made to a State unemployment fund claimed as a credit was or is to be deducted from the payments to employees.

Date ▶   Signature ▶   Title (Owner, etc.) ▶

Form **940** (1979)

A journal entry is made to record the amount deposited.

| FUTA Tax Payable | 2.87 | |
| Cash | | 2.87 |

After posting, the liability account looks like this:

FUTA Tax Payable

| 2.87 | 2.87 |

(This entry is for illustration purposes only. Normally, no quarterly deposit is made unless the tax is over $100.)

An Employer's Annual Federal Unemployment Tax Return Form 940 (fig. 13.4) must be filed on or before January 31. Any FUTA taxes remitted with Form 940 are debited to FUTA Tax Payable and credited to Cash.

State unemployment tax is paid quarterly and must be remitted to the proper state agency during the month following the end of the quarter. The form used for reporting unemployment tax differs from state to state. When the tax is paid, the following journal entry is made:

State Unemployment Tax Payable	11.07	
Cash		11.07

When the entry is posted, the ledger account for the liability appears as follows:

State Unemployment Tax Payable

11.07	11.07

There are two other tax reports for which the employer is responsible each year. A Form W-2, Wage and Tax Statement (fig. 13.5), must be given to each employee by January 31 of each year or, if an employee leaves the job before the end of the year, within thirty days after the last wage payment. This form includes information about the employee's total earnings and the total amount withheld for federal income and FICA taxes. Information regarding state and local income taxes (if applicable) also appears on this form. At least four copies of the form are prepared: two

---

Figure 13.5 Form W-2, Wage and Tax Statement.

Figure 13.6 Form W-3, Transmittal of Income and Tax Statements.

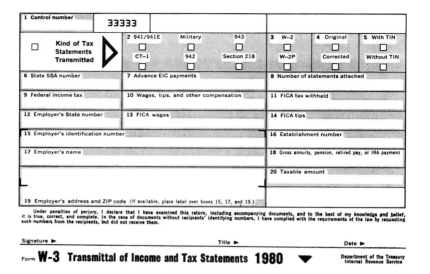

copies are given to the employee, one for the employee's records and one to attach to the employee's federal tax return; one copy is sent to the IRS by the employer; and one copy is retained by the employer. Additional copies are needed if state and local taxes are applicable.

A Form W-3, Transmittal of Income and Tax Statements (fig. 13.6), must be filed with the IRS by February 28 of each year. A copy of each employee's Form W-2 is sent with this form.

The scope of this chapter allows for only a limited treatment of the paying and reporting of taxes; more complete discussions and explanations are usually provided in advanced accounting courses.

Payment of Voluntary Deductions

As stated previously, employees often authorize certain voluntary deductions from their wages each pay period. Voluntary deductions may be authorized for such things as insurance premiums, savings and retirement plans, and charitable contributions. They represent liabilities to the employer until such time as the amounts deducted are remitted to the appropriate parties. At that time a journal entry is made to record the payment. For example, in figure 12.6, $95 was withheld for life insurance premiums. The journal entry to record the remittance of that amount to the insurance company is as follows:

Life Insurance Premiums Payable	95.00	
Cash		95.00

After posting, the liability account appears as follows:

Life Insurance Premiums
Payable

95.00	95.00

Deductions for group hospital insurance premiums amount to $70.20, and deductions for U.S. savings bonds are $30. The journal entries to record the remittance of those amounts to the appropriate parties are as follows:

Group Hospital Insurance		
Premiums Payable	70.20	
Cash		70.20
U.S. Savings Bonds Payable	30.00	
Cash		30.00

When posting has been completed, the ledger accounts for the liabilities appear as follows:

Group Hospital Insurance		**U.S. Savings Bonds Payable**	
Premiums Payable			
70.20	70.20	30.00	30.00

Although all of these transactions have been shown as separate journal entries, they can also be recorded as a compound journal entry. It is also likely that these transactions would be recorded in a cash payments journal rather than a general journal. The general journal is used here for illustrative purposes.

Accrual of Taxes and Wages

Wage expense is typically recorded at the end of each pay period. However, if the end of the accounting period falls in the middle of a pay period, there will be some **accrued wage** expense that has not been paid or recorded because payment is not yet due. When this situation occurs, a journal entry must be made to record the amount of wage expense that has accrued during the current period but that is not payable until the next accounting period.

For example, assume that a company pays wages every Friday for a five-day week ending on Friday. The fiscal year ends on December 31, which falls on a Wednesday. Wages accrued for Monday, Tuesday, and Wednesday, December 29, 30, and 31, total $600. Wages paid on Friday, January 2, of the following year total $1,000. The $600 of earned but unpaid wages is an expense of the year just ended and must be recorded as such. The unpaid wages are considered a liability of the employer. Therefore, in order to show the correct amount of wage expense for the year and the total liabilities, an adjusting entry to record the accrued expense and liability must be made. The adjusting entry is as follows:

Wage Expense	600	
Accrued Wages Payable		600

(This adjustment appears first in the Adjustments column of the work-sheet.)

After this entry is posted, the debit balance of the Wage Expense account correctly shows total wages for the current pay period as well as the current liability for the accrued wages.

Wage Expense		Accrued Wages Payable	
Dec 31 600			Dec 31 600

Later, when the closing process has been completed, Wage Expense has a zero balance and Accrued Wages Payable continues to show a $600 balance.

Wage Expense		Accrued Wages Payable	
Dec 31 600	Dec 31 600		Dec 31 600
(Adjusting)	(Closing)		(Adjusting)

If nothing further is done until the $1,000 payroll is paid on January 2, the journal entry on that date must show a debit to Accrued Wages Payable for $600 and to Wage Expense for $400. Cash is credited for $1,000. This weekly payroll is recorded differently than all other weekly payrolls for the coming year. (Subsequent weekly payrolls are recorded by debiting Wage Expense and crediting Cash for the amount of the payroll.) In addition, the accountant must refer back to the end-of-the-period adjusting entries to determine just how much of the $1,000 must be debited to each of these two accounts.

However, this inconvenience can be avoided if a reversing entry is made on the first day of the new accounting period. The reversing entry for the accrued wages is as follows:

Accrued Wages Payable	600	
Wage Expense		600

After posting, Wage Expense shows a credit balance of $600, and the liability for $600 is removed.

Wage Expense				Accrued Wages Payable			
Dec 31	600	Dec 31	600	Jan 1	600	Bal. Dec. 31	600
		Jan 1	600	(Reversing)			
		(Reversing)					

The reversing entry thus makes it possible to record the January 2 payroll in a routine manner. Wage Expense is debited and Cash is credited for $1,000, the entire amount of the weekly payroll. After the entry is posted, Wage Expense has a debit balance of $400, which represents the actual amount of the wage expense incurred in the new accounting period.

Wage Expense				Cash		
Jan 2	1,000	Jan 1	600		Jan 2	1,000
	400					

Payroll taxes are based on employees' wages; therefore, if an employer has accrued wages at the end of an accounting period, it follows that there are some related payroll taxes that should also be accrued. Logically, both the unpaid wages and the related payroll taxes should be recorded in the period in which they are incurred. Assume that in our example the following payroll taxes have accrued on the $600 of accrued wages: employer's FICA taxes, $39.90; FUTA tax, $4.20; state unemployment taxes, $16.20. If we follow the practice of recording unpaid wages and related payroll taxes in the period in which they are incurred, the following journal entry is made to record the accrued taxes:

Payroll Tax Expense	60.30	
FICA Tax Payable		39.90
FUTA Tax Payable		4.20
State Unemployment Tax		
Payable		16.20

It should be noted, however, that *legally* the payroll taxes do not become liabilities until the related wages against which they are imposed are actually paid.

This circumstance and the fact that the amount of payroll taxes may be immaterial has led some companies to adopt an alternative procedure, which involves recording the total amount of payroll taxes in the year the payroll is paid. If this procedure is followed, the employer's payroll tax expense on the entire $1,000 is recorded at the time the payroll is paid on January 2 rather than a portion on December 31 (on $600) and the balance on January 2 (on $400). Whichever procedure is chosen, it should be followed consistently.

Summary

A series of payroll taxes are levied against employers. These taxes represent expenses to the employer and are based on the amount of the payroll. They include FICA and state and federal unemployment taxes. They are computed by applying a fixed percentage rate to total earnings up to a specified maximum base for each employee for each calendar year. The rate and the maximum limit for each type of tax is specified by the act under which the tax is imposed (pp. 262–64).

The employee and employer payroll taxes must be reported and paid according to time schedules established by the federal and state governments. The schedules for paying the taxes are dependent upon the amounts of the taxes (pp. 265–66). The taxes are deposited with a Federal Reserve Bank or an approved commercial depository.

Employers are required to file various quarterly and yearly tax reports with the federal and state governments (pp. 267–69). They are also responsible for furnishing employees with a wage and tax statement at the end of each year (p. 269).

Any wages that have accrued during an accounting period but that have not been recorded or paid should be recorded in the period in which they are incurred. Logically, payroll taxes relating to accrued wages should also be recorded in the period in which they are incurred even though legally they do not become liabilities until the wages are actually paid. Because of this, many companies prefer to record payroll tax in the year in which the payroll is paid up (pp. 271–74).

Key Terms

accrued wages Wages that have accrued during one accounting period but that have not been recorded and are not payable until the next accounting period.

employer's identification number A number assigned to an employer by the Internal Revenue Service for use in submitting tax payments and reports.

Federal Unemployment Tax Act A federal law that provides for an unemployment insurance program administered jointly by the federal and state governments.

federal unemployment taxes Taxes collected from employers to provide funds for administering unemployment insurance programs.

merit rating A system which permits an employer with a history of stable employment to pay less than the maximum rate of 2.7% of state unemployment taxes.

state unemployment taxes Taxes levied by a state and paid by an employer to provide benefits for eligible unemployed workers.

unemployment insurance Compensation received by employees who through no fault of their own become unemployed.

Upon completion of this chapter, you should be able to:

1. Describe the different methods of processing data.
2. Explain the characteristics that are common to all automated data processing systems.
3. Describe the basic components of an electronic computer.
4. List the advantages to be gained by automated processing of payrolls and other business records.

14 Automated Processing of Accounting Data

5. Define the following accounting terms:

arithmetic unit

automated data processing

COBOL

computer

control unit

electronic data processing

flowchart

FORTRAN

GIGO principle

input

input device

integrated data processing

keypunch machine

manual data processing

mechanical data processing

output

PL/1

program

punched card data processing

storage unit

systems manual

The accounting process includes recording, classifying, and summarizing the financial data of a business. *Data processing* is a term frequently used to describe this part of the accounting process. In earlier chapters, the methods described for processing data have been designed for manual accounting systems. However, these methods are not always the most economical or efficient. In the interest of saving time and money, many companies have advanced to mechanical (automated) methods of data processing. In this chapter, we will discuss some of the basic principles and concepts relating to the automated processing of accounting data.

Introduction to Automated Accounting Systems

A data processing system consists of all the forms, records, procedures, and equipment used in recording and reporting data. It is essential that an accounting system be designed to provide complete, accurate, and current information quickly and economically. The design of a company's accounting system depends to a large extent on the nature of the company's business and the kind and volume of transactions. Other factors that affect the design of the system include the needs of the company, the physical facilities (offices, warehouses, etc.), and the organizational structure.

A company will often "outgrow" its original accounting system, making revisions necessary. A complete review of the present system should be made before any revisions are undertaken. The task of revising an accounting system is divided into three phases: (1) system analysis, (2) system design, and (3) system implementation.

System Analysis

The system analysis usually consists of four steps:

1. A review of the company's organizational structure and job descriptions of the personnel who will be affected by a change.
2. A study of the forms, records, reports, and processing procedures used by the firm.
3. An assessment of the shortcomings of the current system.
4. A projection of management's plans for changes in operations (sales volume, products, etc.) in the near future.

Most companies keep a **systems manual**, which contains much of this information. This manual can prove invaluable in the analysis of the present system.

System Design

The direct result of the system analysis is a change in the design of the existing system. The change may be minor, or it may be a complete revision of the entire system.

Regardless of the magnitude of the change, the systems designer must know about the merits of various types of data processing equipment and be able to evaluate the various alternatives open to the company. A good systems designer must be creative and imaginative while keeping within the bounds of certain general principles:

1. The cost of operating the system should not be greater than the value of the information it produces.
2. The internal control features should be sufficient to safeguard assets and to ensure reliability of data.
3. The system should be flexible enough to accommodate increases in volume of data and changes in operating procedures and data processing techniques without disrupting the existing system.

System Implementation

The final phase of a revised or newly created accounting system is the implementation phase. New or revised forms, records, procedures, and equipment must be installed and obsolete ones removed. Personnel to operate the new system must be trained. A major system change is not implemented immediately; the change generally takes place over an extended period of time so that any weaknesses can be detected and corrected before the changeover is completed.

Methods of Processing Data

In recent years, more and more firms are changing to automated or partially automated methods of processing data. Some firms with relatively small amounts of data to be processed still find manual methods are best suited to their needs. However, as the amount of data to be processed increases, manual processing may no longer be feasible. At that point, companies usually begin to replace manual effort with mechanical equipment.

The term used to describe the mechanical processing of data with a minimum of manual intervention is **automated data processing (ADP)**. When the processing of data is done by electronic equipment (i.e., computers), it is usually known as **electronic data processing (EDP)**. A data processing system in which data is recorded only once in a common language machine and then processed for a number of different purposes by many different machines without being recopied is called **integrated data processing (IDP)**. Integrated data processing is not to be confused with automated data processing. Automated data processing refers to the use of certain machines to process certain types of data. Integrated data processing refers to the entire related system through which data is processed.

There are four methods of data processing: manual, mechanical, punched card, and electronic.

Manual Data Processing

The **manual data processing** method indicates that all processing of data is done by hand. Journals and ledgers are used to classify and sort data. Storage (usually in ledgers or file cabinets), retrieval, and summarizing are entirely manual.

A number of techniques and devices have been developed to facilitate the manual method of processing data. Pegboards, edge-notched cards, continuous business forms, padded multiple business forms, multicolumn journals, forms registers, all help to improve the speed and accuracy of manual data processing.

Mechanical Data Processing

The **mechanical data processing** method replaces manual effort with simple office machines such as typewriters, cash registers, adding machines, calculators, and bookkeeping machines. A bookkeeping machine (also called a posting machine or an accounting machine) is especially useful for speeding up the accounting process and reducing costs. Electronic accounting machines have been introduced that speed up the process even more.

Bookkeeping machines make it possible to prepare several accounting records at the same time. For example, when a bookkeeping machine is used in sales accounting, the sales journal and the customer's ledger sheet and monthly statement can be placed in the machine together. In one operation, the machine enters the sale in the sales journal, posts the sale to the customer's account, and updates the statement to be sent to the customer at the end of the month.

Many smaller firms use a combination of manual and mechanical methods of processing data.

Punched Card Data Processing

Punched card data processing records data on a punched card, which is then processed automatically through machines. Information from source documents is transferred to cards by means of a **keypunch machine.** The cards are then read by other machines, such as sorters, reproducers, collators, and tabulators. These machines convert the data coded on the cards into electrical impulses that cause the machines to sort, post, select, or summarize information and print out reports.

A punched card system is often referred to as a *unit record system,* since each punched card contains all the data for a single transaction. The data on each card is combined with the data on other cards to arrive at a final output.

The punched card method is semiautomatic since human intervention is necessary during various processing stages. Medium-sized businesses often find this method advantageous, although its limited speed and logic capabilities can restrict its use.

Electronic Data Processing

Electronic data processing refers to the processing of data by a computer (fig. 14.1). Computers make it possible to process information at a high rate of speed, to store large amounts of information, and to recall that

Courtesy of IBM.

information in a short time. Computers also possess the capability to perform almost limitless numbers of calculations accurately and quickly.

The accounting system of most large businesses involves the use of at least one type of electronic computer. Furthermore, in recent years, the cost of computer services has dropped, making electronic data processing affordable by many medium- or smaller-sized businesses.

Characteristics of Automated Systems

It is virtually impossible to keep informed about all of the different equipment and procedures being used in automated data processing systems. However, there are some characteristics common to all automated systems with which you should be familiar.

To begin with, the data to be processed originates from a variety of source documents. From that point, there are three basic stages through which data flows in any automated data processing system.

Input Stage

After data has been collected, it must be translated into a form that can be read by the processing equipment. Data that has been translated into a form acceptable for use in automated data processing equipment is called **input.** The form used is the *input medium,* and the unit that conveys the input data into the data processing equipment is called an **input device.** The most common input media include punched cards, punched tape, magnetic tape, magnetic discs, and paper printed with symbols in magnetic ink or optical characters.

Figure 14.2 A data card.

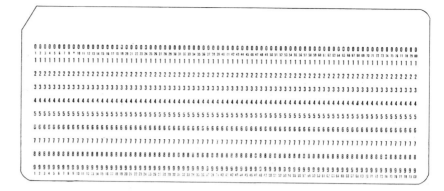

Punched Cards and Punched Tape

The punched card is popular as a form of input media since it can be used not only as input for the processing equipment but also as a basic business document. Many firms use punched cards as invoices and statements of accounts. Punched cards can also be used as payroll checks and dividend checks.

Data is recorded on a card by means of a keypunch, which punches holes in the card. The data is then processed automatically by data processing equipment, such as a computer, which decodes the information contained on the card. One form of punched card, known as a data card, is shown in figure 14.2.

Each card has eighty vertical columns numbered from left to right. Each column is divided into twelve rows. Only rows 0 through 9 are printed on the card. The blank space at the top of the card provides room for rows 11 and 12. Rows 0 through 9 are called numeric rows. Rows 11, 12, and 0 are called *zone rows*. The 0 row can be either a zone row or a numeric row.

When entering numbers only one letter, digit, or character is punched in a column. For example, to record the number 2, use only one column and punch the 2 row in that column (fig. 14.3). For a two-digit number such as 25, use two columns. Punch the 2 row for the first digit and the 5 row in the next column for the second digit (fig. 14.4). The holes punched in the columns are referred to as *codes*.

When a letter of the alphabet is coded, a combination of two holes is punched in the same column. One hole is punched in a zone row and the other is punched in a numeric row. The following combinations are used to code letters:

A through I:	Zone row 12 and numeric rows 1 through 9
J through R:	Zone row 11 and numeric rows 1 through 9
S through Z:	Zone row 0 and numeric rows 2 through 9

Figure 14.5 shows how letters are coded.

Figure 14.3 A data card recording the number 2.

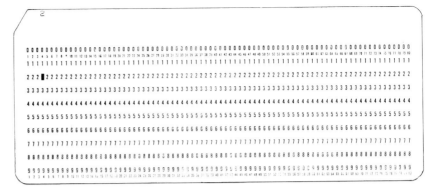

Figure 14.4 A data card recording the number 25.

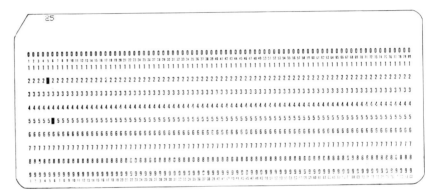

Figure 14.5 A data card showing the punch combinations for recording letters.

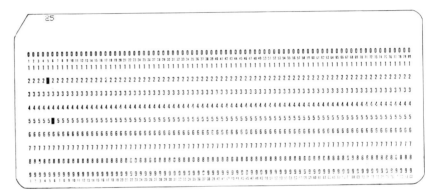

Figure 14.6 A data card containing the fields necessary for a sample invoice.

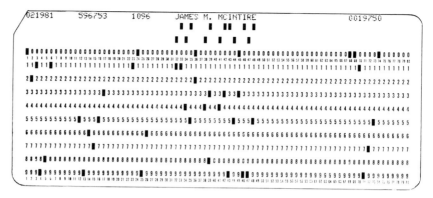

A single item of information, such as an invoice number, is recorded in several columns. The group of columns used to record one item of information is called a *field*. Several fields of information are usually contained on each card.

The first step in using a punched card as an input device is to plan the arrangement of the information on the card. As an example, assume that a punched card to be used for an invoice must contain the following information: (1) date, (2) invoice number, (3) customer number, (4) customer name, and (5) amount. The card is divided into five fields. The length of each field depends upon the maximum number of columns needed to record the data in the particular field. For instance, it is determined that the date should be recorded first and that a maximum of six columns is needed for the date. Columns 1 through 6 are then designated as the date field, and no other data can be recorded in columns 1 through 6. Once a group of columns is assigned as a field, those columns are used exclusively for that particular data (fig. 14.6).

In a numeric field, all columns in the field must be punched. If a number contains fewer digits than columns in the field, the unused column(s) must be filled with zeros. This is not necessary in an alphabetic field.

Another input medium sometimes used in automated data processing, which resembles punched cards, is punched tape. Punched tape can be visualized as a group of data cards joined end to end (fig. 14.7). The basic coding process for the two media is similar; the main difference being that data is punched on tape rather than cards. The code for a punched tape is called a *channel code*.

Magnetic Tape and Magnetic Discs

Punched cards and punched tape are suitable for use with most automated data processing systems. However, they have one limitation that makes them less than suitable for electronic computer systems—they are generally

Figure 14.7 Punched tape.

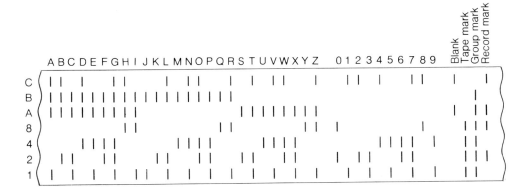

considered too slow for high-speed electronic data processing equipment. Data on punched cards and tape often cannot be read into a system fast enough to keep up with the speed of the computer. Business firms that use electronic data processing most often use magnetic tape as an input medium.

The main advantage of magnetic tape is the speed with which it can process data. Magnetic tape also makes it possible to compress more data into a smaller area so that it is cheaper and easier to store.

Magnetic tape is actually a plastic tape coated with a magnetic metal substance. Data is recorded on the tape by a series of small magnetized spots, known as *bits*. Bits serve the same function as the holes in punched tape.

Magnetic discs are also used as an input medium for electronic computers. As with magnetic tape, high-speed transmission is an advantage of using magnetic discs. The discs resemble a phonograph record. Large amounts of data can be stored since data can be recorded on both sides of the disc. Smaller discs, called floppy discs, are often used as the input medium for smaller computers.

Magnetic Ink and Optical Characters

Data printed in magnetic ink represents another input medium. This method is used extensively by banks in processing checks. The data are printed as numerical symbols in the lower-left corner of the check (see fig. 6.7). The data is read by magnetic ink character recognition (MICR) machines and transmitted to a computer for the necessary processing, such as updating accounts or totaling checks drawn on different banks.

The use of optical characters is growing as an input medium. Optical characters function in a manner similar to magnetic ink in that the characters are readable by both people and machines.

Optical characters consist of a special alphabet, or character set. The characters are printed as standardized angular shapes. They are read directly by an optical character reader (OCR), which eliminates the need to convert the data into a coded input medium. This greatly reduces the time involved in processing data.

Credit card sales invoices and airline tickets are common examples of the application of OCR systems.

Processing Stage

The processing stage could be called the manipulation stage. It refers to the processing equipment that manipulates the data. The four most common types of processing equipment are the punched card machines, MICR processors, optical character readers, and electronic computers. The first three have already been discussed briefly. A more thorough discussion of the electronic computer appears on the following pages.

Output Stage

The final stage in an automated data processing system is the output stage. Information that is produced by the processing system is called **output.** The means for converting the coded information into writing is referred to as an **output device.** The most common output devices are printers, console typewriters, and cathode ray tube displays.

Printers produce a copy, or transcript, of the output. This copy is often referred to as a *printout,* or *hard copy.* The cathode ray tube (CRT) displays the information on a tube similar to a television picture tube. The information displayed on the CRT can also be printed in hard copy. Console typewriters automatically type out a copy of the output.

The flow of data through the stages of an automatic data processing system is illustrated in figure 14.8.

Figure 14.8   Flow of data through an automated data processing system.

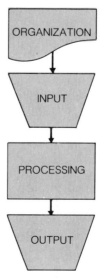

Electronic Data Processing: The Computer

Computers have had a major impact on American business, especially on the handling of accounting data. Even though widespread use of computers did not occur until the early 1960s, there are few businesses today, regardless of size, that do not process part or all of their accounting information by means of the electronic computer. Because the computer continues to grow in prominence in the field of accounting, a more detailed discussion of its use is presented in the following pages.

A **computer** is an electronic device that receives, processes, stores, retrieves, and prints large amounts of data at extremely high speed. It is composed of three basic components: the storage unit, the arithmetic unit, and the control unit.

Storage Unit

The **storage (memory) unit** accepts data to be processed as well as programs of instruction for processing the stored data. This unit is often called the "memory" since it holds the data for periods of time. A computer's main storage system is called the *core storage.*

Arithmetic Unit

The **arithmetic unit** of the computer performs both computing and decision-making functions. It adds, subtracts, multiplies, and divides. The results of the computations performed by the arithmetic unit can be stored and called into use when needed. This unit is also capable of comparing two numbers and determining whether the numbers are equal and, if not, which of the numbers is greater. The results of these comparisons are used as the basis for determining alternative courses of action by the computer.

Control Unit

The **control unit** is so-called because it controls the operations of the other computer units. It directs the processing of data into, through, and out of the computer in accordance with a set of instructions called a program. A **program** is a detailed package of instructions the computer is to follow in completing the processing of data. A separate program must be prepared for each processing job. Each step in the program represents an operation the computer is to perform, and the computer performs its instructions one at a time until the entire program has been completed. It can be directed to repeat the same set of instructions over and over again but each time with a new set of data. Programs can also be stored in the computer until such time as they are needed.

Persons who prepare computer programs are called programmers. They usually prepare the programs first using a graphic device called a **flowchart.** A flowchart makes it possible to visualize or outline the flow of operations that are to be performed in accounting for a particular transaction or a series of closely related transactions. A flowchart shows in graphic form each step required to complete the processing of various data.

Figure 14.9 Some common flowchart symbols.

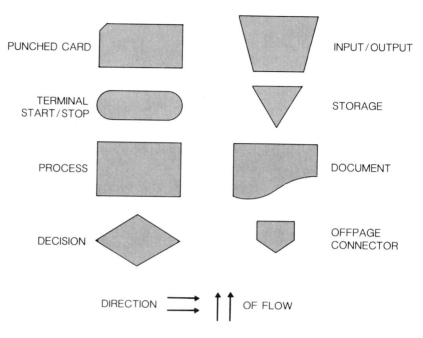

PUNCHED CARD

INPUT / OUTPUT

TERMINAL
START / STOP

STORAGE

PROCESS

DOCUMENT

DECISION

OFFPAGE
CONNECTOR

DIRECTION OF FLOW

Uniform symbols are used to depict certain activities. Some of the most commonly used symbols are illustrated in figure 14.9.

Flowcharts are usually prepared to be read from left to right and from top to bottom. The direction of the flow is indicated by lines and arrows. A brief description of each step of the process is written inside each symbol. Also, if a decision is to be made at one point in the process, the questions to be answered are printed inside or next to the decision symbol. Decisions usually involve the comparison of two items of data. If the items match, the decision is to continue a particular process. If they do not match, the decision is to retrace steps or proceed in some other manner.

After the flowchart is prepared, a program is then written in a special machine language or code. There are a number of program languages available. Some of the more common ones are: (1) **COBOL** (*CO*mmon *B*usiness *O*riented *L*anguage), which is specifically designed for business use; (2) **FORTRAN** (*FOR*mula *TRAN*slation system), which is designed primarily for scientific and mathematical use; and (3) **PL/1** (Programming Language 1), which is gaining popularity for both business and scientific use.

After the program is written in one of the computer languages, it is then entered into the computer by one of the input devices previously

Figure 14.10 Flow of data within a computer system.

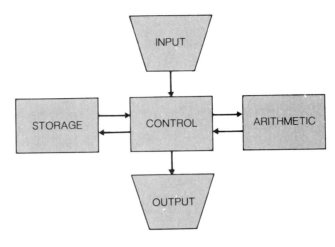

mentioned. The control unit then directs the processing of data according to the program and also controls the output of the computer, telling it what to print and in what form (for people or for other machines).

The flow of data into, through, and out of a basic computer system is diagrammed in figure 14.10.

While computers process data with great speed and accuracy, the human factor is an integral part of the operation. Computers are completely dependent on humans to supply the data that activates the automated system. If the input data is incorrect, the solution will also be incorrect. This is what is commonly termed the **GIGO (garbage-in, garbage-out) principle.**

Automated Processing of Payroll Records

Payroll accounting systems lend themselves well to automated processing. This is true because payroll operations are generally repetitive in nature and involve the manipulation of large amounts of data. Speed and accuracy are also important considerations in payroll accounting.

Much of the data involving payrolls remains unchanged for a number of payroll periods, such as rates of pay and the FICA tax rate. This type of data can be stored in the memory unit of the computer. The computer is then programmed to utilize this data in performing operations necessary to process the payroll. Also, the computer can be programmed to repeat the same set of instructions over and over until the entire payroll has been processed.

Another advantage to automatic processing of payrolls is the ability of computers to make yes-or-no decisions. Consider the employee's FICA taxes as an example. The computer can be programmed to consider the question of whether or not an employee's earnings have reached the FICA tax exempt point. If not, the computer calculates and deducts FICA taxes. If the earnings have exceeded the tax exempt point, the computer is programmed to omit this step.

Automatic processing of payrolls makes it possible to employ the write-it-once principle. The preparation of the payroll register, the paycheck, and the employee's individual earnings record can all be done electronically. Furthermore, data needed for computing the employer's payroll taxes and for preparing various tax reports can also be processed automatically.

Automated Processing of Other Business Records

The use of automation in processing business records is widespread today. The speed and accuracy with which all types of data can be processed make the use of automation practical. This use of automated processing does not change the basic principles of accounting; however, it may affect the form of accounting records and the sequence of processing.

Automated accounting can be used for processing sales and purchases, keeping general and subsidiary ledger accounts up to date, maintaining perpetual inventories, analyzing sales data, and preparing financial statements and other reports.

Data may be recorded on punched cards or tapes or on magnetic tapes or discs for input into the computer, and the computer can be programmed to process the data and produce the desired records. The automated system can be designed so that a minimum of rehandling of data is required.

An automated purchase system can be designed to include not only purchase data but cash disbursements data and inventory data. Automated processing of sales can be designed to include sales allowances and cash receipts and to keep individual accounts receivable up to date. In addition, the data representing sales can be used for detailed analyses of sales by amounts, products, territories, etc. It is also possible to use this same data in maintaining a perpetual inventory system. However, the utilization of the computer to perform these activities is dependent upon proper programming and storage of the data in the memory unit of the computer.

A fully automated data processing system may not be practical for all businesses because of the size of the business or the nature of its operations. In such cases, a semiautomated system utilizing unit record equipment might be more feasible. But with the rapid technological advances being made in automated data processing, it is possible for any business regardless of size to find some means of obtaining the advantages of automated data processing; time-sharing plans or service bureaus, for example.

There are so many systems of automated data processing and so many variations of its use that it is not possible to give a detailed discussion of them here. The brief explanations in this chapter have been presented to help you understand some of the basic concepts and principles of automated data processing.

Summary

Automated data processing has had a tremendous impact on the handling of accounting records. Today almost all businesses process part or all of their accounting records by some means of automated data processing. The changeover to automated data processing usually comes about after a careful analysis of the existing system, followed by the design and implementation of a new or revised system (pp. 278–79).

There are four basic methods for processing data—manual, mechanical, punched card, and electronic. The method a company chooses depends on the size of the company and the nature of its business (pp. 279–81).

The large variety of data processing equipment and procedures in use today makes it impossible to become familiar with all of them. However, there are some characteristics that are common to all automated data processing systems. Data flows through three basic stages: input, processing, and output (pp. 281–86).

The development of the electronic computer has made it possible to process data with greater speed and accuracy than ever before. The computer has the ability to store large quantities of data and to recall data and process it rapidly (p. 286). A computer is directed to perform these activities by means of a program written in a special machine language, but the output of the computer is only as accurate as the instructions it gets from humans. (pp. 287–89).

The use of automation in processing business records is already widespread; but with continual technological advances, automated data processing is within the reach of virtually any business.

Key Terms

arithmetic unit A computer unit that performs calculating and decision-making functions.

automated data processing The mechanical processing of data with a minimum of manual intervention.

COBOL A computer language designed primarily for business use.

computer An electronic device that receives, processes, stores, retrieves, and prints large amounts of data at extremely high speeds.

control unit A computer unit that controls all other computer units; directs the processing of data into, through, and out of the computer.

electronic data processing The processing of data by electronic equipment (computers).

flowchart A graphic device representing each step required to complete the processing of data.

FORTRAN A computer language designed specifically for scientific and mathematical use.

GIGO principle (garbage-in, garbage-out) Incorrect input data results in incorrect solutions from a computer.

input Data that has been translated into a form acceptable for use in automated data processing equipment; the form used is called the input medium.

input device The unit that conveys, or reads, the input data into the data processing equipment.

integrated data processing A data processing system in which data is recorded only once in a common language machine and then processed for a number of different purposes by many different machines without being recopied.

keypunch machine A machine used to punch data into cards used as input media for data processing equipment.

manual data processing A data processing method in which the processing of data is done by hand.

mechanical data processing A data processing method in which the processing of data is done by simple office machines.

output Information that is produced by a data processing system.

PL/1 A computer language designed for business and scientific use.

program A detailed package of instructions the computer follows in completing the processing of data.

punched card data processing A semiautomated data processing method in which data is punched into cards and then processed automatically through machines.

storage unit A computer unit that accepts and stores data to be processed and the instructional programs for processing the stored data.

systems manual A comprehensive manual that contains information about the forms, records, reports, and processing procedures used in a firm's accounting system.

Upon completion of this chapter, you should be able to:

1. Distinguish between a single proprietorship, a partnership, and a corporation.
2. List the advantages and disadvantages of single proprietorships, partnerships, and corporations.
3. Journalize the entries to open the books for single proprietorships, partnerships, and corporations.
4. Explain the differences in the owner's equity for single proprietorships, partnerships, and corporations.
5. Illustrate the methods of dividing earnings in a partnership.
6. Journalize transactions involving the admission and withdrawal of partners from a partnership.
7. Journalize transactions involving the declaration of dividends by a corporation.

15 Forms of Ownership

8. Define the following accounting terms:

appropriation
articles of copartnership
articles of incorporation
authorized capital stock
capital statement
charter
common stock
corporation
deficit
dividends
goodwill
incorporators
mutual agency

no-par-value stock
outstanding stock
par-value stock
partnership
preferred stock
retained earnings
single proprietorship
statement of retained earnings
stockholder
stockholder of record
uniform partnership act
unlimited liability

The three major forms of business ownership are single proprietorships, partnerships, and corporations. Although the preceding chapters have been devoted to explanations and examples of accounting situations relating to single-owner businesses (single proprietorships), we have not specifically discussed what constitutes a single proprietorship—the characteristics, advantages, and disadvantages. Also, up to this point, no reference has been made to the partnership or corporation forms of ownership.

As accounting students, most of you will probably at some time be involved with one of these forms of business ownership. It may be as an owner, an employee, or perhaps an auditor. Therefore, it is essential that you have some knowledge of the nature of these businesses as well as the accounting procedures involved in each. In this chapter, the fundamental aspects of single proprietorships, partnerships, and corporations will be presented.

Single Proprietorships

Organization

A **single proprietorship** is a business owned by one person. It is the most common form of ownership and is the simplest to organize and operate. This form of ownership is common in merchandising and retailing firms and in personal service enterprises. Examples of business enterprises that are usually owned by a single individual include small retail stores, farming operations, and doctor's and dentist's practices.

A single owner may employ other people and depend on banks and other creditors for financial assistance, but the responsibility for operating the business rests solely with the owner. The owner decides what type of business to enter, where to locate it, and the amount of the original investment. The original investment may consist of cash only or of cash and other property, such as equipment or merchandise.

There are few legal barriers to the formation of a single proprietorship. Special permits or licenses are usually necessary for the operation of some businesses, such as banks, liquor stores, and real estate brokerages. Frequently, there are also ordinances that prohibit the establishment of some types of businesses within city limits or certain other areas. In general, though, no formal legal approval is needed to start a single proprietorship.

Advantages and Disadvantages

The single proprietorship offers certain advantages, which include:

1. Ease of organizing the business. A prospective business owner need only to possess sufficient capital or the ability to secure the capital in order to begin operations. No legal agreements with others concerning ownership are necessary.
2. No division of authority or earnings. The owner has absolute control of business operations and makes all management decisions. All earnings belong solely to the owner.

3. No separate taxation of the earnings of the business. All earnings are taxable to the owner.
4. Strong incentive for success. As long as the business is successful, the owner enjoys the profits. If it fails, the owner suffers the losses.

The single proprietorship form of ownership has some disadvantages, the more important of which are:

1. **Unlimited liability.** The owner is personally liable for all the debts of the business. If the business cannot pay its debts, the owner's personal property can be liquidated and turned over to the creditors as payment.
2. Limited capital. It is sometimes difficult for one person to raise large amounts of capital either for an initial investment or additional investments at a later time.
3. Restricted credit. Lending institutions and creditors are often reluctant to extend large amounts of credit to a single proprietor.
4. Limited life. The legal life of the business ends with the death of the owner or the withdrawal of the owner from the business.
5. Limited skills. A single owner may not possess all of the skills needed to operate a business successfully. It is possible to hire employees with the necessary skills, but often the success or failure of the business depends almost entirely on the skills and talents of one person, the owner.

Accounting Procedures

The accounting procedures for handling routine transactions of a business are essentially the same regardless of the type of ownership. The major differences in the accounting procedures are found in the handling of the owner's equity accounts.

The owner's equity accounts of a single proprietorship consist of the capital account, an owner's drawing account, and the temporary owner's equity accounts for expenses and revenue. You are already familiar with the procedure of closing the temporary owner's equity accounts to a summary account and then closing the balance of the summary account (which represents the profit or loss for the period) to the owner's capital account. In a single proprietorship, the profit or loss is solely the owner's.

An individual establishes a business by investing assets—cash or cash and other property. When property is invested, there may be certain liabilities attached to that property; for instance, an accounts payable, note payable, or mortgage payable. Such liabilities represent other claims to the equity of the business, and the fact that they exist must be recorded at the time the business is established.

In formally organizing a business, an owner often prepares a beginning balance sheet to show the assets, liabilities, and owner's equity of the business. If the owner has already been operating the business without

Figure 15.1   Balance sheet prior to opening a formal set of accounting records.

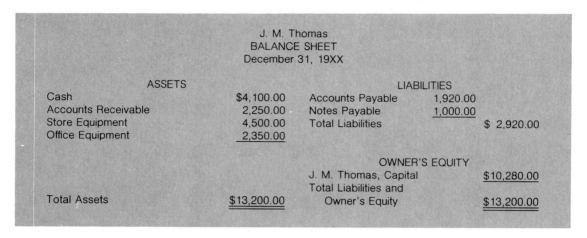

J. M. Thomas
BALANCE SHEET
December 31, 19XX

ASSETS		LIABILITIES		
Cash	$4,100.00	Accounts Payable	1,920.00	
Accounts Receivable	2,250.00	Notes Payable	1,000.00	
Store Equipment	4,500.00	Total Liabilities		$ 2,920.00
Office Equipment	2,350.00			
		OWNER'S EQUITY		
		J. M. Thomas, Capital		$10,280.00
		Total Liabilities and		
Total Assets	$13,200.00	Owner's Equity		$13,200.00

Figure 15.2   Owner's equity section of a balance sheet for a single proprietorship.

OWNER'S EQUITY

J. M. Thomas, Capital, January 1, 19XX		$15,670
Net Income	$3,560	
less Withdrawals	470	
Increase in Capital		3,090
J. M. Thomas, Capital, December 31, 19XX		$18,760

formal accounting records, the task of preparing the balance sheet can be complicated. It may require the services of an accountant to separate business records from personal records and to classify accounts that will appear on the balance sheet. The balance sheet shown in figure 15.1 was prepared by J. M. Thomas prior to opening a formal set of accounting records.

The manner in which the owner's equity is reported on a balance sheet depends upon the type of business for which the balance sheet is prepared. For a single proprietorship, the owner's equity is reported on the balance sheet as shown in figure 15.2.

Some accountants prefer to show the details of the earnings and withdrawals on a separate statement called a **Capital Statement** or **Statement of Owner's Capital.** This statement is prepared from the capital and drawing accounts and shows the changes in the owner's equity and the causes of the changes (fig. 15.3).

If such a statement is used, owner's equity appears on the balance sheet as shown in figure 15.4.

Figure 15.3 Capital statement for J. M. Thomas.

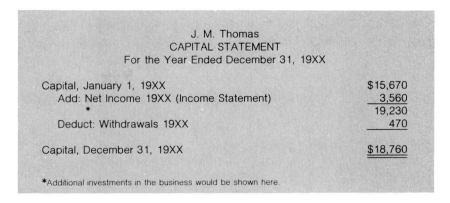

J. M. Thomas
CAPITAL STATEMENT
For the Year Ended December 31, 19XX

Capital, January 1, 19XX	$15,670
Add: Net Income 19XX (Income Statement)	3,560
*	19,230
Deduct: Withdrawals 19XX	470
Capital, December 31, 19XX	$18,760

*Additional investments in the business would be shown here.

Figure 15.4 Owner's equity section of a balance sheet when a capital statement is prepared.

OWNER'S EQUITY
J. M. Thomas, Capital (see attached Capital Statement) $18,760

Partnerships

Organization

A **partnership** is an association of two or more persons for the purpose of conducting a business for profit. A partnership makes it possible to combine capital, skills, and experience for the mutual benefit of all parties.

A partnership is relatively simple to organize and bears many other similarities to a single proprietorship. This form of ownership is used primarily by small business concerns. It is also popular as a form of ownership for professional groups, such as lawyers, doctors, and public accountants.

In most states, the formation and operation of partnerships is governed by the **Uniform Partnership Act.** A partnership is formed as the result of an agreement between two or more persons. The agreement, whether it is oral or written, is a legally enforceable contract. However, it is good business practice to put the agreement in writing. A written agreement, known as the **articles of copartnership,** expresses the intention of the partners and contains the provisions under which the partnership is to operate. Some of the important provisions to be included are:

1. Names of partners
2. Name and location of the partnership
3. Nature and duration of the partnership

4. Duties and responsibilities of partners
5. Investment of each partner
6. Procedures for sharing profits and losses
7. Limitations on withdrawal of assets
8. Procedures for admission and withdrawal of partners
9. Procedures for dissolution of the partnership
10. A provision for arbitration of disagreements

The assets contributed by each member of a partnership become the joint property of all the partners. A partner no longer separately owns any specific resources invested in the firm.

A partnership itself is not a taxable entity. A partnership must file an information return for federal income tax purposes, but individual partners must pay the income taxes on their reported share of the partnership earnings.

Advantages and
Disadvantages

The partnership form of ownership does have certain advantages over other forms of ownership.

1. Greater experience and skills. The talents of several persons can be combined in one organization.
2. Larger amounts of capital. More capital can be raised by combining the resources of one or more persons.
3. Ease of obtaining credit. Credit is usually easier to secure because the liability for all debts of the partnership is assumed by each partner.

The partnership form of ownership has the following disadvantages:

1. Unlimited liability. Each partner has unlimited liability for the debts incurred by the partnership. Creditors can legally satisfy their claims from the personal assets of the partners. Furthermore, one partner can be held fully responsible for all the business debts if the other partners default. Some partnerships contain provisions for the limited liability of certain partners, which restricts their liability to their capital investment.
2. Limited life. A partnership can be terminated for a number of reasons: the expiration of the partnership agreement; the completion of the business for which the partnership was created; the admission of a new partner; the incapacity, death, withdrawal, or bankruptcy of an existing partner. However, the dissolution of a partnership because of a change in partners does not usually disrupt the

continuity of the business. A new partnership can be formed with little or no interruption of the operations of the former partnership.

3. Mutual agency. Each partner acts as an agent for the partnership and can enter into any contract within the scope of its business. Such contracts are binding to all members of the partnership. The partners, however, can agree to limit the right of one or more of the partners to enter into contracts for the partnership. An agreement of this kind is binding on the partnership and on outsiders who have knowledge of the agreement. It is not binding on outsiders unaware of the agreement.

4. Nontransferability of partnership interest. A partner cannot transfer his or her interest in the partnership without the consent of the other partners.

Accounting Procedures

The accounting procedures for a partnership are basically the same as those for a single proprietorship. The differences are in the transactions involving the formation, income distribution, and dissolution of a partnership.

Formation of a Partnership

In partnership accounting, each partner has a capital and a drawing account. Each partner's capital account is credited for the amount of his or her net investment, and a separate journal entry is required for the investment of each partner.

Assume that George Stokes and Rose Farmer decide to form a partnership. Stokes agrees to invest $15,000 cash, office equipment worth $5,000, and a building worth $20,000. Farmer invests $30,000 cash. The following journal entries are made to record their investments:

Cash	15,000	
Office Equipment	5,000	
Building	20,000	
George Stokes, Capital		40,000
Cash	30,000	
Rose Farmer, Capital		30,000

Noncash assets invested in a partnership are recorded at a value agreed upon by the partners. This value is usually determined by the current market price of the assets.

If accounts receivable are contributed to a partnership, only those with a reasonable chance of being collected are transferred. The receivables are debited at their face amounts, and a credit is made to a contra account for possible future uncollectibles.

| Income Distribution | The division of net income or net loss of a partnership is made in accordance with the terms of the partnership agreement. In the absence of such an agreement, the income or loss is shared equally regardless of the amount of capital a partner has contributed. If the agreement specifies the manner in which net income is to be shared but makes no mention of losses, the losses are shared in the same manner as the income. Two common ways of dividing partnership income are: (1) on a stated fractional basis or (2) with salary and interest allowances and the remainder a fixed ratio. |

Stated Fractional Basis

The simplest way of dividing income is on a stated fractional basis. Each partner receives a stated fraction of the total income, such as one-half to Partner A and one-half to Partner B or some other fractional arrangement. For example, if Stokes and Farmer are dividing income based on a fractional ratio of 60 percent for Stokes and 40 percent for Farmer and the net income is $24,000, the distribution of income is computed as follows:

Net Income		$24,000
Division of Net Income	Percent of Total	Total Income
George Stokes	60%	$14,400
Rose Farmer	40%	9,600
		$24,000

The following journal entry is made to distribute the net income:

Expense and Revenue Summary	24,000	
George Stokes, Capital		14,400
Rose Farmer, Capital		9,600

Salary and Interest Allowances

As a way of recognizing differences in personal services contributed by partners and the financial investments of partners, articles of copartnership often provide for salary and interest allowances. These allowances are not to be confused with any salary expense or interest expense appearing in the firm's records. Nor should they be confused with any cash withdrawals the partners may make. Withdrawals of cash are debits to the partners' drawing accounts; allocations of net income are credited to their capital accounts.

To illustrate this method of dividing income, assume that Stokes is to receive a $5,000 salary allowance and Farmer is to receive $7,000. They are each allowed 6 percent interest on their capital balances of $40,000 and $30,000, respectively. The remainder of the net income is to be divided equally.

Figure 15.5 Income statement showing the division of income for a partnership.

Net Income		$24,000
Division of Net Income		
Stokes	$11,300	
Farmer	12,700	
Total Net Income	$24,000	

	George Stokes	Rose Farmer	Total
Net Income	$24,000		
Division of Net Income			
Salary Allowance	$ 5,000	$ 7,000	$12,000
Interest Allowance	2,400	1,800	4,200
Remainder (divided equally)	3,900	3,900	7,800
Division of Net Income	$11,300	$12,700	$24,000

The journal entry closing the Expense and Revenue Summary account and dividing the net income is as follows:

Expense and Revenue Summary	24,000	
George Stokes, Capital		11,300
Rose Farmer, Capital		12,700

If Stokes and Farmer had withdrawn cash equal to their salary allowances during the year, their drawing accounts would have shown debits for $5,000 and $7,000, respectively. Those debits in their drawing accounts would be closed to their capital accounts at the end of the year.

The financial statements of a partnership differ slightly from those of a single proprietorship. A partnership income statement often shows how the income is divided among the partners at the bottom of the statement. Figure 15.5 shows that portion of the income statement for Stokes and Farmer.

The owner's equity section of a partnership balance sheet shows the equity for each partner. The details of the equity are often shown in a supplementary capital statement rather than on the balance sheet (see p. 299).

A new partner may be admitted to a partnership only with the consent of the existing partners. A new partner may be admitted to a partnership either by contributing assets or by purchasing an interest from one or more of the present partners. When the new partner buys an interest of a current partner, neither the assets nor the capital of the firm are affected. It is merely a transfer among capital accounts. However, if the new partner invests assets, both total assets and total capital are affected; the accounts are increased by the amount of the investment.

The following example illustrates the admission of a new partner by the contribution of assets. Assume that Mark Wade invests $20,000 cash in the business of Stokes and Farmer. The journal entry is as follows:

Cash	20,000	
Mark Wade, Capital		20,000

Total assets and total capital have increased $20,000.

To illustrate the admission of a new partner by purchase of an interest, assume that Mark Wade purchases one-half of George Stokes' interest ($40,000) in the firm. The journal entry records a transfer of that amount from the Stokes capital account to the Mark Wade capital account.

George Stokes, Capital	20,000	
Mark Wade, Capital		20,000

There is no change in either the assets or the capital of the firm. The effect of the transaction on the partnership accounts is shown in the following:

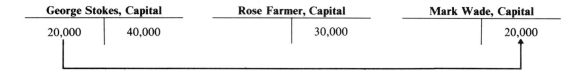

Another factor sometimes considered in the admission of a new partner is goodwill. **Goodwill** is an intangible asset that can be awarded to a new partner who brings some special skill, expertise, or following of customers to a firm. Because the new partner receives credit for the contribution of goodwill, his or her interest in the firm exceeds the amount of tangible assets actually invested. The amount of goodwill allowed the new partner is made up by a reduction in the capital accounts of the current partners.

As an example, assume that Mark Wade is to receive a one-third interest in the firm of Stokes and Farmer by contributing $20,000 cash to the new partnership. The capital of the new firm is increased to $90,000

($40,000 + 30,000 + 20,000); one third of that is $30,000. The difference between Wade's investment of $20,000 and his interest of $30,000 is $10,000. The capital balances of Stokes and Farmer are decreased in accordance with their income- and loss-sharing ratio. Since they now share income on an equal ratio, the entry to admit Wade as a new partner is as follows:

Cash	20,000	
George Stokes, Capital	5,000	
Rose Farmer, Capital	5,000	
Mark Wade, Capital		30,000

Withdrawal of a Partner

A partner may withdraw from a partnership and withdraw assets equal to, greater than, or less than the amount of his or her capital interest in the partnership. If a partner withdraws cash or other assets equal to the balance of his or her capital account, the journal entry to record the withdrawal is a debit to the partner's capital and a credit to the proper asset account(s). Assume that Rose Farmer withdraws from the partnership and the partners agree to her withdrawal of cash equal to her equity, which amounts to $30,000. The following journal entry is made to record the withdrawal:

Rose Farmer, Capital	30,000	
Cash		30,000

Such a transaction does not affect the equity of the remaining partners, but the value of the assets and the total capital has changed—a reduction in each of $30,000.

If a withdrawing partner withdraws less than the value of his or her equity, the transaction represents an increase in the capital of the remaining partners. Assume that Rose Farmer withdraws only $20,000 in settlement of her interest in the partnership. The journal entry is as follows:

Rose Farmer, Capital	30,000	
Cash		20,000
George Stokes, Capital		5,000
Mark Wade, Capital		5,000

The effect of this transaction is to increase the capital accounts of the remaining partners either equally as shown or on a fractional basis as stated in the partnership agreement. In this instance, the terms state that the remaining partners share equally in any gains or losses of equity resulting from a partner's withdrawal.

A withdrawal for an amount greater than the value of the withdrawing partner's equity results in a decrease in the capital accounts of the remaining partners. Assume that Farmer withdraws and accepts $40,000 in settlement. The journal entry is:

Rose Farmer, Capital	30,000	
George Stokes, Capital	5,000	
Mark Wade, Capital	5,000	
Cash		40,000

The excess paid to Farmer represents a loss to the firm and is divided between the remaining partners again according to the terms of the articles of copartnership.

If a withdrawing partner sells his or her interest to a remaining partner or an outside party, a journal entry is made to record the transfer of equity but no entry is made to record the payment of cash. The payment is a private matter between the parties involved.

Liquidation of a Partnership

When a partnership is liquidated, the business discontinues operations. Assets are sold, creditors are paid, and the remaining cash is distributed to the partners according to the balances in their capital accounts. Any gain or loss on the sale of the assets is distributed to the partners' capital accounts before the remaining cash is distributed. In the event the assets are sold at a loss and a partner's capital account cannot absorb the loss, that partner must pay the amount of the deficit into the partnership. If that is not possible, the remaining partner(s) must bear that portion of the deficit according to their income-sharing ratio.

Corporations

Organization

Single proprietorships and partnerships far outnumber corporations as a form of business ownership. Yet corporations far exceed single proprietorships and partnerships combined in terms of dollar volume of business transactions. The corporate form of business ownership is used in a wide variety of businesses; however, it is especially suited to large businesses with very large capital investments.

A **corporation** is an artificial being created by law. It is a legal entity separate and distinct from the persons who own it. It has the right to buy, sell, and own property, enter into contracts, and sue and be sued in its own name. Since a corporation is a separate legal entity, it is responsible for its own acts and debts. The owners of the corporation cannot be held liable for settlement of claims against the corporation. This is a basic feature distinguishing a corporation from single proprietorships and partnerships.

Ownership rights in a corporation are easily transferred from one person to another. Because these transfers do not affect the activities of the corporation, it is said to have *continuous life*. In other words, a corporation continues to operate no matter how often ownership changes.

Figure 15.6   The organizational structure of a corporation.

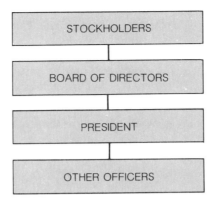

A corporation is formed by securing a **charter** from the federal government or from the state in which the business of the corporation is to be conducted. The charter, known as the **articles of incorporation,** states the conditions under which the corporation can operate. Persons who apply for the charter are called **incorporators.** Usually, each incorporator must subscribe for one or more shares of capital stock. Incorporation requirements vary with the states, but most states require a minimum of three incorporators.

Ownership of a corporation is represented by capital stock, which is divided into shares. The owners of a corporation are those persons who buy the shares of stock. They are called **stockholders,** or **shareholders.** Stockholders receive stock certificates as evidence of the shares purchased and are entitled to one vote for each share of stock owned.

When each share of stock is assigned a definite value, which is stated on the stock certificate, the authorized value is known as the **par value** of the stock. When no authorized value is stated on the stock certificate, the stock has **no-par value.**

The stockholders exercise control, but only indirectly, over the management of the corporation by electing a board of directors. The board of directors hires the officers to manage the corporation. The organizational structure of a corporation is shown in figure 15.6.

The amount of capital stock a corporation may issue, called **authorized capital stock,** is set forth in the charter. The shares actually sold are called **outstanding stock.** Different classes of stock may be issued by a corporation. If only one class is issued, it is called **common stock.** Holders of common stock have the right to attend stockholders' meetings, to vote for the board of directors and on certain business matters, and to share in the distribution of the net income of the corporation. The shares of net income distributed to stockholders are called **dividends** and are distributed in proportion to the number of shares of stock owned.

Another class of stock that is often issued is **preferred stock,** so-called because holders of this type of stock are given first preference on the payment of dividends. Their dividends are paid at either a fixed percentage of the original issue price of the stock or at a fixed amount.

A more detailed discussion of some of the other types of stock, such as treasury stock, is left to more advanced accounting courses.

Advantages and Disadvantages

Limited liability, ease of transfer of ownership rights, and continuous existence are all advantages of the corporate form of ownership. Other advantages include:

1. Capital-raising capability. A corporation has the ability to raise large amounts of capital from the combined investments of many owners.
2. No mutual agency. A corporation owner has no power to bind the corporation to contracts.
3. Professional management. Skilled professional managers are usually employed to direct the activities of a corporation.

The corporate form of ownership also has its disadvantages, some of which are:

1. Taxation. Corporations are subject to a variety of taxes—federal income, state income, real estate, personal property, and franchise taxes.
2. Government regulations. Corporations are subject to greater regulation and control than other forms of business ownership. Many restrictions are placed on corporations by federal and state laws.
3. Limited ability to raise creditor capital. Limited liability is considered as an advantage to corporation owners. Yet it can also be a disadvantage. When creditors cannot look to owners to satisfy their claims, they become reluctant to extend credit beyond an amount for which corporate assets furnish security.

Accounting Procedures

The procedures for handling routine daily transactions of a corporation are much the same as those for a single proprietorship or a partnership. Some differences occur, however, in the accounting procedures for transactions that affect the capital structure and the stockholders' equity accounts.

In a corporation, a distinction is made between invested (paid-in) capital and capital earnings (profit) retained in the business. To preserve this distinction, an owner's equity account called Capital Stock is used to reflect the amount of capital invested by stockholders. Occasionally, a corporation will increase its capital by taking subscriptions to its stock, whereby a subscriber agrees to buy a certain number of shares at an agreed price and to pay for the shares at a later time. In such situations, another owner's equity account called Capital Stock Subscribed may be used. An asset account, Subscriptions Receivable, is affected by a transaction of this kind.

Another owner's equity account, called Retained Earnings, reflects the earnings (profit) retained in the business. **Retained earnings** are earnings retained in the business for use in paying dividends or for financing such things as plant expansion or additional working capital. The balance of this account determines whether or not dividends will be paid to stockholders.

Some of the transactions unique to the corporate form of business ownership are illustrated and explained in the following pages.

Assume that a company is incorporating and has authorized the issue of one thousand shares of common stock at $100 a share. There are five incorporators, each subscribing for two hundred shares. A separate account for each stockholder is kept in a stockholder's ledger. This is a subsidiary ledger that relates to a general ledger control account, Capital Stock.

If all the subscribers pay cash for their shares, the journal entry to record the receipt of cash for the one thousand shares is as follows:

Cash	100,000	
Capital Stock		100,000

As another example, assume that the incorporators paid cash for half of their shares and agreed to pay the balances later. In that case, two journal entries are needed.

Cash	50,000	
Capital Stock		50,000
Subscriptions Receivable	50,000	
Capital Stock Subscribed		50,000

Later, when each subscriber pays the remaining balance, two more journal entries are required.

Cash	50,000	
Subscriptions Receivable		50,000
Capital Stock Subscribed	50,000	
Capital Stock		50,000

The second journal entry is necessary since stock certificates are not issued until the subscriptions have been paid in full. In the event the stock is not paid for in full, the amount of subscribed stock not paid for remains recorded in the Subscriptions Receivable and Capital Stock Subscribed accounts until such time as it is paid in full. Usually if payment is expected relatively soon, the Subscriptions Receivable account is shown as a current asset on the balance sheet, and the Capital Stock Subscribed account is shown as paid-in capital.

Whenever stock is issued for property rather than cash, the proper asset account is debited and Capital Stock credited. In a transaction of this kind, the biggest problem is deciding what amount should be recorded for the property. Normally, the amount recorded is either the fair value of the stock issued or the fair value of the property, whichever is clearer to determine.

Another typical transaction of a corporation is the declaration of dividends. Assume that on March 1 the board of directors votes to pay a cash dividend of $2 a share to holders of stock as of March 1 (called **stockholders of record**). The dividend is to be paid on April 1. When dividends are declared, they represent a liability to the corporation until they are paid. Declared but unpaid dividends are usually recorded in a liability account called Dividends Payable. The journal entry to record the liability follows:

| March 1 | Retained Earnings | 2,000 | |
| | Dividends Payable | | 2,000 |

On April 1 when the dividends are paid, the following journal entry is made:

| April 1 | Dividends Payable | 2,000 | |
| | Cash | | 2,000 |

If no time elapses between the declaration and the payment of the dividend, the journal entry is as follows:

| March 1 | Retained Earnings | 2,000 | |
| | Cash | | 2,000 |

Dividends to stockholders can be paid only out of earnings. At the end of an accounting period, the balance of the Expense and Revenue Summary account is closed to the Retained Earnings account. Net Income is recorded as a credit to Retained Earnings. A net loss is recorded as a debit to the Retained Earnings account. If a loss has occurred and Retained Earnings has a debit balance, a corporation is said to have a **deficit**. In most states it is illegal for a corporation with a deficit to declare a dividend.

The entire balance of a corporation's Retained Earnings account is available for dividend declarations; however, generally not all of its balance

Figure 15.7 Income statement for a corporation.

Net Income before Federal Income Tax	$24,970.90
less Federal Income Tax	5,528.75
Net Income after Federal Income Tax	$19,442.15

Figure 15.8 Owner's equity section of a balance sheet for a corporation.

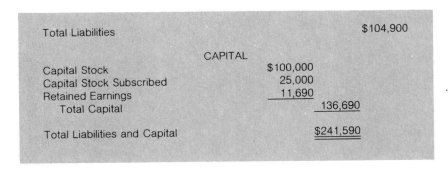

Total Liabilities		$104,900
CAPITAL		
Capital Stock	$100,000	
Capital Stock Subscribed	25,000	
Retained Earnings	11,690	
Total Capital		136,690
Total Liabilities and Capital		$241,590

will be used for that purpose. A portion of the balance may be set aside for a variety of reasons, such as plant expansion or additional working capital. The portion set aside is called an **appropriation.** Money that is appropriated is restricted by a corporation's board of directors from being used to pay dividends. Only the unappropriated retained earnings are immediately available for dividends.

At the end of each accounting period, a corporation prepares an income statement, a statement of retained earnings, and a balance sheet. The income statement of a corporation differs only slightly from the income statements for single proprietorships and partnerships. Corporate income statements show net income before and after federal income tax has been deducted. A portion of a corporation income statement is shown in figure 15.7.

On the balance sheet the section showing owner's equity is usually labeled as Capital or Stockholder's Equity. There may be considerable variations in the Capital section of balance sheets since there are so many differences in the capital structure of different corporations. One example of the owner's equity section of a balance sheet for a corporation is shown in figure 15.8.

Figure 15.9 A statement of retained earnings.

The Hanover Corporation
STATEMENT OF RETAINED EARNINGS
For the Year Ended December 31, 19XX

Balance Unappropriated Retained Earnings, January 1, 19XX			$192,250
Additions: Net Income			63,500
			255,750
Appropriations and Deductions:			
App. for Plant Expansion January 1, 19XX	35,000		
Additional App. during 19XX	20,000	55,000	
Dividends Paid on Common Stock	9,000		
Dividends Paid on Preferred Stock	22,000	31,000	
Total Appropriations and Deductions			86,000
Balance of Unappropriated Retained Earnings, December 31, 19XX			$169,750

The format of the corporate balance sheet shown in figure 15.8 is relatively simple. This format makes it possible to include more detail. If more than one kind of stock is issued, each kind should be listed separately. Also, some corporations include a detailed account of retained earnings in the balance sheet. Generally, though, a detailed account of retained earnings is not necessary since a separate **statement of retained earnings** is prepared for that purpose. A statement of retained earnings is illustrated in figure 15.9. There are also many possible variations in the form that may be used for a statement of retained earnings.

Only a few basic principles regarding the different forms of business ownership are presented in this chapter. An in-depth study is left to more advanced accounting courses.

Summary

Three common types of business ownership are single proprietorships, partnerships, and corporations (p. 296). There are more single proprietorships than any other form of business ownership; however, corporations far exceed both single proprietorships and partnerships in the total dollar volume of business transacted.

Single proprietorships and partnerships have many similar characteristics. Ease of establishing the business and no separate taxation of the earnings of the business are features that these forms of ownership have in common (pp. 296–300). Other less desirable characteristics of both single proprietorships and partnerships are unlimited liability and limited life (pp. 297–300).

Accounting procedures for routine transactions are basically the same for all three forms of ownership. The major differences are found in the handling of the owner's equity of the business. The capital structure and division of income for partnerships and corporations require somewhat more complicated accounting procedures (pp. 295, 300–301, 308–12).

Corporations are separate legal entities with unique capital structures (pp. 306–8). In accounting for and reporting on the stockholder's equity, the invested capital and the earned capital of the corporation must be accounted for separately (p. 309). Dividends must be paid out of the retained earnings. Portions of the retained earnings are also appropriated for other uses. A statement of retained earnings is prepared at the end of each year to show the amount of retained earnings and the distribution of those earnings (pp. 310–12).

Key Terms

appropriation Money that is restricted by a corporation's board of directors from being used to pay dividends.

articles of copartnership A written agreement stating the conditions of the formation and operation of a partnership.

articles of incorporation A document that is filed with a state or the federal government stating pertinent information about the organization of a corporation.

authorized capital stock The amount of stock that a corporation is permitted by its charter to issue.

capital statement A financial statement that reports on changes in the owner's capital that have occurred during an accounting period.

charter A contract between the incorporators and the government, which stipulates the conditions under which the corporation can operate.

common stock One class of capital stock issued by a corporation giving stockholders certain basic rights granted by the corporation charter.

corporation A form of business ownership; an artificial being created by law that is separate and distinct from the persons who own it.

deficit A debit balance in the retained earnings account of a corporation.

dividends A distribution of a portion of the earnings of a corporation to its stockholders; usually a cash distribution.

goodwill An intangible asset that gives a partner or firm a larger interest than the sum of the tangible assets that are invested.

incorporators Persons who provide the initial assets to bring a corporation into existence; persons must subscribe to one or more shares of stock.

mutual agency A characteristic of a partnership in which each partner can bind the partnership to any contract within the scope of its business.

no-par-value stock Stock that has no authorized value stated on the stock certificate.

outstanding stock The total amount of capital stock actually owned by the stockholders of a corporation.

par-value stock Stock that has the authorized value of each share of stock stated on the stock certificate.

partnership An association of two or more persons for the purpose of carrying on a business for profit.

preferred stock A class of stock issued by a corporation, which gives its holders first preference on the distribution of dividends.

retained earnings Earnings (profit) retained in the business that are used for paying dividends or for reinvestment in the business.

single proprietorship A business owned by one person.

statement of retained earnings A financial statement showing the changes in the retained earnings of a corporation during an accounting period.

stockholder A person owning one or more shares of the capital stock of a corporation.

stockholder of record Holder of stock who is entitled to receive a declared dividend.

Uniform Partnership Act A law adopted in most states that governs the formation and operation of partnerships.

unlimited liability A characteristic of single proprietorships and partnerships which makes the owners liable for the debts of the business beyond their original investment; personal assets may be taken to satisfy the claims of creditors.

Glossary

ABA number The number assigned by the American Bankers Association to a particular bank; appears in the upper-right-hand corner of each check.

account Device used to individually record and summarize changes in asset, liability, owner's equity, revenue, and expenses.

account balance The difference between the total debits and total credits in an account.

accounting cycle A sequence of procedures for handling the financial records of a company; the steps followed for each accounting period.

accounting equation The relationship between assets, liabilities, and owner's equity.

Assets = Liabilities + Owner's Equity.

accounting period A period of time for which summaries of a firm's operations are prepared.

accounts payable Amounts owed to creditors.

accounts receivable Amounts due from customers who purchase goods or services on a credit basis.

accrual system of accounting A system of accounting in which revenue is recorded in the period in which it is earned and expenses are recorded in the period in which they are incurred.

accrued expense An expense incurred during an accounting period that has not been paid or recorded; sometimes called accrued liability.

accrued revenue Revenue earned during an accounting period that has not been recorded; sometimes called accrued asset.

accrued wages   Wages that have accrued during one accounting period but that have not been recorded and are not payable until the next accounting period.

accumulated depreciation   A contra account used to record periodic depreciation of long-lived assets.

adjusting entries   Journal entries that record the internal transactions that bring the ledger accounts up to date; usually recorded first on a worksheet.

aging of accounts receivable   The grouping of accounts receivable according to the length of time they have been held.

allowance method   A method of accounting for bad debts that estimates the amount of bad debts expected to result from the credit sales of an accounting period. The expected losses are recorded in the period in which the credit sales are made.

amortization   The process of writing off an intangible asset as an expense.

appropriation   Money that is restricted by a corporation's board of directors from being used to pay dividends.

arithmetic unit   A computer unit that performs calculating and decision-making functions.

articles of copartnership   A written agreement stating the conditions of the formation and operation of a partnership.

articles of incorporation   A document that is filed with a state or the federal government stating pertinent information about the organization of a corporation.

asset   Anything of value owned by a business.

authorized capital stock   The amount of stock that a corporation is permitted by its charter to issue.

automated data processing   The mechanical processing of data with a minimum of manual intervention.

bad debts   Accounts receivable that are uncollectible.

balance sheet   A statement showing a firm's financial condition as of a specific date; often called a statement of financial position; lists the firm's assets, liabilities, and owner's equity.

bank discount   The difference between the principal of a note and the amount of cash received for the note.

bank reconciliation   A statement prepared each month that accounts for or explains the difference between the bank statement balance and the checkbook balance.

bank statement   A statement of the transactions of a depositor's account for a certain period of time; usually sent once each month.

blank endorsement   The simplest means of transferring ownership of a check; includes only the signature of the payee.

book value   The cost of an asset less accumulated depreciation; often called *undepreciated cost.*

business entity concept   The concept that a business is a separate and distinct entity from the person or persons who own it. A separate set of records should be kept for each business.

calendar year   An accounting period that covers one full year and ends on December 31.

canceled check   A check paid by the bank during the month and returned to the depositor with the bank statement.

capital statement   A financial statement that reports on changes in the owner's capital that have occurred during an accounting period.

cash discount   A reduction allowed in the amount of an invoice to encourage prompt payment of the invoice; to the seller, it is a Sales Discount, to the buyer, a Purchase Discount.

cash payments journal   A special journal used to record all transactions in which cash is paid out.

cash receipts journal   A special journal used to record all transactions involving the receipt of cash.

cash system of accounting   A system of accounting for revenue and expenses on a cash basis. Revenue is recorded only when cash is received, and expenses are recorded only when cash is paid out.

charter   A contract between the incorporators and the government, which stipulates the conditions under which the corporation can operate.

chart of accounts   A list showing the arrangement of the accounts in the general ledger by name and number.

check   A written order for a bank to pay a specified sum of money to a designated party.

classified financial statements   Financial statements in which the accounts have been grouped into classifications.

closing entries   Journal entries made at the end of an accounting period that close the temporary owner's equity accounts and reduce their balances to zero; often referred to as closing the books.

COBOL   A computer language designed primarily for business use.

combined journal   A multicolumn journal that provides special columns for those accounts that are often affected in the same way by a number of transactions.

common stock   One class of capital stock issued by a corporation giving stockholders certain basic rights granted by the corporation charter.

compound journal entry   A journal entry that involves more than two accounts or more than one debit or credit.

computer   An electronic device that receives, processes, stores, retrieves, and prints large amounts of data at extremely high speeds.

contingent liability   A potential liability assumed by the endorser of a discounted note if the maker defaults.

contra account   An account that is directly related to another account but that has an opposite or offsetting balance.

control account   A general ledger account that summarizes the information contained in a related subsidiary ledger.

control unit   A computer unit that controls all other computer units; directs the processing of data into, through, and out of the computer.

corporation   A form of business ownership; an artificial being created by law that is separate and distinct from the persons who own it.

cost of goods sold   The total cost of the merchandise that is sold during an accounting period.

credit   The right side of an account.

credit (debit) memorandum   A document given to a customer when merchandise is returned or an allowance in the price is made.

creditor   A person or business to whom a debt is owed.

current assets   Cash and other assets that are expected to be converted to cash or used up within the normal operating period of the business or one year, whichever is longer.

current liabilities   Debts and obligations that must be paid within one operating cycle or one year, whichever is longer.

debit   The left side of an account.

declining balance method   A method of calculating depreciation that assigns a greater amount of depreciation to the early years of an asset's life with a steady decrease in the amount charged to depreciation in the remaining years.

deficit   A debit balance in the retained earnings account of a corporation.

depletion   The process of writing off a wasting asset as an expense.

deposit in transit   A deposit that has been entered on the depositor's books and sent to the bank but that has not been received by the bank at the time the bank statement is prepared.

deposit slip   A printed form used by the depositor to list all items being deposited.

depreciation The allocation of the cost of a long-lived asset over the estimated years of service; a portion of the cost that is charged as an expense of each period of the asset's useful life.

direct write-off method A method of accounting for bad debts that writes off an account as a bad debt at the time the account becomes uncollectible.

discounting a note receivable The exchange of a note receivable for cash or payment of a debt.

dishonored check A check that is not paid when presented for payment; usually for not sufficient funds (NSF) to cover the check.

dishonored note A note that is not paid by the maker on the due date.

dividends A distribution of a portion of the earnings of a corporation to its stockholders; usually a cash distribution.

double-entry accounting Theory upon which the accounting system is based. Every business transaction affects at least two elements of the accounting equation.

drawee The bank on which a check is drawn.

drawer The person who signs a check.

electronic data processing The processing of data by electronic equipment (computers).

employee One who performs a service for payment and is under the control or direction of the business or person for whom the service is performed.

employee's individual earnings record A supplementary payroll record that shows the yearly cumulative earnings and deductions for each employee.

employer A business or person for whom one performs a service.

employer's identification number A number assigned to an employer by the Internal Revenue Service for use in submitting tax payments and reports.

expense A cost incurred by a firm in order to produce revenue.

expense and revenue summary A temporary owner's equity account used as a summarizing device; account to which all revenue and expense account balances are closed at the end of an accounting period.

Fair Labor Standards Act A federal law covering all employers engaged in interstate commerce, which establishes minimum wage and overtime pay requirements.

federal income tax Tax levied by the federal government, which is based on an individual's earnings.

Federal Insurance Contributions Act A federal law taxing employees and employers for support of a national social security program providing retirement, medical, and death benefits.

Federal Unemployment Tax Act A federal law that provides for an unemployment insurance program administered jointly by the federal and state governments.

federal unemployment taxes (FUTA) Taxes collected from employers to provide funds for administering unemployment insurance programs.

FICA taxes Taxes collected equally from employees and employers to support the social security programs.

FIFO method A method of assigning costs to inventory based on the assumption that the first goods purchased are the first goods sold.

fiscal year An accounting period that covers one full year and ends in a month other than December.

fixed assets Assets with a relatively long life that are not expected to be converted to cash or used up in the near future; sometimes called long-lived assets or plant assets.

flowchart A graphic device representing each step required to complete the processing of data.

FOB destination   Transportation arrangements whereby the seller pays the cost of the delivery of goods.

FOB shipping point   Transportation arrangements whereby the buyer pays the cost of the delivery of goods.

FORTRAN   A computer language designed specifically for scientific and mathematical use.

full endorsement   A means of transferring ownership of a check, which includes the name of the party to whom the check is being transferred.

functional depreciation   The loss of usefulness of an asset because of inadequacy or obsolescence.

general expenses   Expenses incurred in the operation of the business that are not a part of the actual process of selling merchandise; sometimes called administrative expenses.

general journal   A book in which a chronological record of all business transactions is kept; book of original entry.

general ledger   A book containing all of a firm's accounts; book of final entry.

GIGO principle   Garbage-in, garbage-out; Incorrect input data results in incorrect solutions from a computer.

goodwill   An intangible asset that gives a partner or firm a larger interest than the sum of the tangible assets that are invested.

gross earnings   An employee's total earnings before any deductions.

gross margin (profit)   The difference between the net sales of a period and the cost of goods sold.

gross profit method   A method for estimating cost of inventory; a percentage of gross profit is applied to the sales of the period.

income statement   A statement showing the results of operations for a period of time; often called a profit and loss statement; lists revenue, expenses, and net income or net loss.

incorporators   Persons who provide the initial assets to bring a corporation into existence; persons must subscribe to one or more shares of stock.

independent contractor   One who sells services to a business for a fee but is not an employee of the business.

input   Data that has been translated into a form acceptable for use in automated data processing equipment; the form used is called the input medium.

input device   The unit that conveys, or reads, the input data into the processing equipment.

intangible asset   An asset that has no physical substance.

integrated data processing   A data processing system in which data is recorded only once in a common language machine and then processed for a number of different purposes by many different machines without being recopied.

interest   A fee charged for the use of money.

journal entry   The formal record of a transaction in a journal.

journalizing   The process of recording a transaction in a journal.

keypunch machine   A machine used to punch data into cards used as input media for data processing equipment.

liabilities   The debts of a business, which represent creditors' claims to the assets of a business.

LIFO method   A method of assigning costs to inventory based on the assumption that the last goods purchased are the first goods sold.

long-lived asset   An asset that is expected to be used in the operation of a business for a number of years.

long-term investments   Securities that are converted to cash eventually but not within the current accounting period.

long-term liabilities Debts that are not due for a relatively long time, usually more than one year.

lower-of-cost-or-market method A method of assigning cost to inventory in which the lower of the cost or market price is applied to the units on hand.

maker The firm or person who signs a promissory note.

manual data processing A data processing method in which the processing of data is done by hand.

maturity date The date on which a note becomes due.

maturity value The amount the maker must pay on the due date of a note; the principal plus interest.

mechanical data processing A data processing method in which the processing of data is done by simple office machines.

merchandise inventory The total amount of goods on hand at the end of an accounting period.

merchandising business A firm whose primary source of revenue is from the sale of merchandise.

merit rating A system which permits an employer with a history of stable employment to pay less than the maximum rate of 2.7% of state unemployment taxes.

MICR number (magnetic ink character recognition) An identification number printed on each check and used to aid the bank in automatic sorting of checks and deposit tickets.

mixed accounts Accounts whose balances are part balance sheet amounts and part income statement amounts.

mutual agency A characteristic of a partnership in which each partner can bind the partnership to any contract within the scope of its business.

net cost The gross cost of an asset less its estimated salvage value.

net income The amount by which total revenue exceeds total expenses for an accounting period.

net loss The amount by which total expenses exceed total revenue for an accounting period.

net pay The amount of pay an employee receives after deductions; often called take-home pay.

net purchases The total purchases—including transportation costs—less any returns, allowances, and discounts.

net sales The total sales less any returns, allowances, and discounts.

nominal accounts Temporary owner's equity accounts whose balances are used for one accounting period only; these accounts are closed at the end of each accounting period.

no-par-value stock Stock that has no authorized value stated on the stock certificate.

normal balance The side of an account on which increases are recorded.

notes payable Written promises to pay a specific sum of money to a creditor or lender on a future date.

notes payable register A subsidiary record containing detailed information about each note payable.

notes receivable Customers' written promises to pay a specific sum of money on a future date.

notes receivable register A subsidiary record containing detailed information about each note receivable.

not sufficient funds A situation that occurs when a person does not have enough funds in his or her bank account to cover a check that has been written.

open accounts Asset, liability, and owner's equity accounts whose balances are carried forward from one accounting period to the next; often referred to as real accounts.

output Information that is produced by a data processing system.

outstanding check A check issued by the depositor but not presented to the bank for payment at the time the bank statement is mailed.

outstanding stock The total amount of capital stock actually owned by the stockholders of a corporation.

owner's equity Owner's interest in the business or claim to the assets of the business; the difference between what the business owns and what it owes. Often referred to as net worth, proprietorship, or capital.

partnership An association of two or more persons for the purpose of carrying on a business for profit.

par-value stock Stock that has the authorized value of each share of stock stated on the stock certificate.

paycheck Check issued by a business as remuneration for an employee's work.

payee The person or firm to whose order a check or promissory note is drawn.

payroll register A supplementary payroll record that summarizes information about gross earnings and deductions of all employees for a specific pay period.

pegboard accounting A manual system of accounting that permits the recording of payroll information on all three payroll records at one time.

percentage method A method of computing employee income tax withholdings.

personal property All assets other than real property.

personal service enterprise A firm that derives the major portion of its revenue from services performed for customers.

petty cash disbursements record An auxiliary record used to record petty cash transactions; classifies payments according to the expense or asset accounts to be charged.

petty cash fund A sum of money set aside to make small daily cash payments.

petty cash voucher A receipt showing the amount paid out of the petty cash fund, the name and signature of the person receiving the money, the purpose of the payment, and the signature of the person making the payment.

physical depreciation A decline in usefulness of an asset caused by use or exposure to the elements.

piece-rate A means of compensating employees based on the number of units an employee produces.

PL/1 A computer language designed for business and scientific use.

postclosing trial balance A trial balance prepared after the temporary owner's equity accounts have been closed; lists only the balances of open accounts.

posting The process of transferring information contained in a journal entry to the general ledger accounts.

preferred stock A class of stock issued by a corporation, which gives its holders first preference on the distribution of dividends.

prepaid expenses Business expenses that have been paid in advance but that are not wholly consumed during the accounting period; they are listed as assets at the time of purchase.

principal The face amount of a promissory note.

proceeds The amount of cash received when a note receivable is discounted.

program A detailed package of instructions the computer follows in completing the processing of data.

promissory note A written unconditional promise to pay a specific person or bearer a specified sum of money either at a fixed future time or on demand.

proving the journal The process of checking the accuracy of the debit and credit columns on a page of a journal.

punched card data processing A semiautomated data processing method in which data is punched into cards and then processed automatically through machines.

purchase invoice A document received by the buyer that contains details about a purchase.

purchase returns and allowances A contra expense account used by the buyer for recording the price for merchandise returned and price adjustments (allowances) on defective merchandise.

purchases Merchandise bought for resale.

purchases journal A special journal in which all purchases of merchandise for resale on account are recorded.

realized revenue Cash or a claim to cash that is received in return for something of value given up.

real property Land and anything that is attached to the land.

restrictive endorsement The safest means of transferring ownership of a check; specifies the purpose for which the check is to be used and restricts any further negotiation of the check.

retail method A method for estimating cost of inventory based on a ratio of cost to retail price.

retail sales tax A tax levied on the gross price of retail sales.

retained earnings Earnings (profit) retained in the business that are used for paying dividends or for reinvestment in the business.

revenue The inflow of cash or receivables in exchange for goods or services.

reversing entry A journal entry made on the first day of a new accounting period to reverse the adjustments for accruals.

salary Remuneration for employees engaged in managerial or administrative work; usually expressed as a fixed monthly or yearly amount.

sales invoice (ticket) A document prepared by the seller containing details of a sale.

sales journal A special journal in which the sales of merchandise on account are recorded.

sales returns and allowances A contra revenue account used by the seller for recording the price of merchandise returned and price adjustments (allowances) on defective merchandise.

salvage value The estimated value of a long-lived asset at the end of its expected useful life.

schedule of accounts payable A list of individual creditors and the amounts owed to each.

schedule of accounts receivable A list of individual charge customers and the amounts owed by each.

selling expenses Expenses incurred in the operation of the business that are directly related to the sale of merchandise.

service charge A fee charged by banks for the services they provide.

signature card A card bearing the signature of each person authorized to sign checks on a certain account; kept on file by the bank as a means of verifying signatures.

single proprietorship A business owned by one person.

source document A printed or written form that contains the facts about a business transaction.

statement of owner's equity A statement showing the owner's net income (or net loss) and the withdrawals during an accounting period.

statement of retained earnings A financial statement showing the changes in the retained earnings of a corporation during an accounting period.

state unemployment taxes Taxes levied by a state and paid by an employer to provide benefits for eligible unemployed workers.

stockholder A person owning one or more shares of the capital stock of a corporation.

stockholder of record Holder of stock who is entitled to receive a declared dividend.

storage unit A computer unit that accepts and stores data to be processed and the instructional programs for processing the stored data.

straight-line method A method for calculating depreciation that assigns equal amounts of depreciation to equal periods of time.

subsidiary accounts payable ledger A book containing individual ledger accounts for creditors.

subsidiary accounts receivable ledger A book containing individual ledger accounts for charge customers.

summary posting The process of posting the total of each special column from a journal to a ledger account rather than posting each amount in the column individually.

sum-of-the-years'-digits method A method for calculating depreciation that assigns greater amounts of depreciation to the early years of an asset's life.

systems manual A comprehensive manual that contains information about the forms, records, reports, and processing procedures used in a firm's accounting system.

tangible asset An asset that has physical substance.

taxable earnings The amount of employees' earnings that are subject to federal and state income taxes. A certain base amount of these earnings is also subject to FICA and unemployment taxes.

time-sharing A way of providing automated payroll accounting to small companies, whereby several businesses jointly own or rent time on a computer.

trade discount A reduction in the catalog or list price of merchandise offered by wholesalers.

trial balance A listing of ledger accounts and their debit or credit balances; a means of proving the equality of debits and credits in the ledger.

uncollectible account An account receivable that cannot be collected.

unemployment insurance Compensation received by employees who through no fault of their own become unemployed.

Uniform Partnership Act A law adopted in most states that governs the formation and operation of partnerships.

units of production method A method for calculating depreciation that is based on the output or production of an asset multiplied by a constant cost per unit.

unlimited liability A characteristic of single proprietorships and partnerships which makes the owners liable for the debts of the business beyond their original investment; personal assets may be taken to satisfy the claims of creditors.

wage-bracket method A method of determining employee income tax withholdings by use of tables furnished by the Internal Revenue Service.

wages Remuneration for skilled or unskilled labor, usually expressed on an hourly, weekly, or piece-rate basis.

wasting asset A long-lived asset that is eventually consumed or exhausted.

weighted average method A method of assigning an average cost to inventory units based on both the quantity and cost of units.

withholding allowance Exemptions allowed on the federal income tax.

worksheet An informal statement that facilitates the preparation of financial statements and other end-of-the-period activities.

Index

ABA (American Bankers
      Association) number,
      112, 113, 126, 317
Account, 20, 43, 317
    balance, 46, 59, 317
    bank, 109
    closed, 101
    contra, 68
    control, 163, 174
    mixed, 83, 105
    nominal, 94, 105
    open, 102, 105
    T, 20
    temporary, 12, 23
Account form
    of balance sheet, 54–55
    four-column, 33
    T, 20
    three-column, 163
    two-column, 33

Accounting
    accrual system of, 148, 174,
      317
    bookkeeping and, 5–6
    cash system of, 62–63, 79,
      319
    cycle, 43, 103, 317
    double entry, 15, 17
    equation, 8, 17, 317
    fundamental elements of, 6–7
    language of business, 5
    for merchandising business,
      149–73
    need for, 4
    payroll, 254–55
    period, 46, 59, 317
    for personal service business,
      62–77
    users of, 5

Accounting cycle, 41, 43, 82, 103,
    317
Accounting equation, 8, 17, 317
    effects of transactions on,
      8–11, 13–15
Accounting machine, 280
Accounting period, 46, 317
    calendar year, 46, 59, 318
    fiscal year, 46, 59, 320
Accounting records, need for, 4
Account number, 34
Accounts
    accounting and accounts, 20
    adjustments for, 82–83,
      222–27
    after posting adjusting
      entries, 84–86
    after posting closing entries,
      97–99
    after posting reversing
      entries, 236–37

balancing, 47
chart of, 34, 43
control, 163, 174
normal balances of, 21,
    46–47
ruling, 101
uncollectible, 178, 197
Accounts payable, 7, 17, 317
control account for, 164
schedule of, 165, 175
subsidiary ledger, 164, 171,
    175
Accounts receivable, 6, 17, 317
control account for, 164
schedule of, 165, 175
subsidiary ledger, 163, 170,
    175
uncollectible, 178, 197
writing off uncollectible,
    178–83
aging of, 182–83, 318
allowance, 180–81, 197,
    317
direct write-off, 178–79
Accrual basis of accounting, 174,
    317
Accrued bank credit card expense,
    226
adjusting entry for, 226, 232
on financial statements, 228,
    230
reversing entry for, 234–36
on worksheet, 224–25
Accrued expense (liability), 194,
    196, 317
Accured interest expense, 194,
    227
adjusting entry for, 194, 227,
    232
on financial statements, 194,
    228, 230
reversing entry for, 236–37
on worksheet, 224–25, 227
Accrued interest payable, 194,
    227, 237
Accrued interest receivable, 194
Accrued revenue (assets), 194,
    196, 317
Accrued wages, 271–73, 275, 318
adjusting entries for, 272–73
reversing entry for, 272–73
Accumulated depreciation, 85,
    105, 206, 318

Additional investments of capital,
    10–11
Adjusted bank statement balance,
    118–19
Adjusted trial balance, 88–90,
    224
Adjusting entries, 83–86, 105,
    232, 318
for merchandising business,
    222–27, 232
for personal service
    enterprise, 93–94
Adjustments, 82–83, 222–27
for accrued bank credit card
    expense, 226, 232
for accrued interest expense,
    194, 227, 232
for accrued wages, 271–73
for bad debts, 180–83, 226
for depreciation, 84–86, 206,
    226
for insurance, 83–84, 223–26
for merchandise inventory,
    223–25
for supplies, 226
for uncollectible accounts,
    226
on worksheet, 87–88, 224–25
ADP (Automated Data
    Processing), 279, 292
Aging accounts receivable, 182,
    196, 318
Allowance
for bad debts, 180–83, 226
purchase, 160
sales, 159
withholding, 246–47
American Bankers Association
    (ABA) number, 112,
    113, 126, 317
Amortization, 200, 219, 318
Appropriation, 311, 314, 318
Arithmetic unit, 287, 292, 318
Articles of copartnership, 299,
    314, 318
Articles of incorporation, 307,
    314, 318
Assets, 6, 17, 318
classification of, 231
current, 231, 239, 319
fixed, 200, 231, 239, 320
intangible, 200

long-lived, 200, 231
depreciation of, 200
discarding, 207
disposition of, 206
selling, 207–8
trading in, 209
normal balance of, 21, 46–47
tangible, 200
wasting, 200
Authorized capital stock, 307,
    314, 318
Automated accounting systems,
    278–79
characteristics of, 281–86
input media, 281
    magnetic ink and optical
        characters, 285–86
    magnetic tape and discs,
        284–85
    punched card and tape,
        282–84
input stage, 281
output stage, 286
processing stage, 286
design of
system analysis, 278
system design, 278–79
system implementation,
    279
for other business records,
    290–91
for payroll, 289–90
Automated Data Processing
    (ADP), 279, 292, 318

Bad debts, 178, 196, 226, 318
adjusting for, 180–83, 226
aging method for, 182, 196,
    318
allowance method for,
    180–81, 196, 318
direct write-off method for,
    178–79
writing off, 178–83
Balance
account, 46, 317
credit, 47
debit, 47
post-closing trial, 102–3, 105,
    234, 323
trial, 46, 50, 59, 325

Balance sheet, 54, 59, 229–31, 318
    account form of, 54
    accumulated depreciation on, 93, 230
    bad debts on, 231
    classified, 229–31
    columns on worksheet, 91–92, 225
    merchandise inventory on, 230–31
    preparing, 54–56, 229–31
    relationship to income statement, 57
    report form of, 56, 230
Balancing accounts, 47
    and ruling, 101–2
Bank deposit, 111
    preparing, 111–15
    in transit, 117, 126
Bank discount on note, 185, 196, 318
Bank reconciliation, 118, 126, 318
    journal entries after, 119–20
    preparing, 118–19
Bank service charge, 117, 127
Bank statement, 115, 126, 318
    reconciling, 117–19
Blank endorsement, 113, 126, 318
Book of final entry, 32
Book of original entry, 26
Book value, 85, 105, 203, 219, 318
Business entity concept, 6, 17, 318
Business ownership
    corporation, 306–8
    partnership, 299–301
    single proprietorship, 296–97
Business transactions, 8
    analyzing, 8–11, 13–14

Calendar year, 46, 318
Cancelled check, 115, 126, 318
Capital, 7
    additional investments of, 10–11
    changes in, 12
Capital stock, 307–11
    authorized, 307, 314
    dividends on, 310–11
    issuing of, 309, 310
Cards, punched, 282–84

Cash
    account for, 108
    basis of accounting, 62–63, 79, 319
    composition of, 108
    discount, 155–56, 318
    petty, 121
    proving, 72
    short and over, 124–25
Cash discounts, 155–56, 174, 318
Cash payments journal, 134–38, 145, 318
Cash receipts journal, 131–34, 145, 318
Cash register tape, 151–52
Charge sales, 150
Charges, transportation, 161–63
Chart of accounts, 34, 43, 319
Charter, 307, 314, 319
Check, 109, 126, 319
    ABA number on, 112, 113, 126
    canceled, 115, 126
    dishonored, 117, 126
    endorsing, 113–14
    magnetic ink characters on, 112, 113, 127
    not sufficient funds (NSF), 117, 127
    outstanding, 117, 127
    payroll, 252
    stubs of, 110
    writing, 110–11
Checking account, opening of, 109
Classified financial statements, 239, 319
Classifying assets, 231
Classifying liabilities, 231
Closed account, ruling of, 101
Closing entries, 94, 96, 105, 232–33, 319
    for expense accounts, 96, 100, 233
    for expense and revenue summary account, 96, 100, 233
    journalizing, 96–97, 232–33
    for merchandising firm, 232–34
    for owner's drawing account, 96, 100, 233
    posting, 97–99, 233

for professional enterprise, 94, 96–97
for revenue accounts, 96, 100, 233
COBOL (Common Business Oriented Language), 288, 292, 319
Combined cash journal, 69, 319
    column headings in, 69
    footing and proving, 72
    posting from, 72–73
    recording in, 70–71
    ruling, 71
Common Business Oriented Language (COBOL), 288, 292, 319
Common stock, 307, 314, 319
Compensation, types of, 243
Composite rate of depreciation, 210
Compound journal entry, 31, 43, 79, 319
Computer, 287, 292, 319
    equipment, 281
    memory of, 287
    planning program for, 287–88
Contingent liability, 189, 196, 319
Continuous life, 306
Contra account, 68, 79, 319
    accumulated depreciation, 85, 105, 206, 318
    allowance for bad debts, 180–83, 226
Control account, 163, 319
    for accounts payable, 163
    for accounts receivable, 164
    for notes payable, 193
    for notes receivable, 191
Control unit, 287, 292, 319
Corporation, 306, 314, 319
    accounting procedures for, 308–10
    advantages of, 308
    board of directors, 307
    disadvantages of, 308
    organization of, 306–8
    stockholders, 307
Cost of goods sold, 172, 174, 319
    calculating, 172
    on income statement, 228–29
Costing inventory, comparison of methods, 214–15

Cost or market, whichever is
     lower, 214
Credit, 20, 43, 319
Credit memorandum, 159, 174,
     319
Creditor, 5, 17, 319
Cumulative earnings, 251, 253
Current assets, 231, 239, 319
Current liabilities, 231, 239, 319
Cycle, accounting, 41, 43, 82,
     103, 317

Data
     input, 281–86
     origination of, 281
     output, 286
     processing of, 278–89
Data processing, 278–89
     automated data processing
          (ADP), 279
     electronic data processing
          (EDP), 279
     integrated data processing
          (IDP), 279
     methods of
          electronic, 280–81
          manual, 280
          mechanical, 280
          punched card, 280
Debit, 20, 43, 319
     and credit rules, 21
Debit memorandum, 160, 174,
     319
Declaration of dividends, 309–10
Declining balance method of
     depreciation, 203–4,
     219, 319
Deductions, payroll, 244, 249
Deficit, 310, 314, 319
Depletion, 200, 219, 319
Deposit slip, 111, 126, 319
Deposit in transit, 111, 319
Depreciable cost, 85, 201
Depreciation, 79, 200–10, 320
     accumulated, 85, 105, 206
     adjustments for, 85–86, 210,
          226
     amortization, 200
     composite rate, 210
     depletion, 200
     expense, 63, 84
     functional, 201

methods of determining,
     202–6
     declining balance, 203–4,
          219
     straight line, 202, 219
     sum-of-the-years' digits,
          204–5, 219
     units of production, 202–3,
          219
     physical, 200, 219
Direct write-off of bad debts,
     178–79, 196, 320
Disbursement, petty cash, 121
Discounting a note, 188, 196, 320
Discounts
     cash, 155–56, 174
     purchases, 157
     sales, 156
     trade, 158, 175
Dishonored check, 126, 320
Dishonored note, 197, 320
Dissolution of a partnership,
     304–6
Dividend, 310, 314, 320
     on capital stock, 310
     declaring, 310
     payment of, 310
Document, source, 25, 43, 324
Double-entry accounting, 15, 17,
     320
Drawee, 109, 126, 320
Drawer, 109, 126, 320
Drawing account, 23
     closing, 96, 233

Earnings
     cumulative, 251, 253
     gross, 243–45
     individual record of, 252–53
     retained, 309, 315, 324
EDP (Electronic Data
     Processing), 279–81,
     287–89, 292, 320
Electronic Data Processing
     (EDP), 279–81,
     287–89, 292, 320
     arithmetic unit, 287, 319
     control unit, 287–88, 319
     programming, 287
     storage unit, 287
Employee, 242, 258, 320
Employee FICA tax, 244–45
     calculation of, 245–46

Employee income tax, 246–49
     calculation of, 247–49
     percentage method, 249
     W–2 form, 269
     W–4 form, 247
     wage bracket method, 247
Employee's individual earnings
     record, 252–53, 258,
     320
Employer, 244, 258, 320
Employer payroll taxes, 262–64
     FICA, 262–63
     FUTA, 263
     journal entry for, 264
     payment of, 265–69
          form 940, 268
          form 941, 266
          state unemployment, 264
Employer's identification number,
     266, 275, 320
Endorsements
     blank, 113, 114, 126
     full, 113, 114, 126
     restrictive, 114, 126
Entries
     adjusting, 83–86, 232
     closing, 94–100, 233
     compound journal, 71
     journal, 27–28
     reversing, 234–38
Equation, accounting, 8, 17, 317
     effect of transactions on,
          8–11, 13–15
Equipment, computer, 281
Equity, owner's, 7, 17, 323
Errors, finding and correcting, 50
Estimated useful life of long-lived
     assets, 63, 201
Expense, 12, 17, 320
     accrued, 317
     closing accounts, 96, 100,
          232–33
     general or administrative,
          229, 239, 321
     prepaid, 226, 239, 323
     selling, 229, 239, 324
Expense and revenue summary,
     105, 233, 320

Face amount, of note, 84
Federal Fair Labor Standards
     Act, 243, 258, 320

Federal income tax, 246, 258, 320
    wage bracket method of
        calculating, 247–48
    withholding allowances for,
        246
    paying, 265–67
    percentage method of
        calculating, 249
Federal Insurance Contributions
        Act, 244, 258, 320
Federal tax deposit forms, 265,
        267
    form 501, 265
    form 508, 267
Federal Unemployment Tax Act,
        263, 275, 320
    calculating employer's
        liability for, 263
    recording employer's liability
        for, 264
FICA tax, 244, 258, 262–63, 320
    deduction for employees, 245
    deduction for employers,
        262–63
Fields, 284
Financial records, importance of,
        4
Financial statements, 46
    balance sheet, 54, 230
    classified, 239
    of financial position, 54
    income statement, 52, 227
    of retained earnings, 312,
        315, 324
First-in, first-out (FIFO) costing,
        212, 219, 320
Fiscal year, 46, 58, 320
Fixed assets, 200, 231, 239, 320
    depreciation of, 200
    disposal of, 206–9
    useful life of, 201
Fixed liabilities, 231
Flowchart, 288, 292, 320
FOB (Free On Board)
    destination, 161, 174, 321
    shipping point, 161, 174, 321
Footing, 47
    accounts and finding their
        balances, 47
    and proving combined cash
        journal, 72
Form 501, Federal Tax Deposit,
        Federal Income Tax,
        265

Form 508, Federal Tax Deposit,
        Unemployment Taxes,
        267
Form 940, Employer's Annual
        Federal
        Unemployment Tax
        Return, 268
Form 941, Employer's Quarter
        Federal Tax Return,
        266
Form SS–5, Application for
        Social Security
        Number, 246
Form W–2, Wage and Tax
        Statement, 269
Form W–3, Transmittal of
        Income and Tax
        Statements, 270
Form W–4, Employee's
        Withholding
        Allowance Certificate,
        247
Forms of ownership
    corporation, 306–8
    partnership, 299–301
    single proprietorship, 296–97
FORTRAN (*For*mula
        *Tran*slation), 288,
        292, 321
Four-column account form, 33
Freight in, 162
Freight out, 161
Full endorsement, 113, 114, 126,
        321
Functional depreciation, 219, 321
Fund, petty cash, 121, 127, 323
FUTA tax, 263

Gain on sale of long-lived asset,
        208–9
General journal, 26, 43, 321
    posting from, 35–36
    proving, 31, 43, 323
    recording in, 27–28
General ledger, 32, 43, 321
    chart of accounts for, 34
    posting to, 35–36
    proving equality of debits and
        credits in, 31, 43
General ledger accounts
    closed, 101
    four-column form, 33
    need for adjusting, 82–83
    open, 102, 105

    three-column form, 163
    two-column form, 33
GIGO (garbage in, garbage out),
        289, 292, 321
Goodwill, 304, 314, 321
Gross earnings, 243–44, 258, 321
Gross margin (profit), 172–73,
        174, 321
Gross profit costing, 216, 219, 321

Heading
    of balance sheet, 54
    of income statement, 52
    of trial balance, 50
    of worksheet, 87
Hourly rate, 243

Identification number, employer's,
        266, 275
IDP (Integrated data processing),
        279, 321
Imprest, 121
Income distribution in
        partnership, 302–3
Income, net, 12, 17, 52, 322
Income statement, 52, 59,
        227–29, 321
    classified, 227, 229
    columns on worksheet, 90–91
    form for, 52–53, 227–29
    multiple-step, 228–29
Income tax
    employees, 246–49
    withholding table, 248
Incorporation, articles of, 307
Incorporators, 307, 314, 321
Independent contractor, 242, 258,
        321
Input, 281, 292, 321
Input media and devices, 281–86,
        292, 321
Insurance, prepaid, 83–84, 223
    adjustment for, 83–84,
        223–24
Intangible long-lived assets, 219,
        321
Integrated data processing (IDP),
        279, 293
Interest, 184, 197, 321
    accrual, expense, 194, 227,
        237–38
    accural, receivable, 194

collection of on note
receivable, 187
computing, 185–86
need for adjustment, 194
payment of on note payable,
191–92
six-day, 6 percent method,
186
sixty-day, 6 percent method,
186
Interest-bearing note, 184
Inventory, merchandise, 149,
211–17, 223
assigning costs to, 211–14
beginning merchandise,
adjusting entry for,
223–25
ending merchandise,
adjusting entry for,
223–25
estimating, 216–17
periodic, 211
perpetual, 211
Investment, owner's
for corporation, 307–8
for partnership, 301, 304–5
for single proprietorship,
297–98
Invoice, purchase, 175
terms, 155

Journal
as book of original entry, 26
combined cash, 69
compound entry, 31, 43
entry, 28, 321
general, 26, 43
posting from, 35–36
proving the, 31, 323
special, 26
cash payments, 134–38,
145, 318
cash receipts, 131–34, 145,
318
purchases, 142–43
sales, 140–42
Journalizing, 27, 321

Keypunch, 280, 293, 321

Last-in, first-out (LIFO) costing,
212–13, 219, 321
Ledger, 32, 43
as book of final entry, 32

general, 32, 43
posting to, 35–36
proving accuracy of, 46
ruling accounts in, 101–2
subsidiary, 163
accounts payable, 164,
171, 175, 325
accounts receivable,
163–64, 170, 175, 325
Liabilities, 7, 17, 231, 321
contingent, 189, 196, 319
current, 231, 239
long-term, 231
Liability
limited, 308
unlimited, 297, 300
Limited liability, 308
Liquidity, 231
Long-lived assets, 200, 219, 321
discarding of, 207
disposing of, 206–8
trading in, 209–10
Long-term investments, 231, 239,
321
Long-term liabilities, 231, 322
Loss on disposition of asset,
207–8
Loss, net, 12, 17, 52, 322
Lower of cost or market, 214,
219, 322

Magnetic ink, 285
Magnetic ink character
recognition (MICR),
112, 113, 127
Magnetic tape, 284–85
Maker of note, 184, 197, 322
Manual data processing, 249,
293, 322
Margin, gross, 172, 174, 228
MasterCard, 150–51
Mathematic Formula Translation
System (FORTRAN),
288, 293
Maturity date of note, 184, 197,
322
Maturity value, 186, 197, 322
Mechanical data processing, 280,
293, 322
Memorandum
credit, 159, 174, 319
debit, 160, 174, 319
Memory unit, 287
Merchandise, 149

Merchandise inventory, 149, 175,
211–17, 223, 322
adjusting entry for, 223, 232
assigning costs to
FIFO, 212
LIFO, 212–13
lower of cost or market,
214
weighted average, 213
beginning, 232
ending, 232
estimating, 216–17
periodic, 211
perpetual, 211
on schedule of cost of goods
sold, 228–29
Merchandising businesses, 148,
175, 322
Merit rating, 264, 275, 322
MICR number, 112, 113, 127,
322
Mixed account, 105, 322
Mutual agency, 301, 314, 322

Negotiable instrument, 184
Net cost, 219, 322
Net income, 12, 17, 52, 322
on balance sheet, 55–56
determining, 53
distribution in partnership,
302–3
Net loss, 12, 17, 52, 322
on balance sheet, 58
determining, 53
Net pay, calculating, 249–50,
258, 322
Net purchases, 160, 172, 175,
228, 322
Net sales, 159, 172, 175, 228, 322
Nominal accounts, 105
Noninterest-bearing note, 185
No-par-value stock, 307, 315, 322
Normal balance, 59, 322
Notes, 184–197
collection of, 187
date of, 184
discounting, 185, 188
dishonored, 189
interest on, 184, 186
interest bearing, 184–85
interest rate of, 184
maker of, 184
maturity date of, 184
maturity value, 186

noninterest-bearing, 184–85
payee of, 184, 197
payment of, 191–93
principal of, 184, 197
proceeds, 188
promissory, 184
time of, 184–85
Notes payable, 7, 17, 190–93,
    322
    accrued interest on, 194
    control account for, 193
    for extension of time, 190
    payment of, 191–93
    register for, 192–93, 197, 322
    to borrow money from bank,
        191
Notes receivable, 6, 17, 186–89,
    322
    acceptance of for extension of
        time, 187
    accrued interest on, 194
    collection of, 187
    control account for, 191
    dishonored, 189
    register for, 190–91, 197,
        322
Not sufficient funds (NSF), 126,
    322
Numeric rows, 282–83

Open accounts, 102, 105, 322
    balancing and ruling, 102
Opening entries
    for partnership, 301
    for single proprietorship, 298
Operating expenses, 228
Optical characters, 285
Other expenses on income
        statement, 228
Output, 286, 293, 322
Outstanding check, 127, 323
Outstanding stock, 307, 315
Overtime, 243–44
Owner's equity, 7, 17, 323
    effect of expenses on, 12
    effect of revenue on, 12
    section of corporation balance
        sheet, 311
    section of partnership balance
        sheet, 303
    statement of, 55–56, 59, 324
    temporary accounts, 12

Ownership, forms of
    corporation, 306–12
    partnership, 299–306
    single proprietorship, 296–99

Partnership, 299, 315, 323
    accounting for, 301–6
    admitting new partners, 304
    advantages of, 300
    allocation of profits and
        losses, 302–3
    articles of, 299, 314
    disadvantages of, 300
    dissolution of, 304, 306
    goodwill, 304, 314
    organization of, 301
    withdrawal of partner, 305–6
Par value, 307, 315, 323
Pay, calculation of, 243–50
    gross, 243–44
    net, 249–50
Paycheck, 252, 258, 323
Payee, 109, 127, 197, 323
Pay plans
    piece rate, 243
    salary, 243
    wages, 243
        accrued taxes, 273–74
        accrued wages, 271–73
Payroll
    accounting for, 254–55
    automated systems, 255–56
    calculating, 244–50
    deductions, 244
        taxes, 244–49
        voluntary, 249
    journal entry for, 254
    net pay, 249–50
    write-it-once principle, 255
Payroll records, 250–53
    automated processing of,
        255–56
    employee's individual
        earnings, 252–53
    paycheck, 252
    payroll register, 250–51, 259,
        323
    pegboard, 255, 323
    time sharing, 256
    write-it-once, 255
Payroll taxes
    employees, 244–49
    employers, 262–64

journal entry for, 264
    paying, 265–69
Pegboard accounting, 255, 259,
    323
Percentage method, 249, 259, 323
Periodic inventory, 211
Perpetual inventory, 211
Personal property, 219, 323
Personal service enterprise, 62, 79,
    323
    business, 62
    professional, 62
Petty cash fund, 121, 127, 323
    establishing fund, 121
    payments from, 121
    proving the fund, 121
    register, 122, 127, 323
    replenishing, 122–24
    vouchers, 121–22, 127, 323
Physical depreciation, 200, 219,
    323
Piece rate, 243, 259, 323
PL/1 (Programming Language
    1), 288, 293, 323
Post-closing trial balance, 102–3,
    105, 234, 323
Posting, 35, 323
    from cash payments journal,
        138
    from cash receipts journal,
        134
    from combined cash journal,
        72–73
    from general journal, 35–36
    from purchases journal, 142
    from sales journal, 141
    summary, 73
Posting reference, 26
Preferred stock, 308, 315, 323
Prepaid expense, 225, 239, 323
Prepaid insurance, 223–24
    adjusting entry for, 83–84,
        223
Principal of note, 197, 323
Principle of conservatism, 214
Proceeds, 188, 197, 323
Program for computer, 287–88,
    293, 323
Programming Language 1
        (PL/1), 288, 293
Promissory note, 197, 323
Property
    personal, 219
    real, 219

Proprietorship, 7
Proving
    accounts payable, 164–65, 175
    accounts receivable, 164–65, 175
    cash, 72
    combined cash journal, 72
    general journal, 31
    notes payable, 193
    notes receivable, 191
    petty cash disbursement record, 121
Punched card, 282–84
    alphabetic data on, 282–83
    columns, 282
    fields, 284
    as input device, 282
    numeric data on, 282–83
    zone rows on, 282
Punched card data processing, 280, 293, 324
Purchase discounts, 157
    invoice, 154, 175, 324
    order, 154
    requisition, 154
    returns and allowances, 160, 324
Purchase returns and allowances, 160, 175, 324
Purchases, 175, 324
    on account, 154–55
    accounting for, 154–55
    cash, 154
    journal, 141–43, 145, 324
Purchases discounts, 157
Purchases journal, 141–43, 145, 324

Quarterly Federal Tax Return and Report (Form 941), 266
Quarterly totals of employees' earnings records, 252–53

Realized revenue, 148, 175, 324
Real property, 219, 324
Reconciliation, bank statement, 127
Reconciling bank statement, 118–19
Report form, balance sheet, 56, 230

Requisition, purchase, 154
Restrictive endorsement, 114, 127, 324
Retail business, accounting for, 149–73
Retail method of inventory, 217, 219, 324
Retail sales tax, 175, 324
Retained earnings, 309, 315, 324
    appropriations and, 311
    dividends and, 310–11
    statement of, 312, 315
Returns and allowances, 158
    purchases, 160
    sales, 159
Revenue, 12, 17, 324
    accrued, 317
    realized, 148, 175, 324
Revenue accounts
    closing, 233
    need for, 12
Reversing entries, 234, 239, 324
    for accrued bank credit card expense, 234–36
    for accrued interest expense, 237–38
    for accrued salary expense, 271–73
Ruling
    and balancing closed accounts, 101
    and balancing open accounts, 102

Salary, 243, 259, 324
Sales, 149
    on account, 149–52
    accounting for, 149
    bank credit card, 150–51
    for cash, 149
    discounts, 156
    net, 172
    returns and allowances, 159, 175, 324
    tax, 158–59, 175
    ticket (invoice), 151–53
Sales discounts, 156
Sales journal, 140–41, 145, 324
    posting to general ledger, 165, 168–69
    posting to subsidiary accounts receivable ledger, 165, 170

Sales returns and allowances, 159, 175, 324
Sales tax, 158–59, 175
Sales ticket (invoice), 151, 153, 175, 324
Salvage value, 84, 105, 201, 324
Schedule of accounts payable, 164–65, 175, 324
Schedule of accounts receivable, 164–65, 175, 324
Selling expenses, 229, 239
Service charge, 127, 324
Shares of stock, 307
Signature card, 109, 127, 324
Single proprietorship, 296, 315, 324
Slide, 51
Social security account number, application for, 246
Social security taxes, 244–46
    calculation of, 245–46
    table, 245
Source document, 25, 43, 324
Special journals, 26
    advantages of, 144
    for cash payments, 134–38, 145
    for cash receipts, 131–34, 145
    combined cash, 69
    function of, 130–31
    for purchases, 141–43, 145
    for sales, 140–41, 145
Special withholding allowance, 247
Standard form of account, 33
Statement of financial position, 54
Statement of owner's capital, 298–99, 314, 318
Statement of owner's equity, 55–56, 59, 324
Statement of petty cash disbursements, 123–24
Statement of retained earnings, 312, 315, 324
State unemployment taxes, 264, 275, 324
Stock
    capital, 307, 309, 314
    certificate, 307
    common, 307, 314
    outstanding, 307, 315
    par value, 307

payment for by incorporators, 307
preferred, 308
Stock certificate, 307
Stockholder, 307, 315, 324
    distributing income to, 310
    of record, 307, 315, 324
Storage unit, 287, 293, 325
Straight line method of depreciation, 219, 325
Subscription to stock, 309–10
Subsidiary ledgers, 163
    for accounts payable, 164, 171, 175, 325
    for accounts receivable, 163–64, 170, 175, 325
Summary posting, 73, 79, 325
Sum-of-the-years' digits method of depreciation, 219, 325
Supplies, adjustment for, 226
Symbols for flowcharting, 288
Systems analysis, 278
Systems design, 278–79
Systems implementation, 279
Systems manual, 278, 293, 325

T account form, 20
Tangible assets, 219, 325
Tape, magnetic, 284–85
Taxable earnings, 251, 259, 325
Taxes
    employee's FICA, 244–46
    employer's FICA, 262–63
    FUTA, 263
    federal income, 246–49
    sales, 158–59
    state unemployment, 264
Tax tables, 245, 248
Temporary owner's equity accounts
    drawing, 23

expense, 12
expense and revenue summary, 96
revenue, 12
ruling, 101
Ten-column worksheet, 87–92, 224–25
Terms, credit, 155
Time-and-a-half, 243
Time of note, 184, 185
Time sharing, 256, 259, 325
Trade discounts, 158, 175, 325
Transaction, 8
Transportation costs, 161–63
    on merchandise purchased, 162–163
    on merchandise sold, 161–62
Transposition error, 51
Trial balance, 46, 50, 59, 325
    adjusted on worksheet, 88–89
    errors in, 50–52
    post-closing, 103, 234
    purpose of, 46
    on worksheet, 87
Two-column account form, 33

Uncollectible accounts, 178, 197, 226, 325
    allowance for, 226
    write off of, 178–83
Undepreciated cost, 203, 318
Unemployment insurance, 263–64, 275, 325
Unemployment taxes
    FUTA, 263
    state, 264
Uniform Partnership Act, 299, 315, 325
Units of production method of calculating depreciation, 219, 325

Unlimited liability, 297, 300, 315, 325
Useful life, 63

Value, book, 85, 105, 203, 219, 318
Voluntary payroll deduction, 249
Voucher, petty cash, 121–122, 127, 323

W–2 Form, Wage and Tax Statement, 269
W–4 Form, Employees Withholding Allowance Certificate, 247
Wage bracket method, 259, 325
Wage bracket table, 248
Wages, 259, 325
Wasting assets, 219, 325
Weighted average costing, 213, 219, 325
Withdrawals, owner, 23
Withholding allowances, 246–47, 259, 325
Worksheet, 87, 105, 222–27, 325
    8-column, 87
    for merchandising firm, 222–27
    for professional enterprise, 88–92
    10-column, 87–92, 224–27
Write-it-once principle, 255
Writing off bad debts, 178–83

Year
    calendar, 46
    fiscal, 46

Zone rows for punched card, 282